BAUDELAIRE

At the Limits
and Beyond

Nicolae Babuts

D1614713

DELAWARE

Newark: University of Delaware Press
London: Associated University Presses

Associated University Presses
440 Forsgate Drive
Cranbury, NJ 08512

Associated University Presses
16 Barter Street
London WC1A 2AH, England

Associated University Presses
P.O. Box 338, Port Credit
Mississauga, Ontario
Canada L5G 4L8

The paper used in this publication meets the requirements of the American National Standard for Permanence of Paper for Printed Library Materials Z39.48–1984.

Library of Congress Cataloging-in-Publication Data

Babuts, Nicolae.
    Baudelaire : at the limits and beyond / Nicolae Babuts.
        p.   cm.
    Includes bibliographical references and index.
    ISBN 0-87413-644-X (alk. paper)
    1. Baudelaire, Charles, 1821–1867—Criticism and interpretation.
I. Title.
PQ2191.Z5B22   1997
841'.8—dc21   97-20434
                                                               CIP

"Je crains bien d'avoir simplement réussi à dépasser les limites assignées à la Poésie."

—Baudelaire

Contents

Acknowledgments

The fifth chapter on Andromache and Baudelairean Exile in "Le Cygne" is a revised version of a lecture given at Princeton University, 8 March 1995. I am grateful to Suzanne Nash and the other members of the Department of Romance Languages for their invitation and warm welcome.

Some chapters appeared previously in periodicals. The first under the title "Baudelaire's 'Le Mauvais vitrier' and 'Mademoiselle Bistouri'" appeared in *Symposium* 49 (Fall 1995), and is reprinted with permission of The Helen Dwight Reid Educational Foundation and Heldref Publications, 1319 18th St. N.W. Washington, DC 20036–1802. The sixth chapter, entitled "Baudelaire's 'Le Voyage': The Dimension of Myth," appeared in *Nineteenth-Century French Studies* 25 (Spring-Summer 1997), and is reprinted by permission of *Nineteenth-Century French Studies*, Thomas H. Goetz, Editor. The Baudelaire quotations come from texts published by Gallimard in the Bibliothèque de la Pléiade series.

I wish to thank Janice Testa, Michael Murphy, and my daughter, Vivian Babuts, for their care in reading parts of the manuscript and for their helpful suggestions. I also must say thanks to the editors at Associated University Presses for giving the manuscript their undivided attention.

BAUDELAIRE

Introduction

A Cognitive Approach

In what follows, I look at Baudelaire in an attempt to define the coherence that is characteristic of his texts. The goal is to distinguish, in their discursive forces, the poet's struggle to meet the constant challenge to his identity, at the limits of his personality, of knowledge, and of poetry. Alongside the assumption that such a coherence exists and that it will always be modulated by the point of view of the critic and by the perspective in which it is viewed, I place the ambition to let the texts that are being considered exert more control over the outcome of the interpretive venture. This is in contrast to the tendency, which has become more evident in the last two or three decades, to appropriate Baudelaire's works and convert him to various ideologically driven beliefs. In pointing out that difference at the theoretical level, I will briefly indicate the assumptions of the cognitive approach adopted here.

The approach is one that coordinates with a cognitive view of literature, which proposes that no discernment and no meaning can occur without an observer or a reader. The perceptually defined relation of the interpreter to the text becomes the dominant factor in the equation of meaning. At one end of this relation stands the text; at the other, the mnemonic potentials, endogenous representational patterns, of the individual reader or critic. Without the text, there would be nothing to interpret; without the mnemonic potentials of the reader/observer, without memory, there would be no interpretation; and without interpretation there would be no meaning.

The Existence of Dynamic Patterns

Interpretation begins with the individual memory's attempt to rebuild or re-create the dynamic patterns, the building blocks of the textual blueprint, that appear in the form of simple images or more complex metaphors, each of them embodied in a clause or a sentence. An indication of the existence of such units in poetry emerged from the study of some traditional patterns of comparison and metaphor in my dissertation (1967), where I defined them as semantic centers, short of realizing that they are the primary units. In an article, I called them dynamic patterns and described their relation to images (see 1977, 187). Other researchers have been moving in the same direction. Although Lakoff and Johnson do not use the same terms, the "orientational metaphors" (see 1980, 14–15) they deal with are clearly dynamic patterns. More recently, Turner demonstrates, in a compelling study, that "metaphor, to which the literary critic is minutely attuned, is not just a matter of literary wordplay, not even just a matter of language—it is a pattern of thought that underlies our cognition and knowledge . . ." (1987, 9–10). The kinship metaphors he focuses on are again excellent examples of dynamic patterns. Evidence that they are basic units of meaning, as I have claimed,[1] comes from various areas of research, including psycholinguistics and the neurosciences. Already in the early nineteen seventies, Jarvella, in an important article on syntactic processing, concludes "that the most recently heard clause and sentence are organized as speech processing structures in memory; the processing of structural semantic information in heard speech operates over these immediate syntactic units" (1971, 415). Seven years later Dillon is able to declare: "Psycholinguists have accumulated an impressive amount of evidence that the clause is a crucial unit of sentence processing" (1978, 30).

What is exciting about these findings is that vision, both animal and human, is also organized in dynamic units, patterns of movement, that correspond to verb dominated clauses. Studies in frog vision show that certain fibers respond in such a way as to create "a context," "a physiological *a priori*," and that what the frog sees is not "a space of simple discrete points," but "every point" "in definite contexts" (Lettvin 1959, 1950). This is how the frog is able to identify, for example, the movement of a bug that is of interest to the frog. More importantly still, tachistoscopic experiments reveal the existence of a first stage of vision in the human retina, which researchers have variously called "the icon" or iconic memory.[2] It may last only from 250 milliseconds to a second, but it represents the form in which the stimulus is available for further processing. Thus, what we see as dynamic patterns, "She opened the front door," "He said hello and smiled," "The train just left," begin with this primitive but powerful organization of the stimu-

lus. When Baudelaire compares "the rain bathed suns" to Marie
Daubrun's "eyes, / Shining through their tears," he models the
new dynamic pattern on a traditional parallelism that we can find
everywhere in European literatures. But the parallelism itself, the
model, is a product of the organizational powers of memory.
When the Gentleman in *King Lear* describes Cordelia's reaction
to the letter bringing news of her father, he appeals to Kent's
ordinary experience to make him understand her "smiles and
tears": "You have seen / Sunshine and rain at once" (1972, 4.3).
Although literary dynamic patterns bear a metaphoric imprint
more often than their everyday counterparts and are often more
complex (constructed of two simple patterns, two clauses, for example), they all have the same organization based on the dynamic
distribution of perceptual forces, a minimum context, and referential power.

Indirect confirmation that dynamic patterns in clauses or sentences are basic units of meaning comes also from an unexpected
source, from the field of traditional oral epic. It appears now that
epic singers knew, before scientists and critics, that a unit in their
songs was not the ordinary word but the "word" in the form of a
clause, a line, or two lines. As Foley says: "Simply put, [the epic
singer's] words are poetic lines, units that epitomize what Parry
called an 'essential idea' and which are governed by the metrical
structure of the tradition" (1990, 44–45).[3] From a cognitive perspective, we now can see that these units are dynamic patterns,
that they occur in written texts as well as in oral ones, and that
Parry's "essential idea" is delineated by the dynamic relation of
forces within each unit. That epic singers, far removed from our
theoretical discussions, should nevertheless confirm our hypothe-
sis about the existence of these basic units of textual fabric is
certainly remarkable.

The Way Dynamic Patterns Function

Cutting across various disciplines, this evidence confirms the
concept's viability. Having a longer and much more complex
coded sequence than a word in isolation, a dynamic pattern creates more precision and depth and is the true unit of meaning.
Generally, the literary patterns have a model, the traditional parallelism, smiles-tears sunshine-rain, for example, which appears
with variations in specific images or metaphors. From the intertextual point of view the pattern may or may not have a specific

source in a similar pattern. For example, Baudelaire's "Et qu'un peuple muet d'infâmes araignées / Vient tendre ses filets au fond de nos cerveaux" 'And when a silent nation of loathsome spiders / Comes to spread its webs deep in our brains' ("Spleen" 1: 75), Rimbaud's "L'Aube exaltée ainsi qu'un peuple de colombes" 'Dawn exalted [rising] as a nation of doves' ("Le Bateau ivre" 1960, 129), and Thomas's "And the shipyards of Galilee's footprints hide a navy of doves" ("On the Marriage of a Virgin" 1952, 127) represent the pattern of the potential, all three having the characteristic tension between oneness and multiplicity. But there is no evidence that the first is the source of the others. We just don't know. The intertextual importance of the concept is simply in the fact that the structure itself appeals to poets. The pattern does not necessarily reveal how a poem was composed.

Moreover, its semantic, syntactic, acoustic, dynamic, metaphoric, and metrical modes act in concert to ensure that each individual pattern can be read in the context of the poem and does not need to be connected to other examples of the basic structure to be understood. The main reason for this relative autonomy is that language has referential power. But if the attempt to establish such a connection as a literary phenomenon is made, it should take into account not only the semantic value of the individual words but also, and more importantly, the pattern's dynamic and metaphoric forces. Thus, unlike the two French poets who use the word "peuple," Thomas uses "navy"; but the tension between "navy" and "doves," between the oneness of the potential and the multiplicity of action, is the same as between "nation" and "spiders" in Baudelaire or "nation" and "doves" in Rimbaud. On the other hand, there are cases in which a key word in one pattern may be semantically similar to a word in another pattern, yet the two patterns may differ in kind and function. For example, in Baudelaire's "Le sifflet, rapide comme un glaive" 'the whistle [catcall] quick as a sword' ("Une Mort héroïque") and in the reference to an Italian despot who would offer a poet of the time "soit une dague enrichie de pierreries, soit un manteau de cour, en échange d'un précieux sonnet" 'either a dagger encrusted with gems, or a court coat, in exchange for a precious sonnet' ("Les Bons chiens"), the words "glaive" and "dague" are semantically similar, but the two patterns are not. The first represents the pattern of cutting to interrupt (a life, a performance); the second belongs to the pattern of gift exchange.

One of the most important—and the most exciting—consequences of this view is to propose that we process literary texts in quanta of energy, in terms of dynamic patterns, which are constantly created to interpret the incoming stimuli.[4] We also use, each moment we think, a dynamic pattern to summarize and assess what has gone before. In other words, we may have read or dealt with a long text containing in its fabric many patterns, but when we think about it, wish to define it, for example, we use one dynamic pattern to do so. We can obviously use more than one pattern for that purpose, but we proceed pattern by pattern. We, thus, transform what appears to be an uninterrupted sequential flow into a series of constantly renewed discrete units, each of which can be viewed as a whole in one unit of time. The "space logic" that Frank saw in modern poetry, according to which the reader has "to suspend the process of individual reference temporarily until the entire pattern of internal references can be apprehended as a unity" (1945, 229–30), and the "time logic" of language, according to which, as Sutton says, apprehension of this unity "develops with the reading of the poem" (1957, 116–17), are reconciled, their antinomy explained if not resolved.

Since all textual building blocks are dynamic patterns, those that interest us in particular are those that contribute the most to the dynamics of the metaphoric field of a poem. The most important among them are those that exemplify or govern the meaning of a text. As this essay attempts to show, many of Baudelaire's poems and prose poems are each governed by a dynamic pattern, one that may be present in the poem itself, as is the "coup de sifflet" in "Une Mort héroïque," or one that can be justifiably introduced as an interpretive gesture to express metaphorically the essence and meaning of a poem (or part of a poem). Such is the case with the mnemonic sea where siren-like voices tempt Baudelaire's travelers, a pattern I introduce to explain section vii of "Le Voyage." Occasionally a pattern may be part of a theme or, less often, connected to what some would call an "archetype," but such connections are incidental. Being more specific, dynamic patterns are equivalent neither to general literary ideas nor to Jungian symbols. And being structures of language and vision, they possess an inner dynamics determined by words—verbs and nouns in particular—and have, on the dynamic and metaphoric levels, harmonic or tension-creating relations to other patterns in the poem or story as a whole.

Since a dynamic pattern may bring, to a poem, intertextual echoes,[5] it may often benefit from a comparison with other texts. Such a comparison would only confirm what the pattern's referentially empowered language and dynamics, in the context, are fully capable of showing. If a pattern governs the metaphoric field of the text, it does so as the fulcrum of the metaphoric and allegoric forces in the poem, as is the case with the pattern of "le crâne incliné" 'the bowed head,' signaling the poet's defeat in the fourth "Spleen." While it may be possible to discover its source or to see affinities with similar patterns in other texts and, thus, confirm its identity, the pattern's meaning and significance do not depend on the exploration of an intertext after the first reading. One reason for this relative self-sufficiency is that patterns have referential power. Their dynamic mode is particularly effective in mimicking events in the visible world. Another reason is that the reader's mnemonic potentials already contain, geared for integration, echoes of other texts with similar dynamic patterns. Note, however, that memory is not an encyclopedia: it can access only the past interpretations of a limited number of texts.

The Metaphoric Mode

Dynamic patterns can be structurally straightforward but many of them are also metaphors. Metaphoric thought is at the core not only of European and American literatures but also of oral songs nurtured in other traditions. An example from "The Djanggawul Song Cycle" of an Australian aboriginal cult is further evidence of the essential metaphoric nature of poetry. The ritual reenacts "the primal birth" (Berndt 1953, 23) of the ancestors of the Aborigines, and the songs themselves narrate the voyage of three Ancestral Beings, the Djanggawul Brother and Sisters, from Bralgu,"the island of Spirits" (somewhere in the northeast) to the Australian mainland. They bring with them many sacred emblems and, during the voyage, meet animals and birds that have or acquire sacred significance. One of the most important of them is the red-breasted parakeet. The Djanggawul introduce it in several songs and the repetition is significant. In Song 33 the parakeet in the sacred tree, "its red breast feathers glistening in the sun,"

> Looked at the sun, and spoke: 'I am drying myself, my
> red breast feathers, my *rangga* feathers—my children!'
> (Song 33, Berndt 1953, 97)

One can distinguish here three simple dynamic patterns: "Looked at the sun"; "Calling softly," repeated in "spoke"; and the highly metaphoric, "I am drying . . . my red breast feathers . . . my children." All three are interlocked in one complex pattern. First the parakeet is identified and given its name by one of the Djangga-wul; then this pattern personifies it, enables it to speak, and, thus, endows it with a sacred attribute. The event reaches its highest power when the parakeet calls its feathers "my children" and shows again that in correspondential thought the sacred and the metaphoric levels are one. The union occurs always when the parakeet's red feathers reflect the sunset (Song 100), and it becomes clear that what makes the metaphor possible is the association of the feathers with the sun's rays. Thus, the feathers and the sun are dynamic forces that interact and produce the parakeet's affirmation in which its identity and character are revealed. The association sunset-(red breast) feathers, repeated in several songs, always occurs when the bird sees the red sunset and leads to the metaphor of feathers as children:

> Feathered string pendants drying, red breast feathers!
> 'Myself (says the bird) I am drying them, my children.'
> (Song 41, Berndt 1953, 104)

The sun has its rays as children, the parakeet has its feathers, and the Djanggawul and the two Sisters have human children symbolically represented by the sacred string pendants made with parakeet feathers. In speaking about the significance of the Djanggawul, Berndt concludes: "There is little doubt, then, that the Sisters, if not the Brother, are projections of the Sun. If they are not Sun Goddesses themselves, they are closely linked with the Sun" (1953, 3). Thus, the array of correspondences comes full circle: from the sun to the parakeet, from the parakeet to the feathered strings and to the Djanggawul, and from them back to the sun. The correspondences translate in visible terms the dominant fertility theme; they explain the presence of the Aborigines, describe their historical origin, and establish the primordial unity of their world. In acquiring sacred attributes, the universe acquires depth, significance, and the capacity to engage the individual in the drama of birth and death, to allow actor and listener to participate in the re-creation of the meaning-giving tradition.

The main impulse for the creation of metaphors is in the assumption not that the visible expresses the invisible but that the visible has a sacred dimension and has links with other referentially identifiable entities. In this case, the justification for the relation between the sun's rays and the parakeet's feathers is plainly visible. But to the untrained eye, most correspondences may remain invisible. It is only the trained eye, of the individual or of a tradition, that reveals them by transposing them onto the level of the text.

What do I mean when I use words like "untrained" or "trained" eye? The trained eye is also a trained memory. It is both vision and sacred words; both magic formulae and syntax of the real. The metaphors in the Djanggawul Songs are not very different from those in modern Western literature. Just as youths in the Aborigine tradition have to be initiated into the mysteries of their religious rituals, so too young readers and poets in ours have to learn existing dynamic patterns (units of meaning) and the principles of their renewal in writing. This is the interpretation one has to give to what Baudelaire learned from Gautier, in particular, and also from Hugo, Balzac, Virgil, Aeschylus, and Saint-Amant. The strong though unstated aesthetic assumption is that correspondences of this sort are not only possible but necessary to a universe that may have lost (though this would depend on the definition of the sacred) its sacred dimension but not the capacity to fashion depth and inspire wonder.

Correspondences

There are, in fact, very few theories that Baudelaire holds in higher esteem than the principle of correspondences. In his article on Gautier, he speaks about an instinct for beauty that makes us consider "la Terre et ses spectacles comme un aperçu, comme une *correspondance* du Ciel" 'the Earth and its sights as a hint of, as a *correspondence* with Heaven' (2: 113–114). He would have no difficulty appreciating the Djanggawul vision of the world. The highest praise he could bestow is precisely to recognize a poet's understanding of correspondences. Thus, after mentioning Gautier's ability to use language, he adds:

Si l'on réfléchit qu'à cette merveilleuse faculté Gautier unit une immense intelligence innée de la *correspondance* et du symbolisme universels, ce répertoire de toute métaphore, on comprendra qu'il puisse sans cesse, sans fatigue comme sans faute, définir l'attitude mystérieuse que les objets de la création tiennent devant le regard de l'homme.

If one reflects that Gautier combines this marvelous faculty [language mastery] with a vast, innate understanding of the universal *correspon-*

dence and symbolism, the repertoire of all metaphors, one will realize that he can continually, without strain as well as without fail, define the mysterious bearing that the objects of creation have before human eyes. (2: 117)

One can without difficulty identify this mysterious bearing of objects with the speaking mode of the living pillars in the sonnet "Correspondances" and also with the symbolic face of the real, which, in the cognitive view, is the only aspect of reality available for coding. And one cannot emphasize enough the fact that the mysterious, outward manifestations of nature are a form of communication and that the capacity to interpret them depends on the poet's innate understanding as well as on his or her language. Coding abilities are a product of both native perceptual talents and language mastery.

In his assessment of Hugo, Baudelaire extrapolates Lavater's theories into the following belief: "[N]ous arrivons à cette vérité que tout est hiéroglyphique, et nous savons que les symboles ne sont obscurs que d'une manière relative, c'est-à-dire selon la pureté, la bonne volonté ou la clairvoyance native des âmes" '[W]e arrive at this truth that everything is hieroglyphic and we know that symbols are obscure only in a relative way, that is, in accordance with the purity, the good will or the innate clearsightedness of souls [minds]' (2: 133). He cites Swedenborg as a confirmation that the unity of the world is correspondential, that is, metaphoric in nature, that form, movement, number, color, perfume, everything in the spiritual as in the natural world is significant and corresponding. Metaphoric and mysterious, hieroglyphic and corresponding are words that hint at the sacred character of the world and bridge the gap between old rituals and the modern poet's "sorcellerie évocatoire" in which language reclaims its magical powers, if not to reenact a religious event then to provoke the enchantment of the metaphoric vision.

Memory and Imagination

While Baudelaire uses words like correspondences, symbol, allegory, and metaphor, not dynamic patterns, in the cognitive perspective, the units he refers to are dynamic patterns. Moreover, Baudelaire's views of the process of painting and of the workings of memory are cognitive in their consequences and very advanced not just for his age but for ours as well.[6] In describing an important principle of drawing, he traces the tight relation between memory and imagination. He tells us that Constantin Guys, faithful to his own impressions, marks the highest or luminous points of an object, in an exaggeration useful to human memory, and that the spectator's imagination will in turn be subject to this tyrannical mnemonic and see clearly the impression things have left on the artist's mind.

This is why the true painters draw not from nature but "d'après l'image écrite dans leur cerveau" 'from the image written in their brain' (2: 698). The image is "written" because it belongs to poets as well as to painters and in cognitive terms represents their mnemonic potentials. The image in these potentials is the end result of an arduous work of interpretation. The painters Baudelaire admires train their memory and fill it with images. Clearly, these images are drawn from the visible universe, but in the process of acquisition they are interpreted, refashioned, and integrated. The cardinal principle is that the whole visible universe is nothing but "un magasin d'images et de signes auxquels l'imagination donnera une place et une valeur relative" 'a store of images and signs to which imagination will assign a place and a relative value' (2: 627). Memory and imagination have the same function and are, in fact, the same faculty.

The Metaphoric Field as a Generative Idea

Painters seek in this universal store, or dictionary to use Delacroix's term, the elements and images that are in harmony with their conception of the world and endow them with "a new physiognomy." The characters, their clothes, the background landscape, in a painting, all must serve to illuminate "l'idée génératrice" 'the generative idea' (2: 625). Just as a dream has to have its own atmosphere, the painter's conception, the composition, needs to move in its own colored milieu.[7] From this view of a generative idea, a characteristic atmosphere, and a milieu, to the concept of a metaphoric field with its own tension and coherence is but a step.

Taking that step, we can see that when a poet composes a text, his or her memory selects elements, or dynamic patterns, either from literary texts or from the visible world, transforms them, and assembles them in a mnemonic space, a metaphoric field, whose creative pressure or coherence is the consequence of the "generative idea," the original need to tell, to write, to communicate a story or a message. This coherence (milieu, color, tension) and the depth it implies are preserved in the patterns on the printed page, a potential that has to be actualized by readers. To do this they have to have enough corresponding materials in their memory, enough mnemonic potentials, to match, to identify, and to integrate the incoming structural stimuli from the text. The matching potentials represent knowledge readers obtain during previous interpretations, knowledge that gives them power to read.

The Power of the Text

Speaking of narrative as performance, Maclean defines the relationship between teller and audience or narrator and reader in the following terms: "Through a narrative text *I* meet *you* in a struggle which may be cooperative or may be combative, a struggle for knowledge, for power, for pleasure, for possession" (1988, xii). This aspect of reading needed to be emphasized. I would add that the central struggle is a struggle for meaning and that both reader and writer have to wage it. Also, while fully acknowledging the similarities between an oral performance and a written performance, one should point out an important difference. In the latter, the text cannot change direction in response to the reader's input. And the struggle between text and reader is an unbalanced struggle. The text is very powerful, in most cases more powerful than the reader. But it has one fatal weakness, which is that it becomes active and makes a riposte with the energy that comes from the reader. It is like the science fiction monster that earthlings attempt to kill; instead of dying, it gets stronger by converting the energy of their phasers.

The power of the text resides in the organization of its signifiers, in the coherence of its patterns, and in the original tension that issued from the act of composition. Nothing can be accomplished without the challenge of those patterns on the printed page and without a reasonable attention to the nuances of that challenge. But interpretation is a mnemonic process, a product of the reading memory.[8] Patterns, depth, and analogies locked in the blueprint of the text, all have to be re-created or rebuilt; they cannot constitute themselves and achieve transparency without the reader's memory as agent of re-creation.

Matching and integrating re-create the original tension, or a facsimile thereof, as a first step toward a comprehensive interpretation. The important thing to note is that our attempts to double the textual patterns do not stop at the shimmering surface of signifiers. After we have entered the field, which is equivalent to re-creating it, we can then go beyond and below its surface, and even step outside it for a final interpretive assessment. In a gesture that is not necessarily chronologically distinct from re-creation, the reader/critic may select other texts that show kinship with the text under scrutiny, that is to say, patterns that help illuminate its original tension and coherence. The last step, the maneuver to gain a more objective perspective and to obtain possible comparisons, is perhaps inevitable, but I maintain that it is not profitable to interpret a text from a certain distance without a re-creation of its field during a first reading.

The Original Coherence

The most obvious way we re-create the original coherence and create depth is by participating in the dramatic conflict as it takes place on the stage or in a text. This means having sufficiently developed mnemonic potentials to appreciate plot developments and reversals, surprises, and ironies and to re-create patterns and relations between patterns. We participate in the development of a poem or narrative when we understand and perhaps sympathize with its characters and situations and when its dynamic patterns appear to mimic our own gestures and preoccupations in the world. If the text is to attract us, its metaphoric field produced during reading must bear a relation to our vision of the world, either by confronting some of its important assumptions with surprising, even shocking, discoveries or by confirming our cherished desires and beliefs. Often a combination of the two is at work. Reading and writing fulfill basic human needs and cannot be reduced to intricate formulas that displace or dilute their goals.

The forces emitted by the text as organization of signs and the forces directed toward the text by the reader's mnemonic potentials are like an interplay of two currents moving to and away from the text. The best model for this type of critical interpretation is a passage in the *Iliad*, singled out by Leitch, in which the Trojans face the Greek encampment over a ditch and see a bird sign.[9] The eagle carrying a snake in its talons may be an omen, and the momentous decision about the conduct of the war will depend on the identification of its meaning. What signs mean or do not mean is dramatically posited by the disagreement between Poulydamas and Hector. The former, relying on his own mnemonic potentials as "an interpreter of the gods" (Lattimore trans., 1951, 12.228), counsels caution and suggests retreat; the latter, in his capacity as general of the apparently victorious army, relying on the text of the message previously sent to him by Zeus, orders the attack against the Achaian battlements. Appropriately enough, the sign suggests its meaning by mimicking, on the symbolic level, the conflict between the Trojans and the Greeks, which occurs on the level of the real. Clearly the coherence of the sign imitates the coherence of reality and simulates its complexity and depth; and the two antagonistic interpreters participate in the semiotic venture because they know that their decisions, instead of being an academic exercise, will have drastic consequences for them in the "real world."

Depth can also be obtained by reproducing the tension inherent in the opposition between past and present, or present and future; between remembering and the pressure of the surrounding circumstances; and between the consciousness of an identity in time and the resistance to it. A third way of attaining depth is through the regeneration of metaphors, through the collision of two simpler dynamic patterns. Complex sequences of metaphoric power engender both depth and precision. These three ways rely on the assumption that critical reading begins with the first reading and the re-creation of the author's vision.

The Question of Imports

There is, however, a fourth possibility to create psychological, ideological, or historical coherence through the reader/critic's textual or intertextual inferences and in the wake of analogies and associations of ideas. In a way that is similar to Hector's reliance on a previous text, contemporary critics import theoretical concepts from outside sources and insert them as a third factor in the equation of meaning, in the relation between mnemonic potentials and text. These concepts are usually ambiguous in nature: they are modified by the mnemonic potentials, perhaps by a desire to give a ludic performance, but they can also accommodate deliberate, politically motivated, ambitions. The danger is that the alien concepts, creating their own tension and agenda, may overwhelm the primary text, that is, the text under scrutiny.

Most critics have to do a balancing act between staying close to the text, that is, interpreting it in the direct light of their own potentials, and ranging far in search of pertinent concepts that will define their methodology and philosophy of approach. And because the preliminary move of introducing any texts to interpret another is already in itself an interpretation, critics have the responsibility of identifying them and clarifying their pertinence to the text under scrutiny. Granted that a critical statement on Baudelaire cannot prove anything, except by evidence and persuasion, we do want to know whether it aims at establishing Baudelaire's or, for example, Freud's coherence. The battle of approaches is crammed within the confines of the choice of comparative texts, whether the choice is deliberate or intuitive.[10]

As Homer's passages show, Hector's error was twofold: first, he was careless in interpreting Zeus's message, forgetting the qualifying clause specifying that the power is granted "'till he makes his way to the strong-benched vessels, / until the sun goes down and the blessed darkness comes over'" (Lattimore trans. 1951, 11.193–94); and second, a misinterpretation connected to the first error, he failed to see the affinity of the first text to the bird sign, to recognize that both the message and the sign were sent by the gods and that both contained temporal and dynamic limits imposed on his success. The accuracy of an interpretation will depend in large measure on the compatibility between the text to be interpreted and the critic's choice and understanding of the outside text or concepts.

Derrida's Gambit

These introductory remarks are far from exhausting the issue of imports but are intended as a clarification of the dilemma that any critic faces, especially in today's literary climate. The problem is rendered more acute by the fact that often critics are either unaware of the implications of their practice or unwilling to admit them. Derrida's analysis of Baudelaire's prose poem, "La Fausse monnaie" ("Counterfeit Money"), is a case in point.

To understand Derrida's interpretive move, it is useful to recapitulate here the short sequence of narrative events. Coming out of the tobacconist's, the narrator and his friend meet a beggar who holds out his cap asking for a donation. The friend gives the man a two franc silver coin [une pièce d'argent de deux francs], considerably more than the narrator's offering. When the narrator expresses his surprise, the friend explains that it was a counterfeit coin. By his explanation, he shows that he is sincere in thinking that he could at the same time perform a charitable act and strike a good deal, acquire paradise and economize at the same time. The narrator is shocked. He cannot forgive his friend for being bad through stupidity.

In the heat of his interpretive argument, Derrida catches himself saying that the narrator "thinks" and immediately is moved to open a parenthesis and explain:

> When we say that he thinks "more or less consciously," we are not probing his soul behind the surface of his utterances ... we are merely analyzing the semantic and intentional possibility of these utterances, such as they are readable on this very surface itself. (1992, 148–49)

The stress coming from his theoretical orientation is such that it forces him to give an explanation that contradicts his own analysis, which does not stay at the surface of utterances. Apparently because Baudelaire translated Longfellow's "The Peace Pipe," Derrida feels justified in stating that in the prose poem, tobacco "is the point of *departure,* to wit, the first partition or sharing [partage]; everything comes out of it, everything issues from it ..." (1992, 115). Although most critics know that Baudelaire translated Longfellow, few would make the connection. The mnemonic potentials are not a mechanical repository of knowledge. But Derrida needs the link between tobacco and sharing because he sees "Counterfeit Money" as a "libidinal drama," "the apparently homosexual duel that is played out not only in the story but in the narrative of 'Counterfeit Money'" (1992, 117).

I prefer to see in the story a variation of the anecdote Baudelaire mentioned in "L'École païenne" in which the villain is an artist who reserves a counterfeit coin for the poor (see 2: 49). "Le misérable" Baudelaire calls him. It is part of the poet's moral concerns, part of his vision of a world shot through with hypocrisy, meanness, and evil. The point here is that the individual under scrutiny could be any of a category of people who are not only evil (in Baudelairean terms) but stupid to boot. The fact that he is here introduced as a friend is incidental and is necessary neither to the moral of the story nor to its dynamics. The moral, like that of a La Fontaine fable, is not that the friend betrayed the bond between them, but that while there is no excuse for being mean, there is some merit in knowing that one is. In other words if there is a bond that has been broken it is between the friend and the ideal human beings conceived by the narrator. If we must have it, the betrayal is of the trust the narrator had in human nature, in his friend as a fellow human being and not just as a friend. I, thus, disagree with Derrida's interpretation, but this disagreement is not at issue.

What I wish to stress is that in his analysis of the prose poem, Derrida does not stop at the surface of utterances but goes far beyond it. Armed with psychoanalytical concepts, imbued with a Freudian view of human mentality, he draws his conclusions not by focusing on the textual fabric but by drawing upon premises originating outside the text. It is this intervention that creates additional depth both at the level of Baudelaire's text and at the level of Derrida's. The readers of the latter follow a bold enterprise in which a keen intellect and rich semantic associations create their own metaphoric dimensions. The conclusion discussing the "secret" "as to what Baudelaire, the narrator, or the friend meant to say or do, assuming that they themselves knew" (1992, 170), contributes further to this depth. While claiming to stay at the shimmering textual surface, Derrida stumbles into pressure points and mnemonic depth without seeing the gap between theory and practice. In the absence of textual signifiers indicating homosexuality, only already formed ideas about human beings, in this case psychoanalysis, could produce the kind of reading he offers and only the existence of the unconscious could justify such a reading.

That as deliberate a critic and philosopher as Derrida should be blind, at least in this particular case, to the implications of his own strategy is an indication that the difficulties are inherent in critical practice. I submit that the unconscious as a concept is just as problematic as the soul. In the past critics used the soul; today they use the unconscious, codes, conventions, effects of language, or mnemonic potentials. It does not matter; they are all part of the critical tools we use. The only advantage we can claim is to know, in a Baudelairean sense to be conscious of, what we are bringing to the text.

The Need for Intertextual Sources

The cognitive view also projects the necessity of bringing evidence from outside sources. It considers intertextual comparisons particularly effective, but insists on the need for a mnemonically detected affinity between the two texts that form the basis of an interpretation. And like other contemporary theories, this view does accept the use of outside concepts when it invokes mnemonic principles to understand the process of interpretation itself. But mnemonic potentials, dynamic patterns, and metaphoric fields are neutral concepts in their functional relation to specific texts, and while they may reveal how a text is organized, they do not specify in advance what its meaning is. The difference is that some approaches offer us ready-made interpretive formulas to apply to any text.

One may recall that, in the past, formalist dogmas prohibited intertextual references and comparisons. Today, going outside the text is not only not prohibited but openly championed. Among the factors that impel critics to make use of outside sources is that the language function of the primary text itself is implicitly committed to intertextual links. In using intertextual comparisons, the cognitive approach, the New Historicist contextual method, and other similar approaches appear as newer variations of the comparative method in literary criticism, which has always relied on the establishment of intertextual relations. But again, it is important that these relations be grounded on the mnemonic affinity of the texts involved.

A second factor in the critical venture's need for outside sources is its inherent tendency toward conceptualization and perhaps philosophical abstractions. At this level, criticism settles itself at the opposite pole from poetry and fiction, which cannot survive for long in the world of abstractions. There is, however, a third factor, more insidious than the rest, which is fed by the desire to impart authoritative aura to our interpretations. As critics we struggle or prosper depending on the manner and extent that our readings are seen as being "powerful," apt, and justified. And the authority of a popular theorist or philosopher is brought in to strengthen our arguments.

I say "are seen" because it is obvious, or it should be obvious, that any new interpretation or critical statement in turn will be interpreted by other readers/critics and that no statement can be efficacious, do the job it is intended to do, without their intervention. In a sense then, the concern with the interpretive efficacy of one's critical statement is a concern with acquiring readers and followers and, therefore, with gaining power.

The Reliance on Memory

The foregoing remarks are meant to point out the inherent problems that plague our interpretive venture. The introductory gesture is also meant to explain why, in the following pages, the main concerns are to detect mnemonically valid intertextual affinities. The decisions of the individual memory are preferable because memory is the most reliable instrument to measure the reality of texts or any other reality. And memory-produced affinities invite appraisals by memory. That is to say, when a new reader has to judge the accuracy of a textual or intertextual relation identified by the critic, that reader can and will rely on his or her memory. But if the critic brought in a concept from outside to help establish that relation, only the outside authority can guarantee its validity. Looking to authorities for guidance can have unexpected and unwanted consequences. Not simply because personal initiative would be lost, but also because in the ensuing power struggle for control, individual freedom would diminish. We need more tolerance for the individual freedom of interpretation.

Properly understood, the concept of individual freedom does not go against tradition but is tradition's essential impulse. As Baudelaire's contribution itself proves it, tradition is not something static, fixed forever in closely guarded archives, but a dynamic current of metaphoric thought, in constant revision and rewriting. I wholeheartedly agree with Brooks's persuasive argument that the canon, or by implication the larger tradition it points to, "is a historically contingent cultural formation" (1994, 521); but precisely for that reason I cannot agree that there are "systems of meaning production" (1994, 522). Meaning is not produced by systems but by individual memory that becomes communal memory when it is incorporated into a tradition. In the cognitive view, individual freedom and tradition are engaged in a struggle for survival; theirs is a force relationship, and the equilibrium they reach is dynamic, in constant flux. Language itself, at the center of this power struggle, though indeed preexisting, is not static but constantly changing: not only because we had Greek and Latin while now we have many languages, but also because English itself is not the English of Shakespeare but the English of Ted Hughes or W. D. Snodgrass, and French is no longer the French of Racine but the French of Yves Bonnefoy and others. And although in confronting reality and literature, in processing and interpreting a myriad of texts, memory undergoes sometimes fundamental changes in its tenor and capacity, as a meaning-producing instrument it remains our most dependable guide.

The reliance on memory implies facing Baudelaire frontally and identifying, through the organization of signifiers, the coherence of his own drive to meaning. It means reviewing the issue of identity in the face of the strong tendency to market a Baudelaire driven by ideology or to promote his works, the prose poems in particular, as the site of self-scattering. Is the self, the self that Baudelaire himself sees, an imaginary self in the Lacanian sense? Is it the product of ideology? If so, it would have to be an ideology that binds such disparate figures as Montaigne, Coleridge, and Baudelaire. That is, one would have to have some reasonable indication that such an ideology exists as distinct from other ideologies. Can we with Hume attribute the notion of identity to pride? Or side with Nietzsche and declare that self-consciousness is a fiction?[11] My claim is that the critical concepts, the instruments of research we bring to the texts in question, will shape our answers and that the self's shifting ground will be a dependent variable of the epicenter of perspective.

A Modest Goal

Does Baudelaire exist then? No, not did he live more than a century ago, but do his works persuade us to believe in the existence of a unified center that inspires and sanctions those forms, passions, and concepts that we consistently call Baudelairean? To see such a center in an instant of time, to capture in one dynamic pattern, in one knot, all the strands that form his works and life, would require a Dantean global perspective, ideal lenses, and a frontal approach driven by superhuman power. Clearly such a goal remains elusive. Instead, the cognitive approach adopted here selects characteristic works, necessarily limiting the exploration to a few chosen texts, which can give an indication of the existence of such a center and of the essential unity of Baudelaire's works. The more modest ambition is to identify textual affinities, distinguish governing dynamic patterns, and define the coherence these patterns create; in short, it is to produce interpretations that stay as close as possible to the primary texts.[12]

In addition to relying on textual comparisons, I have also made use, and deliberately so, of the opinions of other critics on specific points of interpretation. This gesture is not meant to establish a present state of Baudelairean studies, or to say that these opinions are in complete harmony with mine, but to confirm important points of pressure that in a cognitive perspective the text itself is already geared to reveal. Regardless of whether one agrees or disagrees with the views of other critics or readers, the fact that they choose to comment on a textual pattern indicates that the pattern has an important function in the organization of the whole. The procedure of putting side by side different interpretations helps our understanding of the text; it also suggests that a theory can be judged by its interpretive results.

A Brief Summary

The first chapter deals with the unity of the self, its limits, and the manner in which they are transgressed to establish contact with others. Although this transgression appears as an issue of personality, its dynamics tells the story of the constitution of texts. It reflects the manner in which basic needs, namely the desire to obtain concentration, to be the hero "who is immovably centred," and the need to contact the others, to enrich one's personality and creative potential, enter into the equation of meaning. In this view the texts themselves are products of the narrator's interpretation of reality and cannot be conceived as a fulguration of language alone.

The second chapter explores the tension created by the presence of the two allegiances to God and to Satan. It emphasizes that Baudelaire's texts, and "Le Mauvais vitrier" and "Mademoiselle Bistouri" in particular, are evidence of the poet's contact with reality in a world of fundamental limits. In the first of the two prose poems, the transgression of the borders between self and others is prompted by demonic forces, and yet it is a reflection of the narrator's drive toward an ideal, an artificial paradise, accompanied by perils to the unity of the self. The drive becomes, thus, an attempt to transgress the limits imposed upon the human condition. In the second prose poem, these limits become more formidable yet, setting barriers to interpretation and to knowledge.

The third chapter examines the relation to the woman chosen to be celebrated in love poems, in this case Mme Sabatier. In "A celle qui est trop gaie" and "Réversibilité," the Maistrian concept of reversibility modulates the poet's attempt to overcome or transgress the limits separating those who are physically and spiritually privileged and those who are not. Each poem mimics respectively the negative and the positive pole of a theological principle espoused by Baudelaire under the influence of Joseph de Maistre, which makes it possible for the suffering and merits of the innocent to benefit the guilty. Under the influence of Gautier's (and perhaps Nerval's) romantic notion of predestination, however,

Baudelaire modifies the relation: the innocent do not know suffering, while those who are less fortunate can only hope to escape
suffering through the intercession of the chosen.

The fourth chapter studies the strategies of the artist, in "Une
Mort héroïque," to veil the terrors of the abyss and death and,
thus, to discover his limits in time. A comparison with Eliot's "Murder in the Cathedral" and Anouilh's "Becket" reveals that it is
precisely the mime's and Becket's failure to transcend the limitations of the human condition and the knowledge of that failure
that confer upon the mysteries of religion and upon the mystique
of art their most enduring prestige. This chapter confirms once
again the viability of the comparative method and shows that the
main requirement for its success is the existence of affinities
among the texts to be compared.

The fifth chapter reexamines Andromache's role in "Le Cygne"
and her contribution to the creation of the myth of exile. Baudelaire's attempt to transcend exile by the creation of this myth and
to outstrip suffering by gaining access to the suffering of others
reveals a commitment to bind his fate to the destiny of other exiles
and, therefore, to the realm of poetry.

The sixth chapter establishes the mythic limits of the unknown.
Specifically, it shows through intertextual evidence, using again
the comparative method, that the victory of time in "Le Voyage"
does not signify death. What section vii of the poem does is resurrect the tradition of the voyage to the Underworld on the model
of the epic tradition of Homer, Dante, Tennyson and others. "Le
Voyage" emerges as a modern epic, a vast synthesis of sources,
that all speak, echo, and reaffirm a tradition in the very act of
going beyond it.

The seventh chapter takes another look at the all-important
question of Baudelaire's allegories and their relation to the theory
of correspondences. And a final chapter of concluding remarks
offers a view of Baudelaire's struggle to achieve unity in his life
and work.

1

Baudelaire
and the Unity of the Self

The Challenge to the Speaking Subject

Contemporary critics are often moved to see the Baudelairean narrator as a self with a mediated identity or as a fragmented self and in effect to meet on common ground those who have in one form or another proclaimed the death of the subject. Death, however, is not so much an event but a loss of status associated with speaking and writing. Thus, Barthes's claim that the author dies when writing begins is, at least in part, predicated on the belief that a "disconnection occurs" between narrator and narrative and that "the voice loses its origin" (1977, 142).[1] In Lacan's ontology the division is between the subject's ego (*moi*) and the "I" (*je*) of his discourse (1977, 90).[2] For Barthes, it is language that "calls into question all origins" (1977, 146) and for Lacan, "the subject as such is uncertain because he is divided by the effects of language" (1977a, 188). Clearly, though belonging to different theoretical frameworks, death and division are both a consequence of the intervention of language, which appears to appropriate the role of the subject, in the production of meaning.

Other theorists move in the same direction and assign priority to language. Foucault proposes that "the subject (and its substitutes) must be stripped of its creative role and analysed as a complex and variable function of discourse" (1977, 138). For him, the fact "that man has 'come to an end,'" emerges "from within language," "in the play of its possibilities" (1970, 383). Derrida maintains that while it constitutes it and dislocates it at the same time, "l'écriture est autre que le sujet, en quelque sens qu'on l'entende" 'writing is other than the subject, in whatever sense one understands it' (1967, 100).[3]

Against this background, Baudelairean critics have been explor-

34

ing more specific ways in which the narrator's self loses its standing or becomes fragmented. The dangers to its prestige and unity
can be reduced to two closely interrelated categories. One is the
idea, with Lacanian overtones, that the speaking subject in a text
is a mediator whose identity is difficult to separate from, and to
conceive independently of, the objects of mediation.[4] The other
is the application of the rhetorical resources of language to the
creation of texts, a danger coming "from within language," "in
the play of its possibilities."[5] As to the first, since the perceptual
data from the outside world, about other selves or about our own,
are also mediated, that is, coded in the form of images (dynamic
patterns) and submitted to memory by our peripheral organs
of perception, the process of mediation alone cannot justify the
skepticism about the self's ontological reality, unless we are prepared to extend this skepticism beyond literary texts to all knowledge. The danger to the unity (or reality) of the self accrues not
so much from mediation but from the force and multiplicity of
the mediating images. In the second category, the dispersive tendencies of language represent a similar, though perhaps a more
consistent, danger. But these language tendencies are met by
equally strong forces that oppose them and oppose them through
language, through the textual tension engendered by the urgency
to write. I do not deny the centrifugal force, the characteristic
semantic or rhetorical pull in many directions, but point also to
its opposite, a centripetal movement, whose origins are the origins
of language itself.

A Baudelairean Dialectics

In this perspective, prepared and clarified by Baudelaire's own
critical writings, unity and fragmentation (or dispersion) appear
as two interdependent forces opposing each other.[6] In a cryptic
formula Baudelaire proposes a balance between them: "De la vaporisation et de la centralisation du *Moi*. Tout est là" 'Dissipation
and centralization of the *Self*. That sums it up' ("Mon coeur" 1:
676). With Emerson, he understands dispersion and its various
synonyms precisely in relation to a self that exists, that opposes it
and aims to remain "immovably centred" ("Hygiène" 1: 674).
What the poet's proposition suggests is that dissipation can only
be conceived as a function of centralization, in effect, a function
of the existence of the self that can accomplish both. Elsewhere
he says: "Le goût de la concentration productive doit remplacer,

chez un homme mûr, le goût de la déperdition" 'The taste for productive concentration must in a mature individual take the place of the taste for dissipation' ("Fusées" 1: 649).

My claim is that the Baudelairean relation between concentration and dispersion mirrors the opposition between the centripetal force of the creative impulse and the centrifugal movement of language. Concentration means desire to be alone, centralization of the powers of the self, strengthening of its defenses; dispersion, which in its extreme form equals loss of identity, appears as a consequence of the need to contact the crowd, the creative need to multiply and enrich one's personality. As Baudelaire's narrator participates in the conflict between the two opposite tendencies, we begin to recognize, in their interplay, the dynamics and identity of a self, to detect a presence in the speaking voice—not necessarily the image of a historical Baudelaire, but one that stands in a relationship of complementarity with it.

The self, Baudelairean or any other, is projected by a multiplicity of signs, an organization of dynamic patterns, onto a cognitive plane. But this projection is not necessarily defined by static images or patterns in the text; it is defined by the dynamics of the subject's creative impulse, by the transformations and distortions that the self imposes on reality and by other metaphoric and dynamic forces in the text. It is, thus, a dynamic self, which, like fire, cannot be cut with an analytical knife, and which emerges in a dialectical movement of its own birth and death, of transgression and retrenchment, of encounters with others and with itself.

The Tyranny of the Human Face

Traversed by the twin impulses to communicate with the others and to escape their presence, to flee "la tyrannie de la face humaine" 'the tyranny of the human face' ("À une heure," 1: 287 and "Un mangeur d'opium," 1: 483), the Baudelairean self faces the apparently contradictory needs to strengthen the lines that separate it from the world, but also to overcome them as one overcomes obstacles that have to be crossed. In "À une heure du matin," the overwhelming impulse is to defend and fortify the separating borders: "Enfin! il m'est donc permis de me délasser dans un bain de ténèbres! D'abord, un double tour à la serrure. Il me semble que ce tour de clef augmentera ma solitude et fortifiera les barricades qui me séparent actuellement du monde" 'Finally! So I'm allowed to relax in a bath of darkness! First, a double turn in the lock. I think this turn of the key will increase my solitude and fortify the barricades at present separating me from the world' (1: 287, Kaplan 16). A spy or detective narrative could not enhance the suspense of this relief at the realization of being safe from the world. What he fears is not so much a specific event, but the world, the relentless face of the human condition, what in a letter to his mother he calls the degraded Parisian race (see 1973, 2: 254). The others then, with a few exceptions, are not just hostile but inferior, abject, decadent, and capable of invading his room and the borders of his personality, the inner sanctum of the self. And, in fact, the precautions he takes to avert the danger, to assure the strength of the insurrectionist barricades, are themselves evidence that corroborates the existence of the self.

What is particularly Baudelairean as a motivating force in the desire to be alone, and therefore as a force that unifies the self, is not just the horror that the narrator experiences in facing the universal stupidity of his fellow human beings but also the ironic twinges of conscience. Was he contaminated by the contact with the others? He shook hands with many, without the precaution of wearing gloves. The self can be protected from the corruption, lies, and stupidity of others, but it has very little defense against the corruption from within. Having bragged about several nasty actions he never committed and cowardly having denied misdeeds he did perform, he is unhappy with everybody and with himself. While the dispersion of the self and the displacement of moral energy occur during social interaction, either directly from a disruptive contact or from the decisions the self has to make when confronted with the others, the sustained awareness that this interaction marks the boundaries of his personality and defines what he is and who he is takes place in the solitude of the locked room. Here in the "bain de ténèbres," the darkness that blocks the stream of outside stimuli, a memory maintaining the continuity of the voice, linking various moments in time to create an identity, and a flesh and blood human being meet and, in an encounter whose authenticity would be hard to surpass, lay the foundation of the Baudelairean self.

In "Les Foules" opposing the centripetal self-examination, the centrifugal movement toward "un bain de multitude" 'a bath of multitude' extends the limits of the self: "Le poète jouit de cet incomparable privilège, qu'il peut à sa guise être lui-même et autrui. Comme ces âmes errantes qui cherchent un corps, il entre, quand il veut, dans le personnage de chacun" 'The poet enjoys the incomparable privilege of being able, at will, to be himself and another. Like those wandering souls seeking a body, he enters, when he wants, into everyone's character' (1: 291, Kaplan 21).

The dynamic similarity between the centrifugal and centripetal movements is underscored by the use of the same expression "bain de" and, as if that were not enough, the equilibrium resulting from their opposition is underlined: "Multitude, solitude: termes égaux et convertibles pour le poète actif et fécond" 'Multitude, solitude: equal and interchangeable terms for the active and fertile poet' (1: 291, Kaplan 21). Convertible not in the sense that one would take the place of the other and eliminate it, but in the sense that they represent tendencies of equal force that can counterbalance each other. In portraying the Baudelairean dandy, Lemaire points out the contradiction: "haine du monde et besoin de contact avec ce monde" 'hatred of the world and need to be in contact with this world' (1978, 57). But this polarity is an essential paradox of a self whose dynamics can be more accurately understood neither while it joins the crowd nor while it is alone but at the moment when the two movements reveal their interdependence.[7]

In the act of transgressing its limits and entering the body of another, the self acquires new knowledge and experience. The imperative is to remain the active principle that initiates the exchange, to maintain one's identity in a homeostatic equilibrium, and to avoid being engulfed by the others. In the manner of the tragic actors of antiquity who wore masks to identify themselves in their roles, the old acrobat, the mime, the bad glazier are disguised and yet proclaim themselves as Baudelairean alter egos.[8] In each case, the image of a fictional character enters consciousness as a reflection of the self, but the coherence of its relation to the speaking voice betrays the existence of a dynamic center. Despite the impression of fragmentation that the variety of alter egos may create, the self remains capable of recognizing its identity.[9]

A Superior Eroticism

The exploration of what makes the narrator different and unique becomes a strategy intended to heal the moral division within his will and intentionality. In "Les Foules" the act of "the soul" giving itself to others is set against "what people call love" to delineate the borders of his identity. The narrator does not share the common and vulgar notion of love, and his irony is there to draw the line and underscore the difference. Throughout the comparison, however, he maintains the dynamics of a sexual encounter, speaking, for example, of entering the body of another, or of giving oneself completely to the stranger who passes by, to indicate that his contact with the crowd is a superior substitute for the way the egoists experience love. He projects his experience onto a sensual and erotic plane. The operative words are "jouir de la foule" 'enjoying the crowd,' "épouse (la foule)" 'embraces (the crowd),' "ivresse" 'intoxication,' "jouissances fiévreuses" 'feverish pleasures,' "ineffable orgie" 'indescribable orgy,' "sainte prostitution" 'saintly prostitution.'[10] The superiority of this eroticism soon becomes clear; for unlike the common experience of love, which is presumably base and instinctual, the narrator's communion with the crowd attains a higher level. The words "universelle communion" 'universal communion,' "sainte" 'holy,' "poésie et charité" 'poetry and charity,' are indications that the metaphoric dimension of the text has the task of defining that level and of granting the narrator his spiritual depth. When at the end he enlarges his concept to associate it with the experience of founders of colonies and exiled missionaries, he creates a family for himself, a category of persons of genius, to draw the line of his difference from the fortunate of this world, who in their arrogance have no conception of the superior and refined happiness that the elite can experience. Just as retrenchment was characterized by spiritual renewal, so too expansion gives him a sense of belonging, a family in the realm of the spirit. As the prayer at the end of "À une heure du matin" makes it clear, this family comprises not only the souls of those the narrator has loved, but also the souls of those he has celebrated in his poetry. We are here at the core of the Baudelairean self.

The spiritual energy of the prayer in "À une heure du matin" rises from a desire to attain a greater degree of moral purity. But alone in the room, facing his own fallible self, recognizing both his difference and the corruption that makes him like the others, the narrator is forced to see that the drive toward moral purity can be successful only in the context of a superior aesthetic accomplishment. Although he wants to redeem himself, redemption is defined in terms of solitude, in terms of a separation from the others and does not stipulate moral action. Instead it is through the production of "quelques beaux vers" 'some fine poems' that he will affirm his difference and graft desire to identity.[11] And in turn, this literary creation exacts a contact with the others, the union between subject and object, "créer une magie suggestive contenant à la fois l'objet et le sujet, le monde extérieur à l'artiste et l'artiste lui-même" 'creating a suggestive magic containing both the object and the subject, the world external to the artist and the artist himself or herself' ("L'Art philosophique" 2: 598). Thus, the dilemma he faces is that, although they are necessary, both the "bain de solitude" and "bain de multitude" are accompanied by hazards to the equilibrium of the self: The first lacks some elements of its constitution; the second may result in a blurring or loss of personality boundaries. Solitude offers awareness of his biological identity but has no cure for the feeling of inferiority. To "prove" the value of his moral identity in a comparison with others he needs poetry; therein lies his strength. Thus, even more than erotic desire, it is writing conceived as a substitute that forces him to resort to the "bain de multitude," to enter the region of his difference in the presence of the others and to risk identity contamination, corruption, and dissipation. The pressing need is to retain limits and boundaries, the purity and integrity of the self, and at the same time increase its powers of analysis and representation. Let us examine the matter.

The Dynamics of Exchange

"Le Vieux saltimbanque" is a good example of the economy of exchange between the artist and the world. The narrator is again plunged in the "bain de multitude" on a day when the populace is enjoying a Parisian entertainment, acrobats, animal acts, dancing girls, etc. Against the background of universal joy and noise, a poor traveling acrobat appears as the silent image of the man of letters, the poet who no longer can amuse anyone, who is without friends, without family, forgotten. Musset too is haunted at various stages of life by a specter, who is both his mirror image in mourning and the allegory of solitude. But this brother in misfortune appears and disappears with the facility of a hallucination (see "La Nuit de décembre" 41–46). On the other hand, in "Le Vieux saltimbanque" the acrobat and his wretched shack are only too real. But as the narrator watches, the acrobat's own gaze reaches out to him and establishes the cathartic bond that prepares the transformation, the drive toward the allegorical level. As so often in Baudelaire's work, an ordinary spectacle, a swan, an old man, becomes a source of visions and reveals "la profondeur de la vie" 'the depth of life' ("Fusées" 1: 659). The revelation itself is both a transformation of the real and a breaking down of the barriers that separate the self from the other, enabling it to enter the identity of the other and begin the transfer of energies. In the exchange, the old acrobat absorbs some of Baudelaire's own idiosyncrasies and the self acquires some of the qualities of the defeated, but once successful, performer. In this extraordinary text, the poet projects onto the old acrobat's mute gaze his own prophetic future, the aphasia he will be stricken with during the last months of his life.[12] And as paradoxical as that may seem, instead of blurring the contours of the two identities, the process keeps them distinct, but redefines the self to incorporate the consequences of the exchange.

This, then, is a key to the dynamics of identity: a cathartic passport to cross the barriers of difference and establish free trade in an enhanced economy. Catharsis is at once the means to define oneself as subject, as a discrete self, and the privilege to inhabit the object's body and mind. Often as one would expect, Baudelaire has the cathartic experience in encounters with figures of the suffering artist. Just as often, however, he is struck by figures of the widow par excellence: Andromache in "Le Cygne," the widows in "Les Veuves," and the woman in mourning in "À une passante." Perhaps one could include in this category the protagonists of "Les Petites vieilles," and "Les Fenêtres," although there is no overt statement that they are widows.

The Allegorical Other

The anonymous widows who appear in the spotlight distinguish themselves by some qualities that elevate them above the surrounding crowd. But in "Les Veuves" the physical presence and demeanor of the woman, her noble appearance, her sadness and mourning, reflecting her suffering, are attributes that are not meant to draw the portrait of one woman but of a whole category of women.[13] The dejection, the hollow eyes, and the wrinkles are all characteristics of older women as opposed to younger, of poor women rather than rich women, of women as victims. Like "Mademoiselle Bistouri," the text stresses the observer's active role as interpreter. The "innumerable legends" that the narrator deciphers in the features of the widow as victim betray the contours of his own legend and are emblematic of his tendency to read into the perceptual text his own identity. Brugière speaks of Coleridge's instinct "to exist in the form of others" (qtd. 1983, 248) and adds: "cette soif d'altérité masque le désir de se connaître et de s'éprouver par l'entremise d'un objet extérieur" 'this thirst for

alterity masks the wish to know and test oneself through the intervention of an external object' (1983, 248). How this external object
intervenes and how memory processes the text of the world is
crucial to the understanding of the relationship between the self
and the patterns of otherness.

Since the desire is to know oneself, what survives in the radical
transformation of the others is what the narrator discovers at the
moment he confronts them, precisely that part of them that the
dynamics of allegory allows him to call his own.[14] The danger
associated with this enterprise is that the reinscription of one's
own desire allegorically fashioned in the text of reality could render the individualities of the others anemic or could, in a counter-
productive way, deprive them of the power to speak. Chambers
points out that, in "Les Tableaux parisiens," the effect of the
communicational act "is to convey a sense of his speech activity as
lonely, and most often futile, verbal gesturing. The interlocutors
he takes and whom he addresses or questions are unable to hear
him, let alone reply" (1987, 100). One wonders if Baudelaire's
stance, the apparent lack of communication, can be reduced to a
position of radical solipsism that would negate the gains of the
narrator as a Parisian prowler who seeks contact with the new
and, therefore, the others. Thélot has asked the question in connection with poem XXIV ("Je t'adore"): "De sorte qu'il faut demander au poème s'il parle effectivement à autrui, ou s'il n'est pas
un solipsisme" 'So that one has to ask the poem if it actually speaks
to the other, or if it is a solipsism' (1993, 436).

In the context of a psychological realism in which both plot
and character study have to be highlighted, Baudelaire's failure
to grant the others their own desires would mean emptying them
of their freedom, depriving them of the effigy of individuality. It
would be a flaw. However, since the prose poems were not meant
to be realistic short stories in the manner of Balzac or Maupas-
sant, the lack of verbal contribution from the actors of the dramas
may simply reflect the writer's initial choice to produce an internal
dialogue, adapted to the "ondulations de la rêverie" 'ripples of
reverie' (1: 276). Although Baudelaire did make use of dialogue to
create short character sketches (like those in "La Fausse monnaie,"
"Perte d'auréole," and especially "Mademoiselle Bistouri"), he
seems to have relied more often on the exchange powers of the
eyes rather than on the eloquence of the voice. The old acrobat's
gaze, for example, accompanied by an entropy of action and
speech, communicates not less because it is mute but more. The
prophecy foreshadowing the end could not be proffered, if he

were to be given the prerogatives of language. The case of "A une passante" is more problematic.

Precisely why is the exchange between the two limited to the eyes and devoid of voice and in a deafening street, no less? Contrary to what happens in "Mademoiselle Bistouri," here the narrator does not join the woman. And he neither speaks to her nor joins her for the same reason, which can be interpreted in many different ways. There may be those who see this refusal in the context of Baudelaire's identification of the woman with his mother. And to the limited extent that it was superimposed on the woman, the image of the widowed mother may have been the dark attraction, "en grand deuil," of the initial stimulus. For his part, Thélot believes that the refusal is necessary to the work of art itself and that Baudelaire saw again in "A une passante" that form, therefore poetry, is a lie, "une fidélité à l'échec" 'a loyalty to failure' (1993, 492). Yet, in spite of this loyalty or perhaps because of it, one of the greatest strengths of the poem, its ontological tension, is generated by the dilemma of the desire to join the passerby and the unwillingness or inability to do so. The narrator's failure on the existential level is Baudelaire's success on the aesthetic terrain. But is it an experiential failure? Without contradicting Thélot's insight and making abstraction of some practical reasons that may have prevented the narrator from going with the woman, one can argue that he has, in fact, established precisely the kind of contact he desired and that he is living or reliving his dream in the human presence of the ideal beauty, wedding a real face, dress, and leg to the perfect eyes, sex to aesthetics, pleasure to sweetness, and lightning to eternity. The contact may already represent a union and at least a partial fulfillment of sexual desire.

An Uneasy Partnership with Nature

What is certain is that this encounter with a passerby is paradigmatic of Baudelaire's relation to reality. The magic surges from the union of subject and object. The woman is identified, chosen, placed in a correspondential mode, and compelled to yield the mystery of her allegorical face, to reveal "la profondeur de la vie." It is a depth that is at the same time a manner of being in the midst of discovery, the overwhelming input of the other, which sometimes may subsume verbal expression, and a correspondential activity of language, the metaphoric (allegorical or symbolic) power of words lining up their black sequences on the white paper.

Imagining Constantin Guys at work, in the evening after a day of observation, Baudelaire describes this process: "Et les choses renaissent sur le papier, naturelles et plus que naturelles, belles et plus que belles, singulières et douées d'une vie enthousiaste comme l'âme de l'auteur" 'And things are reborn on paper, natural and more than natural, beautiful and more than beautiful, unique and endowed with passionate life like the soul of the author' (2: 693–94).[15] Clearly, the newly created world bears the seal of the author's originality, but Baudelaire leaves no doubt that "La fantasmagorie a été extraite de la nature" 'The phantasmagoria has been extracted from nature' (2: 694). The painter or the poet is the initiator, the governing Logos, while nature remains the mother principle from which the new forms issue forth.[16]

The fact that, perhaps more often than most writers, Baudelaire adopted a dominant, and domineering, approach versus nature does in no way contravene the essence of the relationship. It is not by accident that he sees it sometimes as a duel in which the artist is vanquished and exclaims at the end of a prose poem: "Nature, enchanteresse sans pitié, rivale toujours victorieuse, laisse-moi!" 'Nature, enchantress without pity, rival always victorious, leave me alone!' ("Le *Confiteor*" 1: 278–79) This is an almost-never-equal partnership of self and non-self, in which imagination and nature are inextricably linked in a way that goes beyond questions of who gets credit for what.

In "Les Fenêtres," as in "A une passante," the narrator begins at the point of contact with reality, with an actual person he sees, a poor woman he catches sight of beyond the roofs of Paris. Then his mnemonic potentials come into play: "Avec son visage, avec son vêtement, avec son geste, avec presque rien, j'ai refait l'histoire de cette femme, ou plutôt sa légende, et quelquefois je me la raconte à moi-même en pleurant" 'With her face, her clothing, her gestures, with almost nothing, I have refashioned that woman's history, or rather her legend, and sometimes I tell it to myself weeping' (1: 339, Kaplan 93). It is clear that what he narrates is the process of his own interpretation of reality, the steps of the creation of the prose poem, of the new text. He ends the poem saying: "Qu'importe ce que peut être la réalité placée hors de moi, si elle m'a aidé à vivre, à sentir que je suis et ce que je suis?" 'Does it matter what the reality located outside of me might be, if it has helped me to live, to feel that I am and *what* I am?' (1: 339, Kaplan 93) There are very few passages that express more eloquently the role of catharsis in the definition of one's identity. The prose poem is not about the woman's legend but about the poet's legend, the legend of a Parisian prowler who lives on allegorical (or symbolic) annuities and invests only moderately in the purely objective accounts of the real.

But again, even though the materials at his disposal, the details furnished by the outside world, are sketchy, "with her face," "with almost nothing," it would be a mistake to conclude that the helping reality is unimportant. Whether reality is only a catalyst or the very foundation of the text, subject and object are inextricably linked and the proposition of choosing between invention and disclosure may not be a viable alternative.[17]

Beyond the Courtroom Truth: The Chromosomes of Reality

What is crucial to the understanding of the relationship between subject and object, however, is a look at the opposition between truth and fiction. In this context, Kaplan alertly points out that the woman's legend remained "unwritten" and concludes: "The writer-narrator challenges interpreters to evaluate the paradox that his substance as a person in the world—*what* he is, that is, a writer—derives from untruth" (1990, 125). The question then is, why would an author, engaged in writing fiction, frustrate our expectation and curiosity and leave out this legend, which should be the essence of fiction, of untruth?[18] The omission may suggest that the prose poem is not a piece of pure fiction.

More than anything else, it is a statement about a cognitive experience, which mimics its own production. The narrator is more intent on marking the stresses of the mitotic division between the material and the symbolic chromosomes of reality, that is, the transformations of reality within the bounds of his experience, than of telling the story of the woman. The concern for truth emerges precisely as an essential consequence of the separation, at the heart of reality, of the referent's symbolic constituent from its material component. As soon as the question "Are you sure that this legend is the true one?" is introduced into the act of writing, the counterquestion intervenes, "Does it matter?" No, not does it matter what its symbolic or metaphoric identity is, for if that were the case, he would not shed tears in the telling of it. But does its material identity, which cannot be fully absorbed, the residue left after the original division, matter? And the answer is that if this remnant is available, or still available, for coding, then contrary to the narrator's answer, we would say it does matter. Unfortunately, reality is hardly ever available for processing in its totality, hence the concern for truth, the need for interpretation, and the inevitability of the metaphoric discourse.

In debating the status of truth, the ending of the poem echoes Pilate's question "What is truth?" The irony here is that Pilate challenges the notion of courtroom truth precisely in his role as a judge. To a certain extent the narrator himself adopts a similar role, attempting to decide how much credit the woman herself should receive for the cathartic experience. To have an answer to the question whether or not the legend is true, to assess the value of truth, one has to recall the poet's messianic voice, affirming that poetry is "ce qu'il y a de plus réel, c'est ce qui n'est complètement vrai que dans *un autre monde*" 'the thing that is the most real, that is completely true only in *another world*' ("Puisque réalisme il y a" 2: 59). This statement goes a long way toward explaining why Baudelaire chose not to elaborate on the woman's legend; for if it is only true in another world, her "story" is a matter of belief, an appeal to the power of imagination in the face of the near-impossibility of divulging what one knows about "truth" and about poetry.

This fatigue in the face of interrogation and this refusal to answer or elaborate on a matter, in itself extremely difficult, are further confirmed by the self's fear of being misunderstood. If one looks at Baudelaire's "Projets de préfaces," one sees that his first impulse was to emulate Edgar Allan Poe and to teach his readers the science of poetry in twenty lessons (see 1: 183), in other words, to explain the unexplainable. However, in practical terms, such a step would prove superfluous and he resorts to the stratagem that some people would use to justify their faith in miracles: "Ceux qui savent me devinent, et pour ceux qui ne peuvent ou ne veulent pas comprendre, j'amoncellerais sans fruit les explications" 'Those who know understand me, and for those who cannot or are unwilling to understand, I would pile up explanations without success' (1: 182). For how is one to explain the dynamics of a poetry that can be fully understood only from a perspective beyond the space of the real? How is one to prove a truth whose best evidence is the vision of the invisible? The reference to another world corroborates Raser's conclusion about Baudelaire's art criticism: "The burden of theory and description in art criticism is to prove the unprovable, to put the inconceivable in conceptual terms, and this is also the burden of art" (1989, 88).

Truth and Vision: Anti-Foucault

What is truth then? Or, rather, how can truth be proven? The answer that those who know understand and need no proof is another way of saying that the mind is the only instrument to judge what is true and what is not. Baudelaire's aesthetic is, thus, founded on the vision and cognitive functions of the individual. To Foucault's "truth," produced and sustained by systems of power (see 1980, 133), Baudelaire opposes truth as a function of the individual's freedom from systems of power and from established norms:

> L'artiste, le vrai artiste, le vrai poète, ne doit peindre que selon qu'il voit et qu'il sent. Il doit être *réellement* fidèle à sa propre nature. Il doit éviter comme la mort d'emprunter les yeux et les sentiments d'un autre homme, si grand qu'il soit; car alors les productions qu'il nous donnerait seraient, relativement à lui, des mensonges, et non des *réalités.*

> The artist, the true artist, the true poet, must paint only in accordance with what he or she sees and feels. He or she must be *truly* faithful to his or her own nature. He or she must avoid like the plague borrowing the eyes and feelings of another man or woman, no matter how great the latter is; for then the productions that he or she would give us would be, with regard to him or her, lies, and not *realities.* ("Salon de 1859" 2: 620)

The passage defines the self in terms of its way of seeing, in terms of the difference between one's capacity to see and the capacity of others to see. This is what Proust will later call the qualitative difference in the way the world appears to us (see 1954, 3: 895). And when Baudelaire sees the old woman the way he does he is first and foremost faithful to his own nature, to his own legend, and only secondarily so to her story. To be true to himself as a poet, he has to have a stake in the reality he describes. But his task is to discern the symbolic face of the real and not simply its material profile. Subject and object have to face each other in the dance of interpretation.

Since neither the poet nor anyone else can know all the elements of the woman's actual story, attempting to tell it could be only partially successful. Offering additional details would betray the fact that no matter how great their number, they can never fulfill the promise of completeness and always point to the need for interpretation. Only an absolute being would not need interpretation because it would know everything including the "real" story of the woman. Nevertheless, and despite Baudelaire's hatred for it, reality remains essential to his art, not in the sense that the events he relates took place in real life (some did not; and those that did were transformed by the texts), but in the sense that both allegory and vision (the old woman, the swan, or the seven old men, for example) appear within, and are linked to, his experience of reality. This experience has to be understood as encounters both with literary texts (reading and past interpretations) and with the texts of the visible world. In the cognitive view, literature is also reality and reality also a text.

A Spiritual Family

During the creative enterprise, when transforming the chosen details, the poet-narrator is guided by the needs of his mnemonic potentials, or, as Norman Holland would put it, by the standards of his "personal identity" (1992, 57). In calling the old women in "Les Petites vieilles" "ma famille" and "cerveaux congénères" 'kindred spirits' (line 81), Baudelaire comes closest to defining the factors that govern his choice of allegorical figures. Whether through mnemonic traces of previous experiences or innate (hardwired as it were) knowledge, the poet recognizes them as being spiritually related to him. And he recognizes them because, although they began at the contact with reality, they are projections of his own desires and needs. They are re-created in his own image. That this is true is corroborated by the reference to the exiled missionaries in "Les Foules," who belong to "la vaste famille que leur génie s'est faite" 'the huge family made by their genius' (1: 292). Recognition and re-creation go hand in hand. Defining his family and participating in its possible experience establishes new contours to his identity:

> Je vois s'épanouir vos passions novices;
> Sombres ou lumineux, je vis vos jours perdus;
> Mon coeur multiplié jouit de tous vos vices!
> Mon âme resplendit de toutes vos vertus!

> I see your young passions bloom;
> Dark or luminous, I live your lost days;
> My heart multiplied partakes in all your vices!
> My soul shines with all your virtues!
>
> "Les Petites vieilles," lines 77–80

A multiplied heart, new passions, vices, and virtues are the marks of the expanded personality.

How is this to be understood? Like most poets and writers of fiction, Baudelaire lives vicariously through the characters and narrators of his poetry; but it is equally true to say that they live through him. Though an inveterate visionary, he needs the contact with the painful edge of reality to set in motion his creative desire. Yet, in this contact lurks the risk of exposure to alien stories and desires, to fragmentation and ultimate dispersion. The danger is similar to the one that the hashish user brings down upon himself or herself.[19] The "punishment" that follows the day after is unequivocal: "Vous avez jeté votre personnalité aux quatre vents du ciel, et maintenant vous avez de la peine à la rassembler et à la concentrer" 'You have thrown your personality to the four winds of heaven, and now you have trouble gathering it together and concentrating it' (1: 395). The use of hashish leads to a scattered personality. "Les Petites vieilles" shows a way to resolve the antinomy of the centrifugal and centripetal movements with an expansion that does not equal corruption or dissipation of vital energy.

The reemerging concentration of the self is dependent on a phenomenon associated with the function of language. The self appropriates the revelations at the center of the real, transforms them into allegories and symbols, and through them reaffirms itself as a dynamic center, as the initiator of the interpretive victory over the text of reality, as a consciousness that re-creates or reiterates its own birth. In experiences that repeat themselves again and again, in terms of the choices it makes and transformations it performs, the self redefines its identity as that of *a poet in the process of creating his own family* in the world of poetry (with all the implications that this venture may have on the existential level).

The paradox that poetic narrative maintains is that while the poet is conscious of his kinship, on the metaphoric level, with other men and women, he never abolishes the distance between the observer and the observed. The distance is crossed and the borders are transgressed, but the self retains the power over the conditions under which the acts of transgression are accomplished. In defining the Baudelairean dandy, Lemaire can justifiably speak of "une transgression strictement contrôlée" 'a strictly controlled transgression' (1978, 47). The self does not become lost in the others nor does it allow itself to be totally dominated by them.

Still, the control over the borders of identity does not come easy. Here and there, in different texts, variations emerge. In "Le Peintre de la vie moderne," for example, even though the painter's self resembles the poet's, the polarity of the two impulses, to be alone and to seek the crowd, collapses: "Être hors de chez soi, et pourtant se sentir partout chez soi" 'To be outside oneself, yet feel everywhere at home' (2: 692). The outside becomes less dangerous and becomes home. Because Baudelaire attempts to define Constantin Guys, the tension is no longer identical. Nevertheless, even here, the differences between the self and the world are still maintained, since the painter is compared to "a kaleidoscope endowed with consciousness" (2: 692) and since he is capable of representing the world in images.

In the very act of processing the text of reality, and reinscribing its meaning into a new text, the narrator's strategies reflect the consequences of the moral struggle to write, the struggle against the forces of dispersion and the corrosive and will-dividing irony, against the conflicting pulls of desire and the fractured direction of power and ultimately against death. The care to see the world with one's own eyes enables the narrator to protect his identity and difference and to create his own family, an elite whose accomplishments have been, or will be, recorded in the archives of imagination and exile. But success in this respect would have no meaning, the conflict would lose its poignancy, if Baudelaire did not feel also the overwhelming need to envisage his kinship with those that could understand, to communicate with them, and to become Baudelaire through the act of writing.

2

The Mnemonic Text: "Le Mauvais vitrier" and "Mademoiselle Bistouri"

The Fascination with the Prose Poems

In *Petits poëmes en prose*, Baudelaire casts himself as a Parisian prowler in search of the secret pleasures of the observer, on the lookout for the bizarre, the unexpected, and the paradoxical. The various prose poems that are the product of this activity have been, to use Chambers's words, "a major focus of contemporary criticism." And the assumption is "that 'Baudelaire' is a privileged site for the study of Western culture's historical turn towards 'modernity'. . ." (1990, 169). Inherently complex, Baudelaire's work lends itself to many approaches, each dealing with particular levels of the text.[1]

From the point of view adopted here, the prose poems are exemplary in that they are grounded in the interaction between self and other, between subject and object, and, thus, pose the problem of identity with renewed urgency. Baudelaire's sharp focus on the dynamics of this interaction discloses to what extent the fault lines of the self, its unity and its limits, are determined in encounters with the other. The focus also reveals the role of the observer's mnemonic potentials in interpreting reality and uncovers the cognitive limits to knowledge.

Traces of Mnemonic Potentials

When designing a text, the writer comes to grips with a problem of power or desire, a need to respond to reality and to assess this response in linguistic and perceptual terms. In this struggle the writer has to rely on previous interpretations of other texts, on processed cognitive data, that exist in the form of mnemonic potentials or models, and constitute now a privileged mnemonic text. And since the metaphors and dynamic patterns on the printed page have been modeled on these potentials, if cognitive theory is right, one should be able to detect traces of them and of the tension they generated during the act of writing in the written text. Once the potentials are brought to light and the models identified, one can then confirm and clarify them by their affinities with patterns in other texts.

Internal evidence in "Le Mauvais vitrier" ('The Bad Glazier') and "Mademoiselle Bistouri" ('Miss Scalpel') reveals traces of one such privileged dynamic pattern model: the poet's belief in the existence of two allegiances. Baudelaire defines it in the following manner:

> Il y a dans tout homme, à toute heure, deux postulations simultanées, l'une vers Dieu, l'autre vers Satan. L'invocation à Dieu, ou spiritualité, est un désir de monter en grade; celle de Satan, ou animalité, est une joie de descendre.
>
> ("Mon coeur mis à nu" 1: 682–83)

> There are in every man, always, two simultaneous allegiances, one to God, the other to Satan.
>
> Invocation of God, or Spirituality, is a desire to climb higher; that of Satan, or animality, is delight in descent. (Isherwood 1977, 30–31)

While offering no similar definition, the organization of signifiers in the two prose poems shows unmistakable traces of the tension this belief generated during the creative act.

The first half of "Le Mauvais vitrier" consists of examples of individuals whose actions are driven by uncontrollable impulses that Baudelaire ascribes to demonic forces. The examples impart a particularly Baudelairean twist to the irony of the text and have an auxiliary function to clarify the act that the narrator himself is about to recount. They indicate two things: that the act proceeds from a condition dominated by "ennui" and that it has to be interpreted in the light of its moral implications. While neither moralists nor physicians can fully account for the surprising energy that suddenly takes hold of individuals who are normally dreamers and incapable of action, the narrator himself believes that this unexpected force, which physicians may attribute to hysteria, has a Satanic origin. Thus, "Le Mauvais vitrier" unfolds under the sign of the Satanic pull. But, as we shall see, it is a pull that operates within the structure of the two allegiances.

The Windowpanes of Paradise

Briefly stated, the narrative elements are the following. Waking up to the state of boredom and seeing, from the open window, a glass vendor in the street, the narrator is suddenly overcome by hatred for the man and his discordant cry. He asks the vendor to come up, gleefully thinking of the difficulties the latter will have in reaching the seventh floor. Matter-of-factly he examines the merchandise as if he thought the vendor should have colored glass and then, in an unexpected outburst, reproaches him for not carrying colored panes "qui fassent voir la vie en beau!" 'which make life beautiful!' (1: 287; Kaplan 1989, 15). He then pushes the poor man down the stairs and when the vendor reappears at the entrance, he drops a pot of flowers and breaks the man's "itinerant fortune."

The expression "ivre de ma folie" 'drunk with my madness' (1: 287; Kaplan 1989, 15) describing the climax of this mad act indicates clearly the "joie de descendre" characteristic of the allegiance to Satan. Yet it is also clear that the structure exacts the presence of the allegiance to God. And indications are that certain words and images that shine at the textual surface betray this presence. The first one, the desire to have "des vitres de paradis" 'windowpanes of paradise' (1: 287), is a key to the interpretation of the poem. Both Mauron and Pizzorusso relate the narrator's demand that the glazier should carry colored panes to the desire for a drug-induced paradise.[2] Several passages in "Le Poème du hachisch" show that the relation to hashish is justified. But as is so often the case with Baudelaire, asking for marvelous panes, for a colored vision of the world, is part of a wider drive toward the ideal. The colored panes do not necessarily point to drugs as the source of inspiration, nor do they unambiguously posit an art that would be artificially separated from the real. Rather, they betray the difficulty, perhaps impossibility, of aligning one's dream to reality, the essential antinomy of the poetic enterprise, and serve as a converging point for the narrator's bitterness and sarcasm in a world in which "l'action n'est pas la soeur du rêve" 'action is not sister to the dream' ("Le Reniement de Saint Pierre").

Clearly, the colored panes are in opposition to reality; yet, they forcefully suggest the futility of the artificial paradise. Lemaitre is right to point out that the desire for them is another manifestation of the "«double postulation» baudelairienne, dans cette contiguïté du Paradis et de l'Enfer" 'Baudelairean double allegiance, in this contiguity of Paradise and Hell' (1962, 44n1). Indeed, they should be seen in the light of Baudelaire's drive toward an elusive ideal of spiritual nature. But in the structure of the two allegiances, heaven and hell are not contiguous, and it is an oversimplification to explain the poem as a fable with the moral that those who search for one may end up in the other. Baudelairean heaven and hell are not a matter of distance to be covered; and though they do have spatial extensions, they are characterized by the degree of control exercised by the two allegiances, the two forces that may produce two mnemonic moments, one dominated by eternity, a paradisiac presence, and the other by the victory of time and the domain of spleen. The two moments may belong to two different metaphoric fields; but often, as in "Le Mauvais vitrier," they coexist in the same field and are distorted by the tension of the fundamental conflict.

The Weighing of Pleasure and Salvation

The Satanic force acquires here a virulent form and turns into hatred, sadism, and violence. At the end, the second of infinite pleasure marks an apparent goal that has been reached. Yet, this goal itself is impregnated with words like "éternité," "damnation," and "l'infini," a language that points to the opposing force. And the request for panes of paradise, for a simulacrum of heaven, is not made without the consciousness that real spiritual attainment is possible. And it is no accident that Wall sees the question at the end of the poem as a parody of Pascal's text on the wager. This is the narrator's question: "Mais qu'importe l'éternité de la damnation à qui a trouvé dans une seconde l'infini de la jouissance?" 'But what does an eternity of damnation matter to someone who has experienced for one second the infinity of delight?' (1: 287; Kaplan 1989, 15) And this is Wall's comment: "I find it impossible *not* to read this devilishly ironic text by Baudelaire as some kind of impish rejoinder to Pascal" (1986, 65). The reference to Pascal is right on the mark. But one can also find an argument in favor of eternal life in "Le Poème du hachisch," where Baudelaire himself speaking in his own person condemns the taste for "dangerous substances" and concludes:

> Mais l'homme n'est pas si abandonné, si privé de moyens honnêtes pour gagner le ciel, qu'il soit obligé d'invoquer la pharmacie et la sorcellerie; il n'a pas besoin de vendre son âme pour payer les caresses

enivrantes et l'amitié des houris. Qu'est-ce qu'un paradis qu'on achète
au prix de son salut éternel?

(1: 441)

But man is not so abandoned, so deprived of honest means to reach
heaven, that he has to have recourse to drugs and witchcraft; he does
not need to sell his soul to pay for the intoxicating caresses and friendship of the houris. What is a paradise that has to be paid for with
one's eternal salvation?

The question is a pertinent commentary on, and an answer to,
the question at the end of our poem. Is an artificial paradise
worth more than one's salvation? Is a second of delight not able
to erase the consequences of damnation? Both questions are rhetorical and appear contradictory, the first inviting "no" as an answer, the other, "yes"; but the possibility of interchanging their
answers deepens the irony. The juxtaposition of the two texts,
however, does not lead to undecidability; it does not indicate that
Baudelaire changed his mind; and (unless, like Wall, we understand parody as being potentially all-pervasive) it does not produce a double-edged parody. Rather, the two questions are the
product of two related concerns, in which the allegiance to God
or the allegiance to Satan has the upper hand. One concern is to
fall back on the inner ramparts of belief, where spiritual elevation
is at last possible; the other is to make a sortie in a desperate bid
to reach the illusory freedom of action. In each of the two passages, the weaker of the two allegiances appears to have been
temporarily defeated. As a result, when the two quotations are
juxtaposed, the two dominant arguments, one in favor of gaining
Paradise through spiritual elevation, the other in favor of obtaining infinite pleasure under the influence of demonic impulses
(or drugs), oppose each other and demonstrate the inherent tension of the communicative venture.

The Prison of Allegiances

But the conflict, the clash between the two opposing perspectives, is already present in each individual passage. And the effect
of the dual-allegiance structure in either one can be defined in
the following manner: At the very moment the narrator suggests
an answer in favor of either redemption or damnation, he is conscious of the power of the opposite answer. Thus, in "Le Mauvais

vitrier," the narrator cannot pay his dues to the negative word-association without, simultaneously, contributing to the positive verbal link. Temporarily, he attempts to break the stalemate of this spiritual gravitation by joining with the Satanic forces, in the hope of gaining some degree of freedom. But it is a bluff, a trick play,[3] which can only produce an illusion of freedom and an increased tension and irony from the knowledge of that illusion. He remains subject to the two uncontrollable forces that send their metaphoric attributes to contend for mastery over his being, actions, and thoughts. And the prose poem is a field of conflict, a metaphoric field, which *proclaims the Satanic pleasure with the irony that comes from the memory's inability to forget spiritual elevation.* In the very act of experiencing the brief orgasm of Satanic delight, the narrator affirms the immensity of the consequences of damnation. The verbal patterns of his age are linked to the privileged text in his memory—his mnemonic potentials. He cannot escape them. He is thus free only to the extent that he can understand and channel the tension-creating forces of his metaphors. We can imagine his cry at the end, "Make life beautiful!" accompanied by the smile of one who knows how precarious and short-lived his triumph is. We can surmise the irony of a prisoner who envisages the possibility of freedom in the surrender to the Satanic impulses, the excitement of saying, what if I went all the way down that path? and saying it from the position of one who knows he will neither have the resolve to follow the path nor be able to escape its attraction. The only option or freedom is in the sophistry of its contemplation and, therefore, in the textual fabric; yet that fabric, like a web, conceals risk and danger. The narrator points out the peril that accompanies his prank. But there is danger also in the social consequences of the textual mystification. In his life Baudelaire was often victim of the tendency to hoax the others. And, whether intentionally or not, this particular prose poem did fool those of his contemporaries who believed that Baudelaire was telling a story in which he had been personally involved. Or perhaps it is fooling us, if such an involvement did take place.

There is also a sense that the narrator and his victim are two sides of a divided personality: the bad glazier is "l'autre soi" 'the other self' (Mauron 1966, 117), the creative self, and, thus, victim of Baudelaire's own aggressive impulses. Expressing a similar view, Wing speaks of "the way in which difference divides the acting 'subject'" (1986, 27). As a victim, the creative self is surrounded by the silent eloquence of his broken glass. Finally, there is a tragic aspect of the conflict. For the eternity of damnation does not simply oppose the infinite of pleasure; it also evokes its luminous other: the eternity of the consequences of redemption. And in his lucid moments, and that is to say most of the time, Baudelaire understands that if the spiritual dialectics he is engaged in, and therefore writing, is a game, it is a game in which his own destiny is at stake. Whatever our final assessment of Baudelairean pessimism may be, it would miss the full force of the poet's irony if it emphasized only the pull of the Satanic forces.

A Close Encounter with Madness

The same caution is applicable in reverse to the interpretation of "Mademoiselle Bistouri," in which the allegiance to God appears dominant. The plot is simple but intriguing.[4] Baudelaire presents himself in the familiar role of a stroller. As he reaches the outskirts of a Parisian "faubourg," a woman accosts him, insisting that he must be a doctor and inviting him to her place. He denies being a physician and at first wants to continue his walk. But at her insistence and because he likes mystery with a passion, he lets her have her way. Once in her room, a real hovel, she treats him royally, offering him wine and cigars. Then the game begins in earnest. She recounts vividly the life at the hospital where the narrator himself is supposed to have been an intern. She keeps repeating "Tu es médecin n'est-ce pas, mon chat?" 'You are a doctor, aren't you, my kitten?' He denies it and denies being a surgeon, adding angrily "à moins que ce ne soit pour te couper la tête!" 'unless it would be to cut off your head!' (1: 354; Kaplan 1989, 116) At this point the story could have taken a violent turn as it did in the case of "Le Mauvais vitrier." Instead the narrator begins to play along with her. She then confesses she would go to see certain doctors even though she was not sick. More importantly, she would invite a young intern to her place and would shower him with her compassion. And no, she does not know when this obsession began to haunt her.

As he participates in the textual narration and absorbs the shock of the close encounter with madness, the narrator re-creates and redefines himself. He undoubtedly knew that madmen and madwomen existed, but now madness appears to him with the force of a revelation. And since the observable data about the new reality are incomplete, he is forced to fall back on the familiar dialectics between good and evil, between ecstasy and horror, between compassion and sadism. Thus, the two simultaneous allegiances are brought into play.

Although he speaks in the first person, the narrator, who asks the questions, is not Baudelaire himself. However, he draws closer to the poet, his creator, at the moment when he asks the woman about the beginning of this unusual passion for doctors, and she replies, "I don't know." As the innocence implicit in her answer sinks in, the narrator and the poet appear to merge and, at the same time, turn toward God. While in other prose poems Baudelaire presents an already definitive view of his thoughts, here he presents a narrator at the moment when he veers toward recognizing his limitations and, therefore, accepting the possibility of a higher power.

This acceptance in itself does not necessarily ward off the thought of the absurd. In a letter to his mother, Baudelaire wrestles with the issue of faith: "Je désire de tout mon coeur (avec quelle sincérité, personne ne peut le savoir que moi!) croire qu'un être extérieur et invisible s'intéresse à ma destinée; mais comment faire pour le croire?" 'I wish with all my heart (and no one except myself knows how sincerely!) to believe that an external and invisible being takes an interest in my destiny; but how can I believe it?' (1973, 2: 151; quoted by Pichois 1: 1021–22).

At the end of the prose poem, facing the bizarre and innocent monster, overwhelmed with compassion, the narrator rephrases the question:

—Seigneur, mon Dieu! vous, le Créateur, vous, le Maître; vous qui avez fait la Loi et la Liberté; vous, le souverain qui laissez faire, vous, le juge qui pardonnez; vous qui êtes plein de motifs et de causes, et qui avez peut-être mis dans mon esprit le goût de l'horreur pour convertir mon coeur, comme la guérison au bout d'une lame; Seigneur, ayez pitié, ayez pitié des fous et des folles! Ô Créateur! peut-il exister des monstres aux yeux de Celui-là seul qui sait pourquoi ils existent, comment ils *se sont faits* et comment ils auraient pu *ne pas se faire?* (1: 355–56)

—Lord, my God! You, the Creator, you, the Master; you who made Law and Freedom; you, the sovereign who lets things happen, you, the judge who forgives; you who are abounding in motives and causes, and who have perhaps placed a taste for horror in my mind in order to convert my heart, like a cure at knife point; Lord, have pity, take pity on madmen and madwomen! O Creator! Can *monsters* exist in the eyes of the only One who knows why they exist, how they *were made* and how they might have been able *not to be made?* (Kaplan 1989, 118)

Curiosity leads to discovery and to a high point of existential awareness. A sudden surge of awe within the overwhelming horror of madness redresses the balance in favor of compassion and, at least, the possibility of faith. Her madness is such that it cries out against its own absurdity and in the process exacts the need for comprehension and thus a return to the idea of God.[5]

Yet the prayer is not univocal; its surface is only deceptively unambiguous. In Prévost's opinion, the narrator's fervor in asking for God's pity could be interpreted as the state of meditation before the first step of doubt and perhaps blasphemy.[6] However, if one takes into account the chronology of other Baudelairean texts, one may see in the narrator's address to Providence not the stage before blasphemy but the step after rebellion, not an act of distancing himself from God but perhaps a readiness to envisage the possibility of a divine order. The question whether this movement is a turn or return to faith will probably never be settled.[7]

The depth and complexity of the text are linked to its ambiguity.[8] God created both human beings *and* monsters, and the verb "exist" has to have at least two meanings: the first, asking for a reason why monsters exist, and the second, suggesting that they may not be monsters in the eyes of him who made them. In a historical perspective, Baudelaire is certainly not the first to espouse the spirit of questioning. In "Le Mont des oliviers," Vigny did it with almost as much passion and perhaps with greater skepticism. In a long tradition of French moralists, from Voltaire to Camus, this has been the question: Why do the innocent suffer? Why do punishment and suffering exist in a world created by a forgiving judge? Christian tradition often relates suffering of human beings to the condition of sin. But the answer does not quell the contradictions. And the unresolvable conflict between the two traditions, between acceptance and questioning, brings to mind Ruff's concluding assessment in which he speaks of Baudelaire's awareness of the human condition and its contradiction.[9]

The attributes of the creator, as they are suggested by the text, are all-encompassing. Only an omniscient God can know whether reconciliation of opposites is possible, whether Law and Liberty can be brought into harmony, and whether monstrosity and innocence can spring from the same source. At the beginning of the story, the narrator, in the manner of a detective, spoke of his love of mystery to justify his curiosity. Like the narrator in "Le Mauvais vitrier," he was distrustful, stubborn in his aggressiveness, sarcastic. The tone was light, teasing, bantering. Now, however, as the story comes to an end, horror and compassion saturate the tenor of the prayer. At no time does the narrator remain a detached observer.

The Fundamental Limits

And the stakes are high. Envisaging the possibility of being converted by this experience as a cure at knife point, he seems to be suggesting not only that his faith may need healing but also that this experience with a mad woman was not a chance encounter but part of God's design. Paris is a city teeming with signs; the world is full of signs; but you find them "quand on sait se promener et regarder" 'when you know how to walk about and look' (1: 355; Kaplan 1989, 118). You have to be a stroller, an observer, and, finally, an interpreter. The narrator has fulfilled all these requirements and yet he is far from illumination, from an ultimate understanding, from the final correspondences. Like Poulydamas in the *Iliad*,[10] at the edge of the ditch before the Greek camp, suggesting that the bird omen is a message from the gods, the narrator believes that Miss Scalpel's appearance carries meaning and that divine intention is behind it. But the signs in the text of reality have now become inscrutable, unreadable, despair laden. Like Hector, who relies on the text of Zeus's assurances communicated to him by Iris, he now reverts to a previous text. Asking what this text is involves defining the metaphoric field of the poem.

Although the controlling dynamic pattern is not explicitly formulated, it can be detected in the textual tension and can be defined as the pattern of limits inherent in the human condition. These limits cannot be crossed; but they are not meaningless. They help the stroller focus on things that otherwise would remain obscure and see himself not only against the barriers to understanding evident in the dialogue but also against the frontiers of the human condition as they emerge from the prayer. This mad woman is a monster made by the same creator who made him and other human beings. There is a link then. Not surprisingly Maclean goes so far as to claim that, like the woman, he "is also a monster, an 'innocent' victim of his own drives" (1988, 156). Whether we agree or not, we cannot ignore the closeness of their conditions. The narrator is contemplating the borderlands beyond which human beings become monsters, and monsters become human beings. The metaphoric field of "Mademoiselle Bistouri" exposes *the shifting borders that both define the human condition and set limits to interpretation.*

Aware of these barriers, the narrator makes an extraordinary effort to obtain answers through prayer because prayer is the only human means left when all else fails. The text ends with a question. No answer is forthcoming and no answer is possible in a world of fundamental limits. Or to put it another way, the one possible answer is already contained in the question itself, in its fervor, in its all-encompassing cry. Where do monsters fit in with human beings and human beings with monsters? How can I believe? And therefore, I cannot, yet I want to believe. His concern reflects the need to know and the attempt to reach the side where meaning is possible. The identification with the woman does not occur, at least not the way identifications occur elsewhere. While he has sympathy for her, he does not want to relive her life. Her presence, however, forces him to review his solidarity with other human beings. In her fine analysis of the poem, Maclean draws a parallel between the narrator's cry at the end and Miss Scalpel's "I don't know" (157). And I agree that neither one has the answer. But the difference is fundamental: one is aware of the significance of not knowing, the other is not.

A Structural Chiasmus

The two prose poems have distinctive narrative strategies. In "Le Mauvais vitrier" the narrator sets, from the very beginning, the stage for the dramatic outcome of the story. And just before the appearance of his antagonist, he defines himself as having been more than once a victim of attacks caused by malicious demons. In this manner the text prepares the reader for the crescendo of sadistic impulses moving toward the paroxysm of delight. In "Mademoiselle Bistouri," however, the psychological preparation and evolution toward the final denouement, horror, and exaltation are hidden in the narrative movement. In contrast with "Le Mauvais vitrier," this text does not overtly prepare the reader to anticipate the prayer following the narrative closure. Yet although the depth of the narrator's concern with the moral implications of his experience and the suggestion of shock therapy come suddenly and unexpectedly at the end, they are so characteristic of Baudelairean metaphoric mode that they produce the effect of a powerful revelation. Baudelaire is again Baudelaire, in a reintegration of a conflict that has not been resolved and cannot be resolved.

Both stories are built around the vertical of the two allegiances to God and to Satan. But a chiasmus occurs, an inversion of the two poles: In one poem the dominant force is the allegiance to God; in the other, the Satanic pull. And it is remarkable that in each case the weaker opposite does not disappear. In "Le Mauvais vitrier," while the Satanic force is dominant, we have detected traces of the allegiance to God in the expressions "vitres de paradis," "l'éternité de la damnation," and "l'infini de la jouissance." In "Mademoiselle Bistouri," the narrator's outburst against the woman evinces the sadistic pull of a Satanic force. At the end, this pull has become much weaker, but it continues to be present in the incipient inclination to question God's order and design and in the "taste for horror." Somewhat like a dim star in a binary system, undetectable but for its influence on the motion of its brighter companion, within the prayer itself, the Satanic pull can still be felt.

Interpretation and Figural Language

In "Le Mauvais vitrier" and "Mademoiselle Bistouri," faced with signs that are either difficult or impossible to read, the speaker as Baudelaire's plenipotentiary has recourse to the coordinates in his memory, which function like a mnemonic text. The use of mnemonic potentials and patterns as an interpretive strategy is forced upon the subject by the existence of obstacles to human understanding. If barriers did not exist, we would not need mnemonic potentials. But by the same token if we did not have memory, all texts, including those of reality, would always remain meaningless.

Since, at the moment of writing, the narrator's mnemonic potentials were the product of previous interpretations, containing the metaphoric language he had used to interpret and explain what in experience was not directly available for processing or what needed further precision, it should not be surprising that the two prose poems reveal a mnemonic text, which is, in its very syntax, already figural. This text contains magic panes and monsters, that is, dynamic patterns produced by the metaphoric collision of language. Meaning originates neither in the words suggesting the narrator's desire to reach a higher level nor in the words translating his joy of descending, but in the tension between them. In the first prose poem, the clash of the two allegiances defines the impossibility of escape; in the second, it defines the tension between religious fervor and sadism, between one tendency that would make the narrator ban all doubts from his spiritual impulse and one that would emasculate him and deprive him of all compassion. Re-creating and interpreting responses to reality, figural language defines a self searching for identity and meaning in a space of perpetual division and conflict.

3

The Realignment
of the Love Lyric

The Violence against the Woman's Body

"One fourth of *Les fleurs du mal* are love poems now judged to be among the deepest and most spiritual in all literature" (1960, 12). So begins Henri Peyre's analysis of "Le Balcon." But this assessment once accepted, may be accompanied by the realization that there are poems addressed to women in the tradition of the love poem, poems like "Je t'adore à l'égal de la voûte nocturne," "A une madone," and "À celle qui est trop gaie," which do not retain the traditional sense of love. Are these poems in harmony with Baudelaire's work as a whole? What is the significance of their performances of violence and sadism seldom, if ever, equaled in the annals of love poetry? The best way to understand them is to see them as corresponding, respectively, to the poems expressing an opposite spiritual charge and addressed to the same women: "Le Balcon," "Chant d'automne," and "Réversibilité." I argue that "A celle qui est trop gaie" and "Réversibilité," in particular, oppose each other in a way that recalls the dynamics of the two simultaneous allegiances.

Neither one of the two poems can be fully appreciated without examining the connection between them or without noting the opposition between sadism and a high conception of love, between raging eros and ardent agape, and between the joy of descending and the desire to reach a higher spiritual state. Although the various interpretations of the condemned poem differ in stress, there is general agreement that its violence has an unmistakable sexual substratum.[1]

The poem is grounded on what Emmanuel calls "[le] mystère de l'être, au centre duquel—qu'on le veuille ou non—est la sexualité" 'the mystery of being, which has—whether one admits it or not—sexuality at its center' (1967, 143). Thus, when Baudelaire himself took up arms to defend the poem against his judges, he was led to attribute to them an "interprétation syphilitique," an interpretation which, as Pichois notes (1: 1133), they had not proposed. Unless we are prepared, in the absence of evidence, to imagine that someone had made a false report to him, we have to agree with Pichois that the interpretation is Baudelaire's own. Nevertheless, and despite the fact that one cannot turn aside the association with syphilis, Baudelaire's indignation is amply justified.

Reversibility and Maistrian Influence

The poet's anger is prompted by the conviction that his poetry as a whole should be read in the context of its spiritual attainment. In this perspective, "À celle qui est trop gaie" represents much more than sexual sadism and desire for revenge. Particularly in the last three stanzas, the female body transcends its erotic paraphernalia and its appeal to libidinal instincts to become the focus of a ritual with liturgical connotations. The ritual is prescribed by the negative pole of a theological principle, the idea that the suffering and merits of the innocent can benefit the guilty. The positive pole of this belief is developed in "Réversibilité," which is, not surprisingly, also dedicated to Mme Sabatier. Let us look at it first.

What stands out in the criticism of the poem is the acceptance of Maistrian influence, which is a given, and more specifically the agreement to interpret the poem in the light of Maistre's concept of reversibility. Indeed without this concept the title and much of the poem would remain unintelligible. Crépet and Blin, followed by Adam and Pichois, have laid the foundation for the understanding of the poem and clearly indicated the relevance of Maistrian thought: "La mystique application de ces idées à notre poëme permet de voir en Mme Sabatier un nouveau *Agnus Dei*, un ange intercesseur dont la joie *compense* les angoisses, dont la bonté *contrebalance* la haine, dont la santé *rachète* les fièvres, dont la beauté *répare* le vieillissement" 'The mystical application of these [Maistrian] ideas to our poem allow us to see in Mme Sabatier a new *Agnus Dei*, an intercessory angel whose joy *compensates* anguish, whose goodness *counterbalances* hatred, whose health *makes up for* fevers, whose beauty *restores* the aging body' (1942, 372). Maistre calls his concept of reversibility "one of the greatest and most important truths of the spiritual order" and defines it this way: *"The righteous, by suffering voluntarily, make satisfaction not only for themselves, but for sinners by way of the substitution of merits"* (1993, 251). His purpose in introducing it is twofold. The hermeneutic impulse aims to strengthen Christian dogma by explaining the existence of suffering and demonstrating the way to salvation; the polemic is an effort to convince his public and specifically the Protestants, who have argued against the idea of substitution, that reversibility is simply a weaker form of the concept of redemption, since the latter is *"a great indulgence accorded to humanity through the infinite merits of innocence par excellence, freely immolated for us!"* (1993, 312)

The contact with our poem comes at the moment when Maistre insists that the guilty can benefit only if they cooperate, if they "wish it," for only then "The actions of grace, prayer, satisfaction, assistance, inspiration, faith, hope, and love circulate from one to the other like beneficial waters" (1993, 313). Both "meritorious work" and *"the state of grace"* are needed. One can immediately see that the poet fulfills the condition of wishing it, since he is asking for the woman's prayers, and that perhaps his poem can represent the meritorious work. The "Ange plein de bonheur, de joie et de lumière" may be understood to be in the state of grace or, at the very least, to be the mediator through whom it can be obtained. Yet the salvation paradigm may not correspond completely.

A Critique of the Mystical Connection

In a stunning observation, Hambly points out the discrepancy: "Dans le poème «Réversibilité», pourtant, c'est le méchant qui souffre et l'innocent qui jouit de tous les bienfaits de la vie" 'In the poem "Réversibilité," however, it is the sinner who suffers and the innocent who enjoys all the benefits of life' (1971, 486). Citing a text by Nerval in which reversibility means that virtues are rewarded and sins are punished in this world, Hambly opposes Crépet's and Blin's interpretation and concludes that rather than establish mystical connections between the two persons in the poem, Baudelaire "semble insister sur l'absence de rapports entre elles, sur le contraste entre l'ange radieux et le méchant accablé de malheurs" 'appears to insist on the absence of relations between them, on the contrast between the radiant angel and the sinner overcome by misfortune' (1971, 486).

This view foregrounds the main structure in the body of the poem, which is the contrast, even opposition, between the poet's and Mme Sabatier's conditions, and which was not emphasized by earlier critics. But it does not account for the title or the prayer at the end. Yet the two views are not incompatible. Both the contrast and the intercessory role of the woman are vital.[2] In a way that is linked to a pretextual decision and that may appear arbitrary but is not, casting Mme Sabatier in that role defines her destiny and prepares her to fulfill it. The initial decision does not contradict Maistrian reversibility, since in its strong version, Christ, the model, prepares his life for the ultimate sacrifice. Moreover, even in the body of the poem, the impassioned address to her, the tenor of the vocative, creates, if it does not presuppose, a predestined connection between the two. The balance of contrasting elements, on one side health, joy, and light, on the other sickness, anguish, and old age, generates a textual tension that reaches its high watermark in the last stanza with the image of the dying David, who would have hoped to regain his health from the emanations of her enchanted body.

The Meaning of the Earthly Body

This last stanza reactivates Maistrian vision of various virtues that circulate from the innocent to the sinner (and presumably vice versa, though Maistre is not clear on this point) in the manner of "beneficial waters" and offers a key to understanding the poem itself as a vessel, a container of the potential for salvation. It is, however, extremely important to stress the correspondence between the biological and the spiritual dimensions in the theological polarity established between the innocent and the sinner. Both dimensions are functional and the separating "but I (unlike David) ask only for your prayers" does not negate the physical emanations of her body. Once they are posited, their virtues issue forth from the superior angelic level to the human level and inevitably touch the poet. David is there as a stand-in for the speaker, as a metaphoric dimension and evidence of the unity of vision, the harmony between the rejuvenating power of the woman's body and the angelic capacity of the intercessor to pray for him.

To deny either the intercessory value of the prayer[3] or the efficacy of the body's presence, its physical fragrance, is to neglect one of Baudelaire's most celebrated achievements, the correspondences between the higher concepts of the mind and the perceptual products of the senses, between the spiritual and the corporeal.[4] His poem, built on the interaction between the two, is a pertinent answer to Novalis's question, "Who has divined the high meaning of the earthly body?" (quoted in Hartman 1954, 156)

The Question of Prayer

Whether or not there is evidence that Baudelaire believed in God is not an issue that can be debated here; but there are plenty of indications that he believed in the efficacy of prayer. In "Fusées" he emphasizes its magical, intellectual, and sensory properties: "Il y a dans la prière une opération magique. La prière est une des grandes forces de la dynamique intellectuelle. Il y a là comme une récurrence électrique" 'There is in prayer a magical operation. Prayer is one of the great forces of intellectual dynamics. There is in it something akin to an electrical recurrence' (1975, 1: 659). This passage may justify Blin's idea that we are here on the level of hygiene and organic magnetism rather than of worship. But another notation in "Hygiène" leaves no doubt that Baudelaire goes beyond hygienic concerns: "Faire tous le matins ma *prière à Dieu, réservoir de toute force et de toute justice*, à *mon père*, à *Mariette et à Poe*, comme intercesseurs" '[I resolve] to say every morning my *prayer to God, source of all strength and justice*, to *my father*, to *Mariette, and* to *Poe*, as intercessors' (1: 673). Clearly the strength he refers to here is both physical and moral. It is as if, at this high point on the trajectory of his life, tempered by the lucidity of the approaching end, his consciousness recognizes in the relation between the two levels the essential as opposed to the accidental.

Moreover, Maistre could have taught Baudelaire that "prayer is the *dynamic* granted to men in the spiritual order, of which the material order is only an image and kind of reflection" (1993, 147). Blin acknowledges this likely influence but concludes that for Baudelaire prayer "n'utilise le vocatif que par respect de la Lettre, mais en fait elle n'instaure point de dialogue" 'uses the vocative only out of respect for the Letter, but in fact it institutes no dialogue' (1948, 89). According to Blin, then, prayer is a means of augmenting the potential of human origin but does not issue from a heart "qui s'expose à la grâce par l'acte même de rendre grâce" 'which offers itself to grace by the very act of rendering grace' (1948, 89). Yet, I believe, this is precisely what "Réversibilité" is: a formal but fervent attempt by the poet to gain a state of grace by asking a woman, a privileged being, to intercede for him, in a poem that thus becomes the vessel for the "beneficial waters" and a conductor of "thanks giving." To the extent that Maistrian influence is operative, it only reinforces Baudelaire's parallel alignment of the spiritual and the physical and confirms what is at the core of his view of human nature, the belief in the existence of evil. It is all the more useful to note, then, that for Baudelaire evil should not be identified with the physical; just as the good, or prayer, or the ideal, cannot be divorced from the sensory domain, evil is both a dimension of the flesh and of the spirit.

Vying with Gautier's Monks

Nowhere is that more evident than in "À celle qui est trop gaie." Written a few months earlier (manuscript dated 9 December 1852), this poem stages a perverse metamorphosis of the beneficial waters: it not only reverses the direction of the circulating fluid but also imbues it with a negative emotional and biological charge. But this difference can be understood precisely in relation to the Maistrian metaphor, almost as if the poem had been written in preparation for the positive operating force of "Réversibilité" (dated 3 May 1853). The beauty, exuberance, and happiness of Mme Sabatier, the health that can be transmitted from her arms and shoulders to the despondent passer-by, all foreshadow her enchanted body in the later poem. "À celle qui est trop gaie" can be further clarified by a comparison with a poem by Gautier entitled "Thébaïde," which serves as a sort of background, a metaphoric context.

In it Gautier speaks of the monks of an imaginary Thebaid, calling them "grands voluptueux, sybarites du cloître" 'great voluptuaries, sybarites of the cloister' (1862, 177) who by their devotion gain salvation and also experience the sensual pleasure ("sensual" because it is compared to that of Don Juan and of a lover) of kissing (on the crucifix) the mouth (wound) at the side of Christ. To them he opposes a category of less fortunate human beings, who can neither experience the joys of life nor pray. Gautier claims to be one of them. But although in direct opposition to the monks, he nevertheless parallels their Thebaid by choosing a secret retreat for himself, "D'où l'on n'entende pas le rire des heureux / Ni le chant printanier des oiseaux amoureux" 'From where one does not hear the laughter of those who are happy / Or the spring song of birds in love' (1862, 179).

When Gautier explains, "Car tout son m'importune et tout rayon me blesse" 'Every sound bothers me and every ray of light offends me' (1862, 179), one recognizes the sensitivity to the sun and the insolence of nature in Baudelaire's poem. Moreover, in comparing the pleasures of the monks and declaring them superior to those of a lover, Gautier sanctions the fundamental romantic correspondence (for which there are earlier models, such as The Song of Songs, the poems of Saint John of the Cross) between spiritual love and erotic desire. One can serve as metaphor for the other, empowering it or refining it. As Pommier points out, Baudelaire remembers Gautier's daring comparison of a woman's florid mouth with Christ's wound, "la bouche à son côté livide" 'the mouth at his livid side' and transposes it into "ces lèvres nouvelles" 'these new lips,' like a wound opened in the woman's side (Pommier 1945, 188). If the new context of "À celle qui est trop gaie" does not reintroduce any overt reference to Christ, it does in a subtle way, by the expression "ton sein pardonné" 'your pardoned breast,' endow Mme Sabatier's body with a sacred attribute. She is forgiven or freed from the original sin. Such belief is not alien to the author of "Allégorie," who proclaims the beauty of the woman's body a gift that "de toute infamie arrache le pardon" 'obtains forgiveness for every infamy.' And so when at the end of our poem, he signals the hour of pleasures, unlike the "saintes voluptés" of "Bénédiction," these pleasures appear as a parodic ritual, a sacrilege, designed to defile the body of someone who is in a state of grace. One recalls the poet's claim in a letter to Ancelle that in this book, in *Les Fleurs du mal*, he included "toute ma *religion* (travestie), toute ma haine" 'all my *religion* (disguised), all my hate' (1973, 2: 610). Disguised, this religion is also parodied, as ritual turns into sadistic gesture, respect into fury, and love into hate. And in experiencing the "vertigineuse douceur" 'breathtaking sweetness,' the poet appears to vie with Gautier's monks whose pleasures are superior to those of Don Juan.

As Pichois suggests, "la Présidente" may have seen in this poem "une galanterie, un madrigal" (1987, 319). But to the extent that serious intentionality is at stake, why punish Mme Sabatier? Just as importantly, why begin a series of anonymous poems and letters protesting undying devotion to her with a poem that appears to violate that love in advance? Significantly, it is precisely Apollonie's physical appearance and manner that invited Baudelaire to single her out as the perfect model for both poems. In making her portrait Judith Gautier writes: "Son air triomphant mettait autour d'elle comme de la lumière et du bonheur" 'Her triumphant appearance spread around her light and happiness' (quoted in Pichois 1987, 320). The answers to our questions must have something to do with the original choice.

And perhaps with "Thébaïde." In his poem Gautier distinguishes two categories of human beings: those who cannot pray and are implicitly condemned and those who are admitted to the divine table and are, thus, chosen. The difference is that "Tous ne se baignent pas dans la pure piscine / Et n'ont pas même part à la table divine" 'Not all bathe in the pure pool / Nor do all even have a place at the divine table' (1862, 178). One recognizes here the pool of grace from "Franciscae meae laudes": "Piscina plena virtutis, / Fons aeternae juventutis." Gautier does not assign any priority, but it is clear that there is a tight relation between, on the one hand, the misfortune in this life and the inability to pray and, on the other hand, the health and happiness in this world and the state of grace, the consequence of having bathed in, what he calls, "the ocean of joy." One can see why Hambly was struck by a discrepancy: the idea that the innocent is not subject to suffering does not issue from Maistrian thought; it may come from Nerval or, as I think, from Gautier's text or from both. Reversibility remains operative, but its forces now converge more on the exchange of attributes circulating in the fashion of a fragrance or fluid.

Experimenting with Reversibility

The primary impulse, then, may be to communicate the venom, whether syphilis or spleen or melancholy, to Mme Sabatier, as a being in the category of the chosen, to submit reversibility to a test in the hope perhaps that, if it works, she will then truly become his sister, in both the spiritual and physical senses. Perhaps, indeed, the gap between the chosen and the damned may be thus crossed. This is not intended to minimize the intensity of the sadistic instinct, but to point out the experimental character of the poem. The poem was written, as Baudelaire himself explains in the accompanying letter, "dans un de ces états de rêverie où le jette souvent l'image de celle qui en est l'objet" 'during one of these states of reverie in which he is thrown by the image of her who is its subject' (1973, 1: 205). This state is even more clearly delineated in the letter sent with another poem (8 May 1854): "quand mon être est roulé dans le noir de sa méchanceté et de sa sottise naturelles, il rêve profondément de vous. De cette rêverie excitante et purifiante naît généralement un accident heureux" 'when my being is plunged into the darkness of its natural mean- ness and stupidity, it deeply dreams of you. This exciting and purifying reverie generally generates a happy outcome' (1973, 1: 276). The reverie driven by meanness (sadism) and "stupidity," both temptation and tentativeness, considers various possibilities of approach to reversibility.

"À celle qui est trop gaie" exploits its negative potential. Pro- found feelings, he reminds the dedicatee, "ont une pudeur qui ne veut pas être violée" 'possess a modesty which does not permit that it be violated' (1973, 1: 205). But precisely the act of violating, violence and "viol" 'rape,' occurs in the poem. The idea that in retrospect the poem should be seen as a prelude to "Réversibilité" and the whole series of poems that follow is strengthened by the letter that accompanies "Le Flambeau vivant" (7 February 1854), in which Baudelaire explains the "cowardice" of not signing:

> Quant à cette *lâcheté de l'anonyme*, que vous dirai-je, quelle excuse alléguerai-je, si ce n'est que ma première faute commande toutes les autres, et que le pli est pris. —Supposez, si vous voulez, que quel- quefois sous la pression d'un opiniâtre chagrin je ne puisse trouver de soulagement que dans le plaisir de faire des vers pour vous, et qu'ensuite je sois obligé d'accorder le désir innocent de vous les mon- trer avec la peur horrible de vous déplaire. —Voilà qui explique *la lâcheté*.

> As far as this *cowardice of anonymity* is concerned, what can I say, what excuse shall I put forward, if not that my first offence governs all the others, and that the habit is formed. —Picture, if you will, that some- times under the pressure of a persistent grief (melancholy) I can find relief only in the pleasure of writing poems for you, and that then I feel compelled to grant the innocent desire to show them to you with the horrible fear of displeasing you. —That's what explains *the coward- ice*. (1973, 1: 266)

"My first offence governs all the others" means "not signing the first letter is the decision that had to be upheld in all the subse- quent letters," but also "the first poem I sent you prefigures the others." The extraordinary thing about the letter is that it would have been more appropriate to accompany "À celle qui est trop gaie." Like the letter, the poem emphasizes the movement of ap- proaching her like a coward. The crawling prepares the image of communicating his venom to her and recalls the statue, for which Apollonie was the model, exhibited in the "Salon de 1847," and entitled "Femme piquée par un serpent"; but it also reflects the strategy that the letter discloses and that his behavior confirms. The cowardice is simply an awareness that this strategy conceals his doubts and fears about the consequences of a sexual encounter. The expression "un opiniâtre chagrin" echoes "le passant chagrin" in the poem and specifies that this is the state of mind that gives rise to the creative impulse. Writing the poem, he obtains a "soulagement," both relief and pleasure. But notice that the "innocent" desire to show it to her inevitably leads to an equivalence not so much between writing and having sex, but rather equivalence between, on the one hand, the activity of sending her the poems he has written and dedicated to her and, on the other, infusing his poison into her body.

Spiritual and Biological Needs

The letter justifies the importance we have attached to the original choice of Mme Sabatier and the decision to adopt an anonymous stance: "my first offence governs all the others." Offence of anonymity, but also fear of displeasing her and, more than anything else, fear of profaning the body, the sacred container of all correspondences. "À celle qui est trop gaie" appears to contain a warning that a future encounter would unleash the instinctual forces and would inevitably degrade the ideal. At the core of this fear is the problem of bringing into consonance passion and love, the biological need and the worship of the ideal of beauty. While on the aesthetic level, the drive to deal with the problem has produced some of the most haunting of Baudelairean correspondences, on the level of experience, the drive remains a source of disappointment. Mirroring the poet's awareness that reconciling spiritual and biological needs is as difficult as it is necessary, the poem has predictive powers, in the sense that it points to a future physical contact, which for Baudelaire would remain unsatisfactory. To Mme Sabatier, who as a result of this encounter would fall passionately in love, he sends a warning: The sadistic instincts may gain the upper hand. The poet's letter after the fact (31 August 1857) confirms that, for him, the ideal love has suffered a setback: Mme Sabatier has fallen from her pedestal, a goddess has become a woman. In her answer, echoing his words, "je n'ai pas *la foi*" 'I don't have *faith*,' Mme Sabatier rightly translates them "mais alors l'amour vous manque" 'but in that case you have no love' (quoted Pichois, Ziegler 1987, 362). Yet the striking simplicity of this verdict, so compelling to one in love, and perhaps so true, may not suffice to do justice to Baudelaire's complex erotic tension. It is because he experiences strong emotional pulls toward the two extremes that he cannot unify his orgiastic joy of descending and the pleasure of worshiping the ideal and that he both desires and fears the profanation of the woman's body. Thus, from Baudelaire's perspective, the real life encounter predicted in "À celle qui est trop gaie" fails because the biological tendency is too strong to be overcome by the spiritual and the spiritual too hypnotizing to be negated by the biological. The source of failure is not so much a lack of love, but a fundamental scission in the focus of intentionality.

Mme Sabatier in Cyberspace

Writing poems and sending them to her, however, have not failed. The success is due at least in part to the fact that we are now on the poetic plane, where, like some passionate encounter in cyberspace, this activity replaces the sexual act and brings similar pleasures. When the poet is overcome by fear, hate, and fever, when he falls prey to his natural meanness, he can mimic the violence of the sexual act and obtain relief. He can take revenge on the woman who is free from anxiety and sickness, punish her, and let her know what suffering is.

Yet even in this context, the rich literary background, the Maistre and Gautier tributaries in particular, widen the metaphoric depth of the two poems. The manuscript, containing "T'infuser mon sang" 'infuse my blood,' reflects the sacrificial value of blood in Maistrian philosophy. However, "venin" in the definitive version only increases the religious tenor of the text. It is in keeping with the belief that the existence of evil is a consequence of the original sin, whose emblem is the serpent. To believe, Maistre explains, that men are wicked only when they commit a crime is equivalent to believing "that the viper's venom is engendered at the moment it strikes. The event does not create wickedness, it manifests it" (1993, Ninth Dialogue, 271). For his part, the poet crawls to the beloved, in a parodic, staged repetition of the primal scene in the garden, and mimics the serpent's temptation of the first woman. The change from blood to venom foregrounds Baudelaire's belief that "la volupté unique et suprême de l'amour gît dans la certitude de faire le *mal*" 'the unique and supreme pleasure of love lies in the certainty of doing *evil*' (1: 652). During this parody of love, he communicates not only his spleen and syphilis but also the evil of a corrupted human nature to a woman who has been until then free of the consequences of the original sin. The metaphoric and philosophical dimensions overflow the limited banks of the sadistic fury that informs the ending of the poem.

Mme Sabatier as Intercessor

Moreover, as most of the poems addressed to Mme Sabatier show, her roles of guardian angel, muse, and angelic intercessor prove that they can generate a more refined pleasure, move on higher spiritual ground, and fulfill a need that is related to, yet perhaps even greater than, the sexual drive in its pure state. As Pichois so appropriately puts it, "Mme Sabatier fut sans doute pour Baudelaire une entéléchie" 'Mme Sabatier undoubtedly was for Baudelaire an entelechy' (1975, 1: 908).

A guiding principle toward self-fulfillment, then, a muse, a living torch, a spiritual dawn, Apollonie Sabatier deserves those attributes. If Baudelaire did not list her in "Hygiène" along with his father, Mariette, and Poe, as intercessors, it was perhaps because she would remind him too much of his own drives and would interrupt the positive current. Yet since the poems dedicated to her were part of a spiritual and therapeutic hygiene, reinscribing prayer in the text of daily life, she might very well have a claim to be on that list.

Although Mme Sabatier's specificity as an individual and her freedom of choice were severely limited (and sending her the poems anonymously was precisely a way of preempting her initiative), one cannot conclude that as a real woman she was unimportant or that any woman would have served. The texts we have considered all indicate that the relief would not be obtained, the therapy would not work, if the poet did not have the firm knowledge that this particular woman he knew, whose specific physical and intellectual attributes he could imagine and transform, was there capable of reading and reacting to his poems. Again for Baudelaire, the contact with reality was a source of tension and depth and should not be deleted.

The distinction between those who are physically and spiritually privileged and those who are not, which recalls Gautier's poem, is no less significant. It further clarifies the poet's difference from other men and women, emphasizing a certain predetermination in the fabric of reality. Just as importantly, it confirms that in contradistinction to Jeanne Duval, who played the role of "errante" and "déclassée" and whose destiny was more closely associated with his own, Mme Sabatier belonged to the category of the more fortunate of this world. This may explain why a greater percentage of the poems addressed to her place her on a higher level and inform her with sacred attributes. In spite of the initial act af violence and profanation, she remains an ideal, the power of spiritual heavens, an angelic intercessor, a light emanating guide, in a setting more fitting for a diurnal or evening liturgy than for a nocturnal sadistic orgy.

4

"Une Mort héroïque": Martyrdom and Tradition

An Intertextual Parallel

Contemporary critics, from Mauron to Mehlman and Wing, from Starobinski to Chambers, from Pichois to Kopp and Kaplan, have all placed Baudelaire's "Une Mort héroïque" under intense scrutiny.[1] What makes this prose poem especially attractive is that it delineates Baudelaire's conception of the artist, foregrounds the relation between art and death, and develops an insight into martyrdom and tradition that is as pertinent today as it was in the poet's time. Several studies of the poem have already accurately indicated the inevitability of the mime's death and the inextricable link of art with death.[2] In focusing again on this link, I compare some of the poems's key plot and metaphoric elements to corresponding structures in Eliot's *Murder in the Cathedral* and Anouilh's *Becket*. This strategy, in which "Une Mort héroïque" remains the primary text, is aimed neither at amalgamating the three works nor at proving influence but at illuminating the potential meaning inherent in the textual blueprints.

A parallel between, on the one hand, Baudelaire's prose poem and, on the other, Eliot's *Murder in the Cathedral* and Anouilh's *Becket* confirms the inevitability of death. But it also reveals that death is not the reverse of artistic success but rather its transcendental face, not its hidden side but the guarantor of its authenticity. Killing and reducing the protagonist to silence sets in motion a process whereby the prestige of an artist or of an archbishop is transferred to the public domain and is proportionately magnified. In this view, which is ultimately a view of tradition and history, the triumph of art or religion rises from the cathartic experience of the public, chorus, narrator, and readers. Death and martyrdom reported by one or several witnesses transcend the limits of the individual, reach the metaphoric level, and achieve, in the memories of the survivors, historical significance.

In all three works an unexpected event, the noblemen's conspiracy or the king's decision to name Thomas archbishop, breaks the precarious equilibrium of an uneven friendship and triggers the drama. The jealousy suppressed by the tension of a granted favor erupts into open conflict. In one case, the prince's inability to tolerate a triumph that frustrates his expectations contrasts with Fancioulle's talent and the unswerving dedication to his art; in the other, the king's intense desire to remain first in relation to power and everything connected with power, including women and fame, is set against Becket's ascesis, the steady advance toward incorruptibility, fame, and eventual martyrdom.

Eliot himself, it is true, dealing directly with the last month in the life of his protagonist, does not dwell on the early events that lead to the final outcome. Even so, references throughout the play assume and subsume the relations between the king and Becket. Thus, the first tempter asks Thomas, "What, my Lord, now that you recover / Favour with the King . . ." (1952, 183). Baudelaire uses, at the beginning, the expression "comédien favori" and ends the story saying that other mimes have come to perform before the prince's court but none of them could "s'élever jusqu'à la même *faveur*" 'rise to the same *favor*' (1: 323; Kaplan 1989, 67).

The word connotes the ambiguity of the friendship between the two protagonists and is charged with meaning. Fancioulle is "presque un des amis du prince" 'almost one of the Prince's friends' (1: 319; Kaplan 1989, 63), and "son vieil ami" 'his old friend' (1: 322; Kaplan 1989, 66); he is more than a favorite comedian and less than equal in friendship. While Eliot's text mentions "remembering all the good time past," it does not give us details about the relation between the king and Becket. Anouilh's version, on the other hand, describes their friendship in terms of "amitié" and "aimer," which have homosexual overtones.[3]

In all three works the hero's main antagonist is the despot himself. The knights have a far greater role in Eliot's play, but they remain intermediaries, who are sent by the king and who act on behalf of the king, just as they do in Anouilh's version. Similarly, Baudelaire's prince strikes his rival through an intermediary, his page. Like Anouilh's king, who tries (unsuccessfully) to observe the planned proceedings of Becket's discomfiture and arrest and who upon hearing of Becket's triumph has an ambivalent response, a mixture of admiration and anger, Baudelaire's prince applauds the triumphant mime and at the same time schemes against him.

The Effect of a Death Sentence

But it is the vision of the narrator and the spectators that engenders the uncanny resemblance between Fancioulle's lot and Becket's fate. While the narrator alone sees the mime's halo, the spectators share in the recognition of Fancioulle's achievement against the background of his death sentence. In describing the preparations for the performance, Baudelaire speaks of "l'intérêt moral et mystérieux qui y était attaché" 'the moral and mysterious significance attached to [this occasion by the organizers and the public]' (1: 321). In Anouilh, Becket's martyrdom is defined in the perspective of a historical irony. Having forced the king to acknowledge Becket's sainthood to gain their favor, the Saxon masses have equal praise for the two men, whom they now associate in what will become an inextricable historical link between victim and executioner: "Sire, l'opération est réussie! Il paraît que la foule saxonne hurle d'enthousiasme autour de la cathédrale, acclamant le nom de Votre Majesté, en même temps que celui de Becket" 'Sire, the operation is successful! It seems that the Saxon crowd roars its approval around the cathedral, acclaiming Your Majesty's name and at the same time Becket's' (1959, 190). In defending "l'honneur de Dieu" 'God's honor,' Becket never triumphed in his life as completely as in his death. In *Murder in the Cathedral* Becket accedes to sainthood in an overt and direct fashion. Clearly in all three cases, death does not simply precede spiritual ascendancy and success in the eyes of others and does not constitute a mechanical ligature, but represents a sine qua non of their attainment.

In saying that "l'ivresse de l'art est plus apte que toute autre à voiler les terreurs du gouffre" 'the intoxication of Art is more apt than any other to veil the terrors of the abyss' (1: 321; Kaplan 1989, 65), Baudelaire asserts an unmistakable belief about the function of art and literature. In the economy of this belief, death is not just a threat but also knowledge of a threat, a threat that operates as knowledge. As the narrative events illustrate, the threat does not hamper Fancioulle's performance. On the contrary, the presence of death waiting in the wings grants the mime the special grace of movement, that strengthens his resolve and deepens the intoxicating potency of his art. The parallel with Eliot and Anouilh suggests that the awareness of death influences both performer and spectators or chorus. It is no accident that Anouilh begins his play with the end of the story, the scene in which the king has to do penance before Becket's tomb. The effect of knowing has cathartic implications, and as such it may be universal.

This awareness manifests itself most clearly in the clown's halo, which becomes the metaphoric predictor of Fancioulle's martyrdom: "Ce bouffon allait, venait, riait, pleurait, se convulsait, avec une indestructible auréole autour de la tête, auréole invisible pour tous, mais visible pour moi, et où se mêlaient, dans un étrange amalgame, les rayons de l'Art et la gloire du Martyre" 'The buffoon went, came, laughed, wept, contorted himself, with an indestructible halo around his head, a halo invisible to everyone, but visible to me, and in which were blended, in a strange amalgam, the rays of Art and the glory of Martyrdom' (1: 321; Kaplan 1989, 65). The halo, like halos in some Renaissance paintings, is an incontrovertible sign not only of the highest artistic achievement but also of the impending martyrdom. At the very instant when the public is under the spell of Fancioulle's genius when no one thinks "de mort, de deuil, ni de supplices" 'of death, of mourning, or of torture' (1: 322), the clown's martyrdom and death are foreordained, his essence extracted, his renown proclaimed, and his mourning assured. Dramatic irony is engendered by the tension between the projected execution the public in rapture denies and the martyrdom the metaphoric dimension asserts.[4] In Baudelaire's view, art, though not illusory as Starobinski would have it (1967, 409), is necessarily performed near the edge of the abyss. Like Eliot's or Anouilh's Becket, perhaps like all martyrs, Fancioulle knows he has to die. During the moments of exaltation, those seeing his performance do not think about death; but it is their knowledge of the death sentence that helped them reach the exalted state.

The "Coup de Sifflet" Pattern

If then we accept death as the driving force in the performance itself, the question still remains, why does Fancioulle die at the moment of the "coup de sifflet" 'whistle' or 'catcall'? If the ending of the story exacts death, an execution, as initially suggested, would have provided a proper outcome. It would have satisfied the prince by allowing him to enjoy both the performance and the sadistic pleasure of watching his "comédien favori" die on the scaffold. That, however, would not have satisfied Baudelaire and, in our effort to see why, we come across the controlling dynamic pattern of the catcall.

The effect of the "coup de sifflet" is confirmed by a text that Crépet cites as a possible source, in which the author points out that it is common for artists to experience despair and to wish to die when they no longer have the favor of the public. In the case of a particular artist, a whistle (catcall) he thought he heard was his death warrant (see Kopp 1969, 290–91). Other texts could be adduced here to sustain the relation between death and the public's disfavor, and, as Kopp points out, the idea must have been common. However, in Fancioulle's case, the catcall comes in the middle of his triumph, as a result not of the public's but the prince's disfavor. As in Anouilh's or Eliot's play, it comes when the protagonist has reached the foreordained point in the design of the textual tapestry. While crossing the English Channel, Becket knows that he will not die in the storm before reaching the Cathedral: "Dieu s'amuse. Il sait bien que ce n'est pas comme ça que je dois mourir" 'God is having fun. He knows well that this is not the way I must die' (Anouilh 1959, 172). Death is anticipated but not before its predetermined time. Yet the converse is also true. Although preset, the time does not come without its unexpected elements. And in Eliot's version, Thomas tells the priests: "However certain our expectations / The moment foreseen may be unexpected / When it arrives" (1952, 203). Both the archbishop and Fancioulle have scheduled performances: vespers for the former and pantomime for the latter. In both cases, what is scheduled is interrupted by what is foreordained. Dynamically, the sharp whistle in Baudelaire's poem resembles a rapid sword that rends and divides time, and with a violent earsplitting sound interrupts the performance: "un coup de sifflet aigu, prolongé, *interrompit* Fancioulle dans un de ses meilleurs moments" (my italics) 'a shrill drawn-out whistle blast interrupted Fancioulle at one of his greatest moments' (1: 322; Kaplan 1989, 66). The whistle identifies the world of the poem as *the metaphoric field of an interrupted performance.*[5] The knights and the catcall are both inappropriate and necessary, unseasonable and opportune, untimely and, yet, timely.[6]

The untimely/timely event occurs as a break precisely at the moment when religion and art are held in high esteem by the public. Is it an arbitrary authorial intervention? A basic mechanism in the human condition? A rhetorical device linked to discursive functions? Or finally a consecration of palimpsestic traces of events in memory? They all have a hand in the artist's downfall. In a cognitive perspective, however, the mnemonic imperative is the strongest. Death occurs as a scission in the metaphoric field of the performance itself. In mythological terms, the page's catcall, as the agent of the Fate (Atropos), cuts the thread of life. While death comes when the spectators (and readers in the role of spectators) least expect it, it also arrives as an answer to their anticipation. The dynamics of the story has constantly reinforced its necessity. Baudelaire has woven, at the metaphoric level, into the texture of ritual and sacrifice, a view of art in which the artist has to die to accede to "l'héroïsme de la vie moderne" 'the heroism of modern life' ("Salon de 1846" 2: 493).

The Knowledge of the Chorus

A related way of anticipating death is modulated by foreknowledge.[7] Traditionally the knowledge of the chorus is mantic, meaning that it has predictive powers. In *Murder in the Cathedral,* the chorus has a strong premonition: "I have smelt them, the death bringers, senses are quickened / By subtle forebodings . . . (Eliot 1952, 207). In "Une Mort héroïque," there is no chorus as such but the role is shared by the narrator and spectators. The "mysterious" importance the public attaches to Fancioulle's performance indicates that, like the narrator, the spectators have foreknowledge. If this foreknowledge does not come from a "mantic heart" as the fear of the chorus in *Agamemnon* (Aeschylus 1953, 65), it may originate in their memory of other texts of martyrdom and, consequently, may obey a mnemonic imperative as strong as the textual constraints themselves. But like the ancient chorus, who cannot understand Cassandra's prophecies (Aeschylus 1953, 69), and unlike the narrator, the spectators can, and do, misunderstand what they see.

The ease with which Fancioulle comes on the stage appears to fool them and strengthen their idea of clemency. The idea began with rumors defined by impersonal expressions like "le bruit courut" 'the rumor circulated' and "disait-on" 'they were saying.' Perhaps those rumors were, at least initially, fed by an intentional leak coming from the prince himself. Now the spectators appear to believe that since Fancioulle is so natural and light in his demeanor, he must know more about the likelihood of clemency than they do. This is one fallacy of observation. Another fallacy is the fact that it is difficult for spectators to believe that an individ-

ual who is performing so well, who does what under normal circumstances a mime is expected to do, and more, before their very
eyes, could be executed, could be dead in short order. In this
respect the narrator does suggest by the veiled irony of words like
"le noble public" that he is above committing this error. Of course,
it would be a mistake to believe that the idea of death has been
neutralized by these hopes. The text does not imply that the mime
believes the prince will pardon him; rather, it suggests that the
pantomime movements require such concentration and focusing
that they screen him from the fear of death.

What the Protagonist Knows

At the moment of death the protagonist appears to have a sudden revelation about the significance of the drama. The nature
and function of this understanding are not always obvious.[8] In
Eliot, Becket's vision of martyrdom has been steady from the beginning. The something new at the moment of his death is perhaps a greater emphasis on blood. In Anouilh, just before they
kill him, Becket appears to waver when he turns to God and
exclaims: "Ah! que vous rendez tout difficile et que votre honneur
est lourd!" 'Oh! how you make everything difficult and how heavy
your honor is!' (1959, 294) In Baudelaire's story there is no statement explaining what Fancioulle's thoughts are before he dies.
However, we can infer from the tension of the text that the whistle
summarily censures and mocks his consummate art and delivers
a message: his time is up and there will be no pardon.

Here a fundamental difference may appear between Becket
and Fancioulle. Eliot and Anouilh both stress Becket's faith
whereas Baudelaire does not dwell on the mime's aesthetic beliefs.
Perhaps that is the reason why critics have spoken of the illusory
character of art in "Une Mort héroïque." Fancioulle cannot be
saved. An existential doubt hits him and overwhelms all hope. The
"coup de sifflet" appears as the sharp edge of a massive irony that
transforms performances and lives into playthings. No aesthetic
or religious faith can shield our consciousness from the inexora-
bility of death.

The Difference between Actor and Spectators

But in such circumstances is death a failure? Or how can the
inability to transcend the limitations of the human condition end

in triumph? How can failure confer upon the mysteries of religion and upon the mystique of art their most enduring prestige? The question rephrases success and failure in a dialectical paradox and exposes the fundamental duality of perspective. The martyr and the artist confront death, succumb, and fail to complete the immediate task at hand. Yet, in the eyes of those who are still living, the apparent failure turns into triumph. An abyss opens to separate the actor who is engaged in a dangerous enterprise, and who struggles on the perilous stage, and the spectator, who is invaded by the tragic emotions of catharsis but remains on the sidelines of the semiotic space. The loneliness of the actor can never be duplicated in the spectator.

Not only is the spectator's interpretation decanted by the cathartic distance, it also takes place under fundamentally different conditions. Nietzsche suggests that there is a difference of viewpoints, primarily, I suppose, in the sense that the victim does not want to be a victim: "The sacrificial animal does not share the spectators' ideas about sacrifice, but one has never let it have its say" (1983, 210, Bk. 3 sec. 220). Baudelaire, on the other hand, believes the victim's consent is essential: "Pour que le sacrifice soit parfait, il faut qu'il y ait assentiment et joie de la part de la victime" 'For a sacrifice to be perfect, it has to have the victim's consent and joy' (1: 683). What the two assessments have in common is the question whether or not the victim is empowered to communicate. And in this respect each case may have to be judged separately. Although he has no chance to speak before dying, Fancioulle's performance itself conveys a silent but eloquent message. In Anouilh's play, Becket speaks, and his words carry in their everyday denotation the explosive knowledge of ironic fission. In Eliot's play, Becket allows very few doubts about his supreme lucidity in the midst of conflict.

Nevertheless, important cognitive differences between the individual on the stage and the spectators persist. Both Becket and Fancioulle must have profound insights into the events that overwhelm them; but, engaged in mortal struggle to control the unfolding metaphoric field, they face a danger that does not allow time for a leisurely interpretation. The spectators, on the other hand, free from the physical danger, can deploy more of their energy in an attempt to control the field by interpreting its recreation. They arrogate to themselves the privilege of a sheltered position. And in "Une Mort héroïque," the narrator enjoys additional privileges. Shielded by his position, he not only interprets the events, in the manner of a spectator, but also hints that he may have inside knowledge about the motivation behind them.

However, the decisive difference between one who is, or is assumed to be, on the playing field and the spectator who remains on the sidelines occurs at the moment of death. For the former, action ceases and interpretation falls silent; for the latter, interpretation and possibly action are at their highest potential. In trying afterwards to describe the pantomime, overcome by the tears of "une émotion toujours présente" 'an everpresent emotion' (1: 321; Kaplan 1989, 65), the narrator again feels pity and fear, as a continuation of the original cathartic exhilaration he experienced as a spectator.

Death as the Ultimate Measure

The question one has to ask is this: Should art or religion protect the artist or believer against death? And the answer is that no human value can protect us from physical death. To be consistent then, since both Fancioulle and Becket die, we would have to call all our values and beliefs illusory. And perhaps, in an absolute sense, they are. But in a historically defined context, we have to conclude that the emerging principle in "Une Mort héroïque" is the precarious yet immense value of art: an art that is impregnated by death. The performance put on by "l'étrange bouffon, qui bouffonnait si bien la mort" 'the strange clown, who was clowning so well the ways of death' (1: 322) is a ritual that veils "the terrors of the abyss" and obliterates the chasm that separates character and actor, by the ineffable leap from the vague ideal of beauty to its incarnation on the stage. The ritual's narration is silent, but its meaning is unmistakable: what Fancioulle mimes is his own life and death.

The Narrator

While assuming awareness in the minds of the mime and the spectators, Baudelaire's narrative excels in highlighting the consciousness of the narrator. There are in fact two narrators. The first one is the persona, the speaking voice, the "I" of the story, who remains subordinated to the authority of the text. Wing expresses a well defined belief that through irony and "multiple or indeterminate points of view" "the [prose] poems deconstruct" his authority (1979, 24). Still, within the fabric of fiction, he is a privileged observer and the metaphoric language only reinforces his position. The second narrator is the poet himself, seen as a historical figure, who is the constructor of the text, the writing voice as it were. This narrator appears to stand aloof in a position to have a one-to-one relation to the text. His authority is higher than that of the first narrator but it too has to be submitted to the textual constraints. Moreover, defining it or ascertaining its efficacy is sometimes elusive, since it can only be formulated through the textual evidence and in a more comprehensive attempt by means of intertextual comparisons. In his first role as persona, the narrator joins the spectators at the performance; in his second, as writer, he attempts to communicate with his readers.

As an observer in "Une Mort héroïque," the narrator belongs to the tripartite structure of the poem, but he enters a world dominated by the polarity of two powers: the authority of the prince and the prestige of the artist. The narrator looks at the spectacle before him and measures the distance that separates the despot, who believes the world is there for his own entertainment, and the mime, who believes art is the last answer on the way to salvation. The vast space that separates them is marked by the tension between two radically opposed points of view. On the surface, at least, the narrator attempts to be objective; not only does he not openly condemn the prince, but often his descriptions betray a certain admiration born out of the existential affinity between the prince and Baudelaire. In the ironic dimension of the text, one has the impression of discerning the implication that being cruel, emulating a Nero, is part of being a prince. The narrator's greater sympathy, of course, does go to the performer, who embodies the essence of the poet's striving;[9] but comprehensive meaning emerges from the tension between the two antagonists.

Some Cognitive Implications

More than a reflection "on the nature of poetic language" (Johnson 1983, 79), the prose poem is a demonstration of the dynamics of the cognitive relation between subject and object and of the limitations of the process of cognition itself. In the perspective of the stage, the mime remains somewhat at a distance. Yet at critical moments the intense focus brings him closer and the narrator notes his eyes "démesurément agrandis" 'inordinately widened' and other facial expressions. The narrator also looks at the prince and tries to read his face as a text. The prince's face, as a consequence of his own observations, offers some observable data: a new pallor added to the habitual pallor, the narrowing lips, and the blazing eyes. They are signs but they have to be interpreted. Moreover, there are many things that the narrator simply cannot see, many things in the prince's mind that are not susceptible to being seen. And while an observer can be successful in reading someone's mind, the attempt is more often than not fraught with uncertainty. The narrator's questions illustrate how the process of cognition works in the absence of sufficient data. What must the prince be thinking? Does he feel defeated in his power? Does he feel frustrated in his expectations? Beyond the perceptual level, the questions the narrator asks remain far flung enigmas. They reinforce the difficulty of knowing and create a degree of suspense. The narrator gives the impression that he knows more than the others in the audience but is careful not to state unequivocally his conclusions: he implies them and suggests them.[10]

Critics agree implicitly that the narrator's comments are essential in interpreting Fancioulle's story. But the participation of the other spectators, their applause in particular, is also necessary to the effectiveness of the performance. Here again the comparison with *Murder in the Cathedral* can help. The "scenes of frenzied enthusiasm" (Eliot 1952, 178) with which the people of Canterbury receive the archbishop parallel "[l]es explosions de la joie et de l'admiration" the '[e]xplosions of joy and admiration' (1: 322; Kaplan 1989, 65) that greet Fancioulle's performance. In the play, having completed the murder, the knights address the audience, explain their action, and suggest "that you now disperse quietly to your homes," adding: "Please be careful not to loiter in groups at street corners, and do nothing that might provoke any public outbreak" (Eliot 1952, 219). The irony is that the priests, the chorus, and implicitly the theater audience respond in a way that is contrary to the spirit of the knights' admonition. If in the prose poem the spectators, after applauding Fancioulle's performance with boundless enthusiasm, appear to "disperse quietly to [their] homes" and so fade away from the fabric of the story, they subsequently refuse to grant other mimes the favor enjoyed by Fancioulle. The way the human game is played they have no choice but to participate in the ritual of martyrdom.[11]

Does History have a Meaning?

What "Une Mort héroïque" reveals may be the most traditional yet the most radical paradox: the transformation of the violent break in linear chronology into a concept of timelessness. Only through death can art outstrip time and gain some measure of freedom, some modicum of immortality. Both the mime and the prince are in time, but by being the instrument of the mime's death, the prince incarnates a determinism that introduces timelessness into the scheduled chronology. The poem's fable[12] suggests a view of history in which historical time is in perpetual crisis. For art exacts a rupture in time and repeatedly triggers off a conflict between power and the ideal, between history and timelessness. At this point Foucault's belief that "history has relations of power, not of meaning" regains its irony. And when he exclaims: "History has no 'meaning'" (1980, 114), we would have to agree, but only if we imagine historical events without their interpreters, Fancioulle's (or Becket's) martyrdom without spectators and narrator.

"Une Mort héroïque" asserts that the artist has to die and that death is inherent in the triumph of art. True, this state of affairs cannot be generalized: not all artists are martyrs. However, the prose poem suggests a principle that can be extended to all. Not only is there no real success without a public and a narrator: there is no meaning without them. The struggle for meaning takes place on the level of texts and their interpretation. Tradition and history, each dealing with the same material but differing somewhat in method and focus, are propagated and written by those who survive historical events. Although they do not determine the outcome of these events, the survivors as spectators and narrators settle the issue of meaning. Knowing this, the victors on the playing field spare no effort to cajole or compel writers to interpret events in a way that is favorable to their image. As Baudelaire's prince, who cultivates rumors, and Henry II, who manipulates public opinion, demonstrate, the tendency of modern rulers and groups that rule to have their versions of history and truth is not new. Lattimore points out that even Homer tipped the balance in favor of the Greek heroes and against Hector to the point that "we sense deception" (1951, 36).

In the light of our texts, history and tradition emerge from the dialectical interplay between power and meaning, between the physical and moral forces that contend on the stage and the producers of metaphors that define the conflict and assign value to victory and defeat. Though Fancioulle and Becket die, the spectators see their works as triumphant achievements and refuse respectively to grant other mimes the same high "favor" and to disperse quietly without ensuring the martyr's fame. The cognitive view, opposing Foucault's, asserts that both relations of power and relations of meaning are essential to the constitution of history but that the two kinds of relations are separated by the distance between actor and observer, between protagonist and reporter. And inevitably the dialectics has to be carried one step further. The creators of metaphors and paradigms in turn enter the conflict of interpretations and are in need of spectators, readers, and narrators to take their place. A tradition comes into existence as long as there are survivors to interpret the events they witnessed and lives as long as there are descendants to renew it.

5

Andromache and Baudelairean Exile in "Le Cygne"

The Critics and the Question of Origin

Baudelairean exile acquires its definitive attributes in the space of a familiar city square, a mnemonic zone where despair and auto-hypnosis meet and allegory suddenly rises in the midst of reality not as a simple trope but as a fully armed obsession, unavoidable, and overwhelming:

> Andromaque, je pense à vous!
>
> Andromache, I think of you!
>
> ("Le Cygne" line 1)

Like all great beginnings, this apostrophe holds a strong fascination for readers and critics precisely because it is sudden, appearing unexpectedly, seemingly *in medias res*, presupposing a preexisting world and a narrative already in progress.[1] But in referring to the tradition of Andromache in Homer and Virgil and to the account of how the poem came to be experienced, the text remains difficult to interpret. Why begin with an address to a legendary Trojan princess, if "Le Cygne" is, as its title indicates, about the allegory of a swan, a swan being "its main image" (Leakey, 1992, 81)? Why create another allegory? And even more fundamentally, why choose Andromache to begin with? In attempting to answer these questions I look again at the metaphoric field of the poem, its chronology, its time and space, and its possible origins.

The difficulty stated or implied by critics can be formulated in the following manner: which one of the three candidates, the swan, Andromache, or Carrousel Square, has the privilege of being the point of origin? Chambers suggests that all three have

90

equal claim (see 1987a, 167–68). Houston speaks of "an elaborate tangle of unexpected analogies" (1969, 100). Leakey believes that "the poet voices his thoughts exactly as they will have occurred to him, when into his mind there came suddenly the image of Andromache" (1992, 82). That would be the point of origin. And Burton echoes the same belief that the poem foregrounds "its own genesis" (1988, 155): "The first section of 'Le Cygne' re-enacts the process of its own formation from moment of conception . . ." (1988, 162). But the same year that Leakey first proposes his view (his essay on the originality of "Le Cygne" first appeared in 1973), Brombert points out the undecidability of the first line and writes: "La chronologie du poème implique des structures en apparence contradictoires de stratification et de circularité" 'The poem's chronology implies apparently contradictory structures of stratification and circularity' (1973, 255). And MacInnes categorically disagrees with Leakey: "The narrative that follows the opening apostrophe as if to justify it, in fact makes it impossible to declare an 'actual moment' at which the poem comes into being" (1988, 95). And more recently, Terdiman goes even further. If he appears to assume that the apostrophe is the beginning, the point of origin, it is only because for him the text is the product of the arbitrariness of the semiotic: "*Nothing* in the poem gives itself out as the product of immediate experience or perception. *Everything* is already semiotized . . ." (1993, 141).

The disagreement in these critical passages is ample evidence that the poem resists any attempt to decipher its point of departure and that this resistance can be felt during reading. The speaker's walk is really not the first crossing of the Carrousel Square. An earlier crossing becomes the object of meditation during the later walk and, thus, becomes the story of the swan. While it is normal to suppose that of the two (or at least two) crossings of the Carrousel Square, the second crossing, as more recent, brings to mind the first, it is difficult to know if that scenario, supported by the title, guarantees that the image of the swan came before the image of Andromache, precisely because in the body of the poem Andromache comes first. The opposite scenario, that Andromache came first, is also problematic. It is supported by the initial apostrophe but negated in the second part of the poem by the sequence Louvre (Carrousel Square)—the swan—Andromache.[2] Brombert can justifiably ask: Is the thought of Andromache a coincidence, being simply evoked by certain sensations and impressions, or is it "un appel, partant d'une intentionalité" 'an appeal, coming from an intentionality,' a voluntary

effort of invoking the royal widow in the hope of obtaining conso-
lation? (1973, 254). One has to allow for the possibility that the
key to the mystery is in the intertwining of insistent mnemonic
traces and the voluntary effort to write a poem. And once the
correspondences have been swept into the orbit of the metaphoric
field, its urgency would then determine the order in which they
should be presented.

Clearly Andromache is addressed and therefore appears to
mark the beginning of a semiotic chain. She rises as a fully armed
figure above the white void of the printed page but does not
originate in a void. She has a history, which begins in a distant
city in a distant time and carries a strong echo of the alien tongues
of Homer and Virgil. Consequently, the poem's story, the story of
its composition, is a gesture of erasing the distance between the
past and the present, between the dawn of myth and the birth
of allegory.

The Influence of the French Tradition

Nelson Jr. and Hampton have both masterfully studied the
poem's links to the classical epic. What has passed unnoticed is the
debt that Baudelaire owes to the French tradition. Saint-Amant's
melancholy in "Les Visions," which associates a deer he encounters with the death of Acteon, transforms swans into ravens swimming in blood and the Louvre into an asylum, bears a striking
resemblance to Baudelaire's melancholy, which apotheosizes a
swan into myth.[3] The obsessive character of the seventeenth-
century poet's vision is transferred to the modern poet's repetitive
return to the same image: "une image m'opprime / Je pense à
mon grand cygne" 'an image oppresses me / I think of my great
swan.' Moreover, the apostrophe to Polyxena, "O belle Polixene!
amante infortunée!" 'O beautiful Polyxena! unlucky in love!' ("Les
Visions" 1855, 1: 83), parallels Baudelaire's address to Andromache. Classical literature corroborates the extraordinary association
between the two women, two sisters-in-law. In Euripides' *The Trojan Women*, Andromache contrasts her fate with that of Polyxena:
"Polyxena is dead, free of the misery where we are trapped"
(1993, 37). And in *The Aeneid*, Andromache whispers: 'Happiest
of us all was Priam's daughter, / The virgin picked to die at the
great tomb" (1990, 3.438–439).

Polyxena had been sacrificed on the tomb of Achilles; Andromache was making her offerings, in ecstasy, before the tomb of Hector. If Baudelaire read these passages (we know he read Virgil and perhaps he read Euripides), he could not fail to be impressed both by the similarity and contrast they evoke. And since Saint-Amant lamented Polyxena's fate in a poem where swans and the Louvre are transformed into virtual allegories, why not celebrate Andromache's destiny in connection with an allegory of a swan that appears near the Louvre? Obviously we can never be sure. Saint-Amant's possible influence only deepens the mystery and strengthens the resistance of "Le Cygne" to any attempt to determine the chronology of its composition. But we can note that such a scenario does not contradict the possibility that the thought of Andromache and the swan, prompted by reminiscences of "Les Visions," came to the poet precisely as he says while crossing the Carrousel Square.

In the context of Saint-Amant's possible influence, we begin to suspect that the impetus for the composition of the poem, the origin, the illumination, may have come not separately from any of the three images, the new Carrousel, the swan, Andromache, but from the sudden discovery of the allegorical link that unites all three, a discovery made while crossing the new Carrousel, or afterwards while at his desk reading Virgil or Saint-Amant or simply trying to write a poem. "Dans certains états de l'âme presque surnaturels, la profondeur de la vie se révèle tout entière dans le spectacle, si ordinaire qu'il soit, qu'on a sous les yeux. Il en devient le symbole." 'In certain states of mind [which are] almost supernatural, the depth of life is revealed in its entirety in the spectacle, no matter how ordinary, before one's eyes. It becomes its symbol' (1: 659). Baudelaire firmly believes in the existence of these privileged moments; they are as authentic insights into the meaning of reality as the poet will ever be granted, but we as readers can hardly be certain about their exact location in time and space. Notice, for example, that, in the poem, the final mythopoeic touches are given to the swan in the present tense, "Je vois ce malheureux, mythe étrange et fatal, / vers le ciel quelquefois . . ." 'I see this hapless creature, sad and fatal myth / Sometimes towards the sky . . .' (lines 24–25; McGowan 175). "Sometimes," like "an image oppresses me" in the second part, is an indication that the present is invested with the power of repetitive vision, that the past transfers to the present its energy of leit motifs, of inevitable returns. Rather than remaining isolated in time, the moment of revelation is unending obsession.

The Poem's New Chronology

Still, it remains legitimate to ward off "the intentional fallacy" fear and learn as much as possible about the circumstances surrounding the composition of a poem. As many studies of "Le Cygne" attest, intertextual references may help us better understand the process of forging correspondential links. What is important to recognize is that the urgency of the metaphoric field of a poem restates the chronology of its figures and patterns. During composition all dynamic patterns are submitted to the new coherence of the developing field; they are now neither pure rhetorical patterns nor images wholly of reality. As the links to their origins weaken and the new relations among themselves grow stronger, the dynamic patterns can be made to obey the chronology of the new text, which may not reiterate the steps leading to its composition. Chronology is not abolished but it is submitted to the exigencies of writing. And the question, why begin with Andromache, comes back with renewed insistence. The poet's choice may have been dictated by strategic factors, by a desire to facilitate the entry of readers into the metaphoric field of the poem. Both images, Andromache and the swan, are privileged, but Andromache is instantly recognized as the Trojan princess in exile; the swan, on the other hand, would need an introduction. And precisely the first stanza is there to introduce the readers to the condition of exile and, thus, prepare them for the appearance of the swan.

Moreover the choice is appropriate in other ways. Andromache's memory is the prototype, the founding dynamics, of the poet's own memory at work. Her tears augment the waters of an artificial Simois, an artifact of memory, just as the poet's melancholy and suffering create the poem. As Kaplan aptly puts it: "Andromaque herself appears as an artist who has constructed an emblem of her exile, the artificial Simois which reminds her nostalgically of fallen Troy" (1980, 244). Her figure sets in motion the complex system of linkage in memory in which a concatenation of events spells separation from the native river and life in exile. Beginning with Andromache's illusory Simois and waiting until the fifth stanza to introduce the swan of the title represent a strategy of delay employed for suspense purposes but also for the preparation of the image of the swan bathing its wings in the dust of the gutter, in which dust is equivalent to fake water.

The Appeal of Widowhood

The second of our two initial questions remains to be answered. What is the determining factor in the choice of Andromache as the first model (and perhaps the ultimate model) of the individual in exile? The attempt to explain why, in "Le Cygne," Baudelaire chooses to address a widowed woman may give us a key to the understanding of the concept of exile in the poem. In a fundamental way his preference can be explained by the fact that, for him, a feminine figure lends itself more readily to the movement of empathy. Critics have been more specific. Speaking about the second widow in "Les Veuves," Mauron asks: "n'évoque-t-elle pas . . . un souvenir cher entre tous: l'image de Mme Veuve Baudelaire à Neuilly?" 'doesn't she evoke . . . the fondest of memories: the image of Mrs. Baudelaire the widow at Neuilly?' (1966, 52). Burton picks up the idea, applies it to "Le Cygne," and makes it even more specific, by pointing to "the image of the thirty-four-year-old woman [Baudelaire's mother] in widow's weeds, veiled and weeping, in a candlelit Paris church, heavy with incense" (1988, 166). This view is further buttressed by the belief that the "figure of Hector" should be read "as an emblem of the poet's long-dead father Joseph-François Baudelaire" (1991a, 8).[4] And there is no doubt that both the death of his father and the image of his mother in mourning must have left an indelible imprint on the son's memory. Still, with its dynamic and complex set of valences, the allegorical image transcends the one-to-one relationship with historical reality. The textual language imposes its own demands on the associations that either the author or the reader can make. And that not only because the image of Andromache has links with other texts, but also because a strong textual coherence, the tension of the metaphoric field, reinforces the widow's solidarity with the other exiles and weakens whatever connections it may have with the poet's mother and father. This does not mean a denial of the original cataclysmic event, represented by the mother's mourning. Emmanuel is not far from the mark when he says: "Privé de sa mère, il se veut damné" 'Deprived of (abandoned by) his mother, he wants to be damned' (1967, 142).[5]

Mnemonic deposits of images, however, do not occur in the manner of fossils, that is, they do not remain inert; both the old and the new continue to be active and undergo important modifications that come from reciprocal influences. Gradually they begin to reveal in their palimpsestic dogma that life is exile and suffering. In "Le Masque" the poet explains the mysterious sorrow of the statue of a woman saying: "—Elle pleure, insensé, parce qu'elle a vécu!" '—She weeps, fool, because she has lived' (line 32) and lives, because life itself is an exile, and our response to art and poetry is evidence "d'une nature exilée dans l'imparfait" 'of a [human] nature exiled to the imperfect' ("Étude sur Poe" 2: 334 and in "Théophile Gautier" 2: 114). A first answer that suggests itself is that the choice of a widow in "Le Cygne" appears to have been determined by the crosscurrents of a nostalgic past and an increasingly impassioned conviction that by the mark of suffering shall you know the elite.

That is why, although often mourning becomes their misfortune, widows do not have to wear black and other trappings of mourning to be recognized: "Qu'elles soient en deuil ou non, il est facile de les reconnaître" 'Whether or not they are wearing mourning, they are easy to recognize' ("Les Veuves" 1: 292; Kaplan 23). They are recognized by the correspondential signs of suffering on their faces and in their eyes, by their stylized gestures, by Andromache's bearing before the empty tomb of Hector. Since suffering is universal, however, one may justifiably ask, why select women and widows (or old women) in particular? The memory of the poet's mother in mourning may not be sufficient to explain his preference. Two other factors, the aesthetic and the sexual, add their share of influence.

A "Fusées" fragment offering a definition of Baudelaire's own concept of beauty makes a distinction between beauty in a woman's face and beauty in a man's. Ignoring the latter and concentrating on the former, the poet defines aesthetic modernism in terms of the association of beauty and misfortune, declares that Melancholy is beauty's illustrious companion, and adds: "Je ne conçois guère ... un type de Beauté où il n'y ait du *Malheur*" 'I hardly can conceive of ... Beauty without *Misfortune*' (1: 658).[6] Beauty in the face of a woman inextricably linked with melancholy and bearing the imprint of misfortune raises questions that go beyond its romantic character.

But is melancholy simply an indication of the poet's aesthetic preference? Or is it a hint of a greater degree of accessibility to the woman's precincts forever desired yet more often than not denied to him? Is it, in other words, the obverse of his exile from the feminine other? Thélot believes that her widowhood renders Andromache inaccessible. She may indeed be inaccessible to Hector, since he is separated from her by death and by a different kind of heroism, and to Pyrrhus and Helenus, since she married them not by choice but by necessity. Perhaps that is why some believe that she evokes not only Virgil's Andromache but Racine's as well.[7] On the other hand, the poet's access to her inner being is sanctioned by the dynamics of a cognitive projection of desire. Misfortune reassures the poet of his affinity with the elite of sorrow, granting him access to the domain of myth and fulfilling, thus, the promise of overcoming loss. But the poet also reads woman, and therefore Andromache, as a text where misfortune is allied in some fundamental way not only to beauty but also to sexual desire.

This alliance is especially striking in the portrait of the old women whose eyes fascinate him: "Ces yeux mystérieux ont d'invincibles charmes / Pour celui que l'austère Infortune allaita!" 'Those enigmatic eyes have compelling charms for whoever was suckled on the milk of austere misfortune' ("Les Petites vieilles" lines 35–36; Scarfe 197). The use of the expression "invincibles charmes" to describe them betrays the sexual nature of their appeal. The stylistic power play fuses their past—their suffering and loss—and their sexual potential into the present fascination. In "Les Fenêtres," Baudelaire claims that he could have reconstructed the story of an old man just as easily. And that is true (the old acrobat may be an example), but why bring it up at this juncture, if not to avert the accusation of being sexually attracted to the woman he observes? Moreover, in other texts, in "À une passante" for example, the attraction that the widow holds for him is clearly sexual in nature. In "Le Cygne" neither the swan nor the orphaned children militate in favor of this interpretation, but the presence of the black woman, a subdued reference to Jeanne Duval, which may have been introduced to facilitate the poet's admission into the circle of exiles, corroborates the sexual link. One has to conclude that, at least in some important cases, the desire to belong to the category of those who suffer exhibits strong sexual overtones.

In a sense, Baudelaire can identify himself with a widow because he too is a widower in mourning, refusing to compromise his solitude. Again, biographical evidence could be adduced to show that Baudelaire felt alone. In "Mon coeur mis à nu," he notes: "Sentiment de *solitude*, dès mon enfance" 'Feeling of *solitude*, since my childhood' (1: 680). To his mother (in 1861) he writes: "Je suis seul, sans amis, sans maîtresse, sans chien et sans chat, à qui me plaindre" 'I am alone; I have no friends, mistress, dog or cat to complain to' (1973, 2: 152). However, it may not be necessary to turn to biography, since in "Le Cygne" itself, the poet speaks of "ma mélancolie." Solitude is not a specific event: it is a state of mind dominated by the belief in one's existential loneliness and characterized by an inability or unwillingness to abandon one's dreams or to compromise one's uniqueness.

The Exilic Stubbornness

In "Le Cygne," Andromache's appeal, in Racinian fashion, is precisely in her refusal, since her marriage was imposed on her, to accept either Pyrrhus or Helenus as her legitimate husband. Without this crucial determination, the full force of the textual urgency is lost. An example of what can happen comes from Marxist approaches. Following in Dolf Oehler's footsteps, Goldbaek identifies Pyrrhus with Napoleon and Andromache with France: "De même qu'Andromaque s'accomode allègrement de son nouvel époux au pouvoir sans borne, de même la France s'accomode de Napoléon III" 'Just as Andromache cheerfully puts up with her new husband who has unlimited power, so too France is content with Napoleon III' (1990, 79). The poem's historical context tells a different story. It is Hugo, not a submissive France, that best epitomizes the attitude of the poem's exiles. In a letter to him, dated 23 September 1859, the year of the composition of the poem and just after Napoleon's declaration of amnesty, Baudelaire writes: "Il y a quelque temps, l'amnistie mit votre nom sur toute les lèvres. Me pardonnerez-vous d'avoir été inquiet pendant *un quart de seconde?* . . . Votre note est venue qui nous a soulagés. Je savais bien que les poètes *valaient* les Napoléon, et que Victor Hugo ne pouvait pas être moins grand que Chateaubriand" 'Not long ago the amnesty made everyone talk about you. Will you forgive me for being worried [unsure] for *a quarter of a second?* . . . Your note arrived and made us feel better. I knew that poets *are a match for* the Napoleons of this world, and that Victor Hugo could not be less great than Chateaubriand' (1973, 1: 598). In the note Hugo is unyielding: "Personne n'attendra de moi que j'accorde, en ce qui me concerne, un moment d'attention à la chose appelée amnistie . . ." 'No one will expect me, as far as I am concerned, to pay a moment of attention to the thing called amnesty . . .' (qtd. 1973, 1: 1037). Hugo would return, when liberty returned. This is precisely the stubborness that characterizes the exiles in the poem. Thus, if there is an analogy to be made, it is between Victor Hugo, a present exile, and Andromache, an exile of the past. For it is through her refusal to submit that Andromache accedes to her essence, to her widowhood, as it is now preserved in tradition.

The Time and Space of Exile

Exile as such is especially susceptible to being modulated by a temporal relation. In *The Iliad*, Andromache foresees her widowhood at the moment when Hector takes leave of her to go battle: "you have no pity / on your little son, nor on me, ill-starred, who soon must be your widow" (1951, 6.407–8). And she foretells her exile (see 1951, 24.725–34). Thus, in the scene in Epirus, Virgil allows Andromache to bring back into time the timeless essence of loss, mourning, and exile and to fulfill her destiny. What was a foretold future becomes a haunting present; the promised widowhood ends in eternal identity. What was once the river of a celebrated city turns into a stream that directs the mimetic impulse toward the permanence of exile. Building the "little Troy," the replica, creating the fake Simois are simply indications, signs, that there will be no return to Troy.

Yet even in *The Aeneid*, turned toward the past, living from the strength of her memories, Andromache has not lost all contact with the present. In this she is torn between two metaphoric fields. One field is generated when, immersed in thought, she pours her offerings before the empty tomb of Hector and the purified past holds her captive at its center. The other suddenly opens when Aeneas and his men arrive and interrupt her captivity, violate the purity of her chosen past, and destabilize the enchantment of the cathartic experience. Seeing the men "in Trojan arms, her mind misgave" and "she swooned" (1990, 3.415–418).

Andromache's shock and disbelief, her impression that the Trojans are part of a delusion, emerge from the collision of two metaphoric fields: a mnemonic stasis and an inexorable succession of events in time. One is nurtured by her memories of a selected and exalted past; the other is sustained by the presence of Aeneas and his men, embodying no longer a past but a historical present. In the first, arrested history is metamorphosed into myth; in the second, the exigencies of myth become the mainsprings of history. When she comes to, she asks, "Your face, / Can it be real?" and "Where is my Hector?" (1990, 3.420–24) She means that if they are dead, ghosts, Hector should be among them. But the text may also suggest that if they are alive, who should be dead by her reckoning, if the past in her memory has become real, then perhaps Hector should be among them. Andromache has to make a great effort of the will, as the expression "And it was long / Before she spoke" indicates, to negotiate the passage from one field to the other. The text bears traces of the struggle and of the tension between the two fields. Once she has crossed the field barriers, she steps into the dynamic present, and although she laments her fate, she inquires about Aeneas's son, Ascanius, and is able to behave more or less the way a woman would when meeting a close relative she has not seen in a long time.

In "Le Cygne," Homer's visionary future in exile and Virgil's tension between past and present have now been transfigured into a condition of loss, appropriately described by Nash as a "state of permanent exile" (1976, 30). Almost immediately after the initial "I think of you," the present is engulfed in a flashback of visual patterns emerging from memory and generating a narrative time and a tension between a city square and a tradition, between personal experience and literary intimacy. The voice of the speaker, then, shuttles between the narrative time and the present, aiming to erase the gap between meditation and the words on the printed page. Thus, after "comme je traversais" 'as I was crossing' (line 6) comes "Le vieux Paris n'est plus" 'Old Paris is no more' (line 7); after "Là s'étalait" 'There was set up' (line 13) and "Là je vis" 'There I saw' (line 14), the poet returns to "Je vois" 'I see' (line 24), a present that becomes dominant in the second part. But the textual complexity goes beyond verb tenses; the present time itself contains the past in a correspondence that stands at the center of the poem.

Subsuming both past and future in a homeostatic present, Baudelaire's time resembles *The Iliad*'s mythic time, in which the characters know both their past and their future but always move in an eternal present. The difference appears to be that Baudelaire's figures cannot conceive of a future except as a repetition of the present. Time in *The Aeneid*, envisioned as the chronological movement toward the future fulfillment of Aeneas's destiny, contrasts sharply with the present that in "Le Cygne" has leveled all hope. In this respect the future oriented present in *The Aeneid* parallels the present that moves inexorably toward a denouement in *The Odyssey*, while the endless present in "Le Cygne" mimics *The Iliad*'s mythic present. In the first category, the text relates a series of chronologically modulated events; in the second, the text narrates the story of the birth of allegory and myth.

Chronology and memory modulate the three figures of An-

dromache. Virgil's and Baudelaire's come after Homer's but they
are not simple repetitions. Each is an avatar that aspires to the
memory of its previous embodiment or embodiments. The modern setting, the Baudelairean "hélas," and the poem itself make
Baudelaire's Andromache unique; but it is the mnemonic links
with Virgil's and Homer's heroines that generate the task of reaf-
firming her identity, of completing her destiny. As a corollary, and
perhaps paradoxically, part of her difference resides in the fact
that readers cannot help perceiving her in terms of their memory
of the earlier figures. That is to say, one can conceivably read
about Andromache in a passage from Homer without relating it
to Virgil and Baudelaire, but it would be difficult to read "Le
Cygne" without thinking of Virgil and Homer. This, of course,
is not an absolute distinction. There may be readers for whom
chronology of this sort is abolished early and the intertextual links
work in all directions.

From the narrator's perspective in "Le Cygne," the present field
and the past are intersecting at the point of allegory. Baudelaire's
Andromache is wholly absorbed in thought and her rapture before the empty tomb comes after the two originally irreconcilable
fields have settled into an allegorical balance of a single metaphoric field. Exile is now the land where an artificial river, an
empty tomb, a city gutter, a fog, everything is a simulacrum of
the lost harmony with the environment, a sham, an illusion of the
native splendor calculated to revive and tease the consciousness of
loss. Exile is the space where water is the measure of life and
where there is no water, the point where autohypnosis and despair
come together, the site of hopelessness of suffering.[8] Exile is also
the place where choices are made, a list of models drawn, and
someone is designated to break ground, to begin building the
allegorical city for the elite of misfortune.

The Poet and his Allegorical Figures

Aware of the close relationship between the poet and his allegorical figures, critics formulate a delicate balance. Mauron points
out that the exiles "ne sont pas Baudelaire, mais mêlés à lui" 'are
not Baudelaire but are mingled with him' (1966, 81); and Burton
suggests that "The poem's emblematic victims both are and are
not himself" (1988, 165). The relation to the historical Trojan
princess is perhaps less than complete commingling but more
than simple imitation.

It is initially a projecting of ambitions and desire onto a historical figure, a gesture that does not blur the boundaries of the two
identities. That is why Terdiman can speak of "the materialization
of Andromache at dawn in a demolished square" (1993a, 182),
and Bonnefoy can call her "une passante lointaine, une femme
réelle" 'a distant passerby, a real woman' who exists "hors de la
conscience" 'outside consciousness' (1959, 160–61). Yet Andromache before her husband's empty tomb is also a dynamic pattern
that belongs to the poet's memory and, as such, is part of his
identity. That is to say, we as readers see and interpret Baudelaire
by the patterns he produced; we have no other way to perceive,
or make contact with him (biographical texts are simply patterns
produced by others or by Baudelaire himself on other occasions).
Thus, to define the Baudelairean self in relation to his allegorical
figures is to apprehend him in his function as a poet: "Le propre
des vrais poètes . . . est de savoir sortir d'eux-mêmes, et comprendre une tout autre nature" 'The peculiar gift of true poets . . . is to
know how to come out of their selves, to understand a completely
different person' (1973, 1: 334). The act of understanding is also
a gesture of transforming the person into one who is like the
poet; it is a strategy of remaking another human being in his
image, a need to obliterate difference and obtain the essence of
what unites them. In this process through which the poet pays
his dues for membership in the club of exiles, both he and the
figures he appropriates incur losses to their specificity, to their
delineation in the dimension of the real. But they also gain a great
deal; for while individually each exile may flounder in the midst
of defeat, and knowledge of defeat, as a member of the elite
each refuses to yield and continues to proclaim his or her own
inalienable right to a native and primary dream in memory. And
in joining them, in projecting onto them his spiritual hope and
despair, Baudelaire celebrates his kinship with them. His poetry,
then, is not a static image but the celebration of a self engaged in
the drive to go beyond fragmentation and reestablish its lost unity.
The rhythm is one of access not of denial; and though the identification is permeated by sexual energy, its impulse is not primarily
sexual but cathartic in function and purpose.

The Mnemonic Relation

No concept or image alone can adequately account for this
function because the poem is not about a concept or an image

but about a mnemonic process. Memory unifies the self, linking one moment of vision to the next and paving the way for the construction of meaning. The allegorical figures, the swan, Andromache, the black woman, and Victor Hugo as dedicatee, may appear at first disconnected, shards of a fragmented vision, and from a semiotic perspective the decision to use them in the poem may seem arbitrary.[9] But the semiotic relation, while long and potentially endless, is controlled, defined and, thus, limited by the mnemonic relation. Far from being arbitrary, the choice of the intertextual references has been mnemonically determined through what Baudelaire calls "le grand criterium de l'art," "le souvenir" ("Salon de 1846" 2: 455). It has obeyed the demands of the mnemonic potentials whose obsessive and autohypnotic character reflects the primary need to write the poem.

In the final analysis, the individual dynamic patterns, the allegorical figures, appear stylized and brought into a new mnemonic space whose chronological dimensions have been overriden by a new necessity. This is the dominant need of the self to break the taboos of the elite of sorrow, to achieve mnemonic unity with them, and to lay the cornerstone of his identity. Baudelairean exile is not a simple affirmation of difference, "I am not like other men," but an impossible hope to transform the others into brothers and sisters, or failing that, an ambition to find others like him in the realm of the imaginary. Clearly even that ambition is tainted by the cognitive reality that to find exiles in other texts is equivalent to reading one's own alienation into those texts. It is an attempt to draw from misfortune's meager rations a more potent milk, to transcend exile by the creation of the myth of exile, and to outstrip suffering by gaining access to the suffering of others. The remarkable achievement of Baudelairean allegory is not in establishing an arbitrary commerce on the semiotic highways but in sanctioning access to the markets of memory and myth; not in issuing a limitless number of semiotic (allegorical) coins but in adopting suffering as a common currency for the city of exile. Baudelairean allegory does not appear ex-nihilo, "in the void that separates intent from reality" (de Man 1971, 34), but springs fully armed from the head of history; it does not constitute itself "on the far side of the existential project" (de Man 1971, 35), but originates in the memory of other interpretations.[10] Baudelaire does not argue for the separation of literature and reality but narrates the reality's mitotic division in material history and legendary vision. The poet's allegorical project produces, thus, a more painfully experienced duality of language, a renewed tension between the material and visionary realities, between, on the one hand, the awareness of loss, despair, and suffering, and on the other hand, the hypnotic desire to belong, to join those who have already joined, and to experience exile as a new form of mnemonic exhilaration. One must imagine "Andromaque en extase courbée" happy, transgressing mourning to attain a higher joy "qui n'est complètement vrai[e] que dans *un autre monde*" 'which is completely true only in *another world*' ("Puisque réalisme il y a" 2: 59).

6

"Le Voyage":
The Dimension of Myth

Echoes of Epic Sources

"Le Voyage," Baudelaire's longest poem, ranks among his most complex and enigmatic. As long ago as 1945, Pommier confessed that, at least up to that time, he had not been able to untangle the poem's complexity (1945, 344). And Leakey begins his analysis by describing its structure as "elaborate, even devious" (1969, 294). Complexity and enigma surround not only the structure but the principal figures and symbols as well. While asserting their inalienable difference, their uniqueness in a modern context, the poem's figures, Circe, the drunken sailor, Time, Electra, and Pylades, nevertheless weave intricate echoes of their traditional epic sources. And one way to interpret them is to situate them in relation to their mythological counterparts.

Critics have assumed that such a relation is justified but have not pursued its implications. Burton, for example, acknowledges that "'Le Voyage' deploys a wide range of mythological, historical and literary allusion . . ." (1988, 72), but sees it "as an anti-*Odyssey*" (1988, 73), which "preserves the movement and energy of epic while undermining their teleological justification" (1988, 153). He thus stresses the contrast with the classical epic. I focus instead on the resemblance, on the way the relation to traditional structures discloses the mythic attributes of Baudelaire's symbols. This strategy proves helpful in solving a crucial difficulty of interpretation and in accounting for the difference between the voyage in section vii and the one in section viii.

The Victory of Time

The difficulty occurs after two stanzas in which human efforts to escape Time are shown to be futile: "Lorsque enfin il mettra le pied sur notre échine . . ." 'When in the end he sets his foot on our back . . .' (line 121).[1] Calling this "the dramatic turning-point of the poem," Austin begins his analysis by identifying Time with death: "When at last Time, now identified with death, has laid us low . . . what then?" (1961, 29) Expressing a similar view of this line, Adam comments: "Ce sera la Mort, la Mort qui n'est elle-même qu'un dernier voyage" 'That is Death, Death which itself is but a last voyage' (1961, 431n25). But are critics justified in believing that death intervenes at this moment? They acknowledge with Austin the "entirely new and original note" (1961, 30) of the last two quatrains but believe sections vii and viii speak of the same voyage. Thus, when Burton notes a shift in meaning, he points to the contrast between section vi and the "concluding stanzas" (1988, 86) and not between section vii and those stanzas. The question that arises is this: If the voyage that follows the victory of Time signifies Death, why would the speaker need to call on Death in the last section and ask for a new voyage?

To say that the last section, which clearly marks a new departure, continues the previous one without a break, that the two constitute only one voyage, is not satisfactory. The only answer that is consistent with the organization of the poem is that after the victory of Time there are two voyages, one in section vii, one in section viii, and that the first does not signify the death of the speaker. The two-voyage interpretation explains why during the first voyage the travelers hear voices with a familiar accent (line 133) whereas in the second voyage they seek "du *nouveau*" 'something new' (line 144; Scarfe 1964, 190).

Intertextual evidence corroborates the view that the victory of Time does not signify death. At the end of "La Chambre double," Time reappears and resumes its dictatorship telling the speaker, "Vis donc, damné!" 'So live, damned one!' (1: 282; Kaplan 1989, 8). In "Chacun sa chimère," the image of several men, the narrator calls travelers ("voyageurs"), walking with chimeras on their backs and being condemned always to hope is dynamically similar to the one of the travelers in "Le Voyage," who, now that Time is on their backs, can hope and cry, "En avant!" 'Forward!' (line 122) In both cases they are very much alive although moving in an intermediary space between life and death, a Baudelairean Underworld or twilight zone. How then can we explain the fact that in "Le Voyage," though they are old, they remain young at heart? Is their joy in accepting the consequences of Time's reign another form of Baudelairean irony? Above all, if the new voyage does not represent death, why are they embarking on the Sea of Darkness? And what is the significance of the voices they hear?

Ulysses's Last Voyage

The first two questions have already been answered by Austin and Leakey, who stress that the "child, with his vast appetite, has never died within us" (Austin 1961, 30) and that at this point of the poem "the prospect lightens, paradoxically, to one of joy and hope" (Leakey 1969, 306). I will attempt to answer the other two questions. In Crépet's opinion, the reference to the Sea of Darkness has its source in Baudelaire's translation of Poe's *Une Descente dans le Maelstrom,* and "La *Mer des Ténèbres* c'est l'Atlantique" (1932, 12: 448). If it does designate the Atlantic, it does not necessarily imply death. I argue, instead, that the voyage on the Sea of Darkness is in fact a modern version of Odysseus's journey to the Underworld and of his subsequent encounter with the Sirens.

As has been pointed out by many (see Kopp 1969, 297–98), the dynamic pattern of the afternoon without end comes from "The Lotos-Eaters," but in some ways this section resembles the last voyage of Ulysses invented by Dante and taken up by Tennyson in "Ulysses." The journey is undertaken before the death of the speaker and explores a transitional zone that marks the limits of human power to probe the Unknown. Although apparently Dante did not read Homer, and Tennyson did not follow him, the structures of their narratives recall the archetype: Odysseus's visit to the Underworld, which occurs long before his death.

In Tennyson's poem, Ulysses and his mariners contemplate embarking on a last voyage and sailing "beyond the sunset" (line 60) at a moment in their lives when they, like Baudelaire's travelers, are old and Time has made them weak in body but "strong in will" (line 69). The sea that awaits them resembles the Sea of Darkness: "There gloom the dark, broad seas" (line 45) and the possibility of reaching "the Happy Isles" and seeing Achilles points to the land of the dead. In Dante, Ulysses sails past the Pillars of Hercules to the Atlantic, the Sea of Darkness, and, almost instinctively, attempts to break the barrier separating this world and the next. His attempt fails because, unlike Homer's hero, he has no divine guidance. Yet his ambition is to go beyond the sun and to reach the land of the dead (the mountain of Purgatory).

Ulysses begins his account with the words "When I left Circe" (1954, 26.86), even though the implication appears to be that he saw his family before leaving. This initial allusion to Circe resembles the dynamics of Baudelaire's reference to Circe at the beginning of the poem, which is clearly intended to mark the departure of a whole category of travelers. Circe's presence in "Le Voyage" and in canto 26 of *The Inferno* foreshadows the need to undertake a journey similar to the one Odysseus accomplishes in *The Odyssey* when he leaves Circe, on her advice, to visit the Underworld. Functioning as a catalyst to facilitate the reader's entry into the metaphoric field of the two newer texts, Circe's image betrays the master pattern of *The Odyssey*. (In "Le Voyage" the other catalyst is the child with its maps and prints, who prefigures the passion for knowledge and the desire to explore the world.)

Baudelaire's Circe is, of course, stylized in a modern version of the ancient goddess. As Burton says, she "is no daughter of the Sun and Sea but an all-too-human woman" (1988, 73). Yet the metamorphosis does not erase the traces of the ancient pattern or the source of her power. Her perfume is dangerous and she still has the capacity to transform men into beasts. The marks of her kisses can be effaced with time, but her appeal and the prestige of the tradition she exemplifies may never be lost. Baudelaire's insight, confirmed by Pound (whose first canto begins with a reference to Circe and summarizes Odysseus's journey to the Underworld), Stevens, Bonnefoy, and others, is that mythical models are susceptible of being transformed to fit a modern context.

The Siren-like Voices

With the victory of Time, the expressions "En avant," "Les yeux fixés au large," "Par ici," and "là-bas" simulate a decisive voyage, a movement in time. But a second and stronger impression is that the travelers are moving not on an empty sea but in a space peopled with familiar figures and voices:

> Nous nous embarquerons sur la mer des Ténèbres
> Avec le coeur joyeux d'un jeune passager.
> Entendez-vous ces voix, charmantes et funèbres,
> Qui chantent: «Par ici! vous qui voulez manger
>
> «Le Lotus parfumé! c'est ici qu'on vendange
> Les fruits miraculeux dont votre coeur a faim;

Venez vous enivrer de la douceur étrange
De cette après-midi qui n'a jamais de fin?»

À l'accent familier nous devinons le spectre;
Nos Pylades là-bas tendent leurs bras vers nous.
«Pour rafraîchir ton coeur nage vers ton Électre!»
Dit celle dont jadis nous baisions les genoux.

We shall set sail on the sea of Darkness with the joyful heart of a young passenger. Do you hear those ravishing and mournful voices singing: "This way! you who would taste of the perfumed Lotus! it is here that you pick the miraculous fruits which your heart craves; Come to get drunk on the strange sweetness of this endless afternoon"? The familiar tones betray the specter; over there our Pylades stretch their arms to reach us. "To refresh your heart swim toward your Electra!" says she whose knees we once embraced.

(lines 125–36)

What these voices offer to the travelers is not something new but the fulfillment of the desires they have always had: the desire to be intoxicated with some impossible fruit that suggests the preoccupations with "artificial paradises" and the need to find Electra, the ideal wife, mother, sister, and mistress. The gesture resembles the temptation of the Sirens in *The Odyssey*. By singing about the hero's exploits in the Trojan war (see Lattimore 1965, 12.189–90), the Sirens offer Odysseus knowledge about everything that happens on earth, but the appeal to the memories of his past is the essence of their temptation. Similarly, Baudelaire's travelers are tempted with highlights of their own past. And the quoted stanzas define the metaphoric field of the poem as *a mnemonic sea, where alluring voices tempt the travelers with their own memories.*

The Electra mystique

In "Le Voyage," as in the dedication to "Les Paradis artificiels," Baudelaire's tendency to identify himself with a literary model resurfaces in the reference to Electra and Orestes. As I have tried to show elsewhere, the couple defines his identity and close relationship with a woman, who is most likely Jeanne (see 1979, 4). In De Quincey's *Confessions*, translated by Baudelaire in *Les Paradis artificiels*, Electra is not simply Orestes's sister, but the ideal wife and companion. After comparing his state to that of Orestes, De

Quincey addresses his wife Margaret and tells her that she was kind and humble enough "to refresh [his] lips when parched and baked with fever" (1856, 153). Baudelaire picks up the verb "to refresh" both in the dedication and in the text, translating it with the French "rafraîchir" (1: 400 and 463). In the dedication, Baudelaire addresses the woman for whom he writes the translation and after speaking of the consoling role of De Quincey's Electra, he adds: "*et tu devineras la gratitude d'un autre Oreste dont tu as souvent surveillé les cauchemars, et de qui tu dissipais, d'une main légère et maternelle, le sommeil épouvantable*" 'and you will guess the gratitude of another Orestes, because you often kept watch over his nightmares and dispelled his dreadful sleep with a light and maternal hand' (1: 400). In the Greek drama and tradition, Electra may have been fanatic and savage in her vengeance, but her devotion to Orestes was not in doubt. And it is around this trait of her character[2] that a whole romantic tradition converges to transform her into the woman who brings compassion and love to the suffering hero.

If De Quincey's wife is maternal in her affection, she is also like a sister, not only because Electra is Orestes's sister, but also because there is contamination already in *The Confessions* with the "noble minded Ann" (1856, 136), an orphan companion, a street walker, who helped him when he was sick, and whom he loved "as if she had been [his] sister" (1856, 144). In the dedication to *Les Paradis artificiels,* the affinity between De Quincey's two heroines, Ann and Margaret-Electra, increases and Baudelaire's J. G. F.-Electra unites both maternal and sisterly attributes. And if one accepts that J. G. F.-Electra in the dedication is Jeanne, one will not be surprised that in "Le Balcon" dedicated to Jeanne, the poet calls her "mother of memories" and, with the expression "my fraternal hands," suggests a brother-sister relationship. Nor should one be surprised that the image of nestling on the knees of the beloved in "Le Balcon" resembles embracing Electra's knees in "Le Voyage"; both suggest a strong sexual worship tempered by the need for maternal and sisterly compassion.

The elements of worship are reinforced by a transfer of Circe's divine attributes to the image of Electra. In telling his story, Homer's Odysseus explains that, eager to return home, he approached the goddess, begging her to keep her promise: "but I, mounting the surpassingly beautiful bed of Circe, / clasped her by the knees and entreated her . . ." (Lattimore 1965, 10.480–81). The affinity between the pose of Homer's hero as a suppliant and the position of Baudelaire, the traveler, embracing Electra's knees shows once again that the strength of the Electra model resides in its mnemonic associations.

The Ghosts of the Underworld

It is true that as a consequence of various strata and mnemonic deposits, Baudelaire's images are no longer in their pure classical state. Yet as myth is filtered through personal memories, it is reinvested with magic powers, and the voices in "Le Voyage," having regained their Siren modulations, become attractive, irresistible. And for the travelers they are also elusive, since the danger here is not so much in being lured to death, but in always remaining just on this side of the outstretched hands, in dealing not with real people but with specters. Thus, like the impotent dead crowding around Odysseus, the shades, who drink the sacrificial blood to be able to speak, Pylades, faint at first, needs the infusion of creative energy to stretch out his arms toward the individual traveler. It is not even certain whether his outstretched hands offer welcome or ask for help. Beyond his symbolic function, Pylades does not have any attributes that would permit us to identify him with one of Baudelaire's friends.[3] And Electra-J. G. F. is now stylized as the essence of the beloved wife and sister whose knees the poet embraces in a distant, purified, and stylized "long ago." The use of the possessive adjectives, "nos Pylades" and "ton Électre," is perhaps a reminder that they are not the Greek friend and sister but our friends and our Electra. Despite their "spectral" character or perhaps because of it, these images become vivid markers of a glorified past and have the aura of what has been chosen from a long experience to be preserved in the archives of discourse.

Like the ghosts in the Underworld of *The Odyssey*, the specters dwell in a mnemonic space that is not beyond the reach of the living, in a transitional region between life and death,[4] and function as symbols or emissaries carrying messages. Their voices, however, are not "les signes qui parfois semblent venir de l'Inconnu" (Galand 1969, 427).[5] Nor are they demons of a completely uncharted world. Like Homer's Sirens, they are figural representations of the traveler's own desires and identity and their temptation does not suggest "the Forbidden Knowledge of Genesis" or "the occult knowledge of the Faust legend" (Clarke 1967, 64); rather, it offers certain coordinates to locate the point where one's own life and myth converge.

The Search for Knowledge

The mythic imagination has always invited the question: Why do heroes have to make this visit to the Underworld?[6] The basic goal of the voyage, the search for knowledge, allows for variations. In a leitmotiv older than *The Odyssey*, Gilgamesh, grieving for his dead companion, Enkidu, begins a journey to "cross the waters of death" (Sandars 1972, 104), to see Utnapishtim, and "to question him concerning the living and the dead" (Sandars 1972, 98). Similarly Odysseus, in the land of the Kimmerians, consults with Teiresias and others about his destiny and the return home. Dante's hero undertakes his voyage "to seek virtue and knowledge" (1954, 26.120); Tennyson's hero is enticed by the appeal of the act of striving and seeking.

As the expression "Amer savoir" 'Bitter knowledge' indicates, in "Le Voyage," the travelers also seek knowledge, but Baudelaire's text redesigns the issue: it substitutes implied inquiry and unstated alternatives to overt questions and clear-cut responses. Yet these differences, I suggest, pale before the palimpsestic need to weigh the value of life against the thought of death. The task is all the more urgent because his travelers journey with the burden of Time on their backs. At this crucial stage, the imperative is to move along in a space where tasting the miraculous fruit and reaching the land of the inoperative Time become mirror-like patterns of the experience the self has always sought. However, the permanent quality of the illusion/disillusion sequence foredooms any hope of success and the overall tone remains ironic, inconsolable.

The differences in the way the heroes make the final decision to opt for life or for death is also revealing. After his visit to the Underworld, Odysseus is steeled by what he learns from the ghosts of his friends, Achilleus in particular, and he resolves to live and return home to his wife and son. Aeneas too is more determined after his stint in the Underworld where he sees his father's shade and has a glimpse of the future of Rome. Their experiences simply reinforce their original intentions. In appreciating the decision made by Baudelaire's travelers, one has to take into account the negative dynamics of their drive, the fact that they began their voyage to flee "une patrie infâme" 'a despicable homeland' (line 9). As a consequence, when during the contact with the voices from their past, they understand that the charm of the afternoon without end, friendship, and love are all deception, vanity, and disillusion, they are ready to make the decision to seek the Unknown. There is no one with the wisdom of Teiresias to advise them how to get home because, one senses, there is no home to return to.[7] These travelers have no choice but to summon Death and to get ready for another departure.[8]

"Lo conocido / es lo desconocido" 'That which is known / is the unknown' (Pablo Antonio Cuadra, "El Maestro de Tarca" III, 1979, 33)

And it is at this point that the fundamental theme of the poem stands at epiphanic alignment. The travelers now realize that the only "unknown" that is within human grasp is in Time, in their own past. However, while the past can be explored and better understood, it does not in any ontological sense of the word disclose "something new." This proposition is mirrored in the textual surface. Looking back at what we have read, we can see that all the previous images of exploration, Icaria, Eldorado, Americas, the drunken sailor, and other references, are all part of a past familiar to Baudelaire and his generation and do not represent the unexplored but the explored. Because they are here stylized, downgraded, and wholly traversed by irony, they are not always easy to identify. Columbus, for example, the Admiral of the Ocean Sea, becomes a "drunken sailor, inventor of Americas" (line 43).[9] A few silhouettes and short exclamations condense a whole literature of explorers, conquistadors, and three-masted caravels driven by storms against Caribbean reefs, a whole mythical past as it is preserved in memory.

The engrams and their rich associations strengthen the metaphoric tension of the field and form the foundation of the new epic. In the mnemonic context, the new allegories, the foolish lookout on the foremast, the dreamer, the drunken sailor, and the vagabond acquire some of the symbolic prestige of heroes. And although it does not reinscribe in its development a historical chronology,[10] the poem organizes historical fragments into new myths that reflect what must have appeared to Baudelaire's contemporaries as the familiar side of history. The expression "aux yeux du souvenir" 'in the eyes of memory' appearing in the first stanza is a forewarning to the reader: the poem is about memory and its creative and "resurrectionist" prerogatives (see "Le Peintre de la vie moderne" 2: 699). In the eyes of memory the Mediterranean Sea and the Atlantic become the *mare nostrum* of a tradition. Unlike Rimbaud's "Le Bateau ivre," which begins with the unexplored and ends up in familiar surroundings, Baudelaire's voyage of exploration recalls the familiar figures of the past throughout and only in the conclusion allows a confrontation with the unknown.

The Second Voyage

Exacting the death of the speakers, the last voyage begins on a sea that has no buoys, no seamarks, no pillars of Hercules, and no voices. The only reality is the rays of light in their hearts, the inner reality, then, no longer available for further differentiation. When they set their new course, the travelers see the Unknown in its purest version, without contours or characteristics.[11] The description is minimal, its chronology compressed, and its visions hidden in the last enigma: "pour trouver du *nouveau!*" 'in quest of *something new*' (line 144; Scarfe 1964, 190) This new reality marks, by definition, the far side of the boundaries of human power and is not open to human understanding.

Clearly the two voyages are related. The first voyage sanctions a commerce between the living and the shades of the Underworld as a basis for making a decision about life and death; the second uses the lesson of this commerce to justify its new ambitions involving the death of the speaker. At times, the distinction between the two voyages is ambiguous. Dante's Ulysses, for example, cannot reach the Underworld without dying, but Dante and Virgil do and obtain knowledge. In Tennyson the distinction, though not clearly stated, remains in effect.

The second voyage marks the point of greatest separation between ancient epics and "Le Voyage." In the first the arrow of orientation points toward life; in the second toward death. Death, true Death, is the only release from the dimension of Time, and in contemporary terms, the only way to reach the outside of the Western discourse. Thus, "Enfer ou Ciel, qu'importe?" 'what matter if it's heaven or hell?' (line 143; Scarfe 1964, 190) may not mean that the choice between the two does not matter, but that neither of them matters.

Although, thus, a tabula rasa may appear as a precondition for the discovery of the new, caution is needed here lest we interpret the poet's desire in terms of a total rejection of life. Baudelaire insists that, before embarking on the journey into the Unknown, his travelers take some rays of light with them, carry a small baggage of memories from this world to the other. All the bitterness and irony of the previous sections are gathered in a powerful élan, a synthesis of desire, which, like a favorable wind that fills the ship's sails, drives the poem to its inevitable end. And though far-reaching pessimism permeates the textual fabric, the impression one has in reading the poem is one of forward momentum, vigor, light, and beauty that overcome pain and despair. These qualities and the tension of the complex metaphoric field, its mythic power and mnemonic depth, all create an appeal to counterbalance the pull of the poem's dark message.

An all-encompassing scope, a far-flung mythic vision, and pessimism then. But a pessimism that is not outside the scope of the western tradition. The paradox is that the poet has to attempt to go beyond the experience of the past to produce a final assessment of it. The implications of Baudelaire's critique of human societies and of the belief in progress reverberate on social, political, philosophical, religious, and historical levels; but the poem's reorganization of signs is neither an attempt at deconstruction nor a politically motivated intention to subvert the bourgeois society, even though he loathed its power and its nefarious effect on the artist. The need that the text releases is to submit a tradition to the filter of memory for the purpose of rewriting it, to humble it, and then to resurrect it in a form that can belong to his generation and our own. There are many approaches to Baudelaire's poem and many ways to appreciate it. A most profitable one is to replace it in the perspective of the tradition it seeks to define, demoralize, deny, and ultimately, in the written text, reaffirm. There is no myth and no history without a witness, without a singer of tales, and no poem without memory. "Aux yeux du souvenir," 'in the eyes of memory,' Troy has to be destroyed for the tale to begin, one has to leave Circe to obey her commands, one has to resist and leave behind the seductive voices of memory to immortalize them, and country and communal beliefs have to be abandoned so that some ultimate hope be reinscribed in the poem's vertiginous trajectory of bitterness and despair.

7

Allegory and Correspondences

Allegory and Symbol

Few ideas have been as apt to reflect the particular temper, the ontology, and the aesthetics of a literary period as the concept of allegory. From the Middle Ages when writers used it to design bridges to the transcendental world of the spirit to the Romantic period when they held in contempt its abstractions to the present day's tendency to recirculate its energy under Benjamin's auspices and direction, allegory has offered spectacles of the power of tropes to fascinate and to engage. Baudelaire is fully aware of what literature has lost when it allowed inferior painters to trivialize it and to lower its prestige.

We know the importance attached to the difference between symbol and allegory by Coleridge[1] and other Romantic theorists, who stress the existence of a "natural" link between symbol and the idea symbolized as a reflection of a fundamental unity. But during a long period beginning with Pommier's *La Mystique de Baudelaire* (1932) and ending with Leakey's *Baudelaire and Nature* (1969), while emphasizing the overall significance of Baudelaire's correspondences, twentieth-century critics make no concerted effort to distinguish between symbol and allegory. Pommier devotes a chapter to the poet's allegories, but his excellent discussion is textually oriented; it does not touch upon the Romantic distinction. Most studies define Baudelaire's symbolism in light of its aesthetic and philosophical aims, its teleological drive toward a final, or original, unity.[2]

In the early 1970s, however, perhaps with de Man's *Blindness and Insight* (1971), under the influence of Walter Benjamin, allegory's stock begins to rise. Benjamin's first step is to downgrade the "idea of the unlimited immanence of the moral world in the world of beauty," the conception of the symbol, which he calls "romantic and destructive extravaganza" (1977, 160). "Whereas

116

in the symbol destruction is idealized and the transfigured face of nature is fleetingly revealed in the light of redemption, in allegory the observer is confronted with the *facies hippocratica* of history as a petrified, primordial landscape." What allegory offers the observer is nature "subject to the power of death" (1977, 166). And since it involves a temporal dimension, history in its sorrowful aspect, this dialectical, allegorical view of the world is superior to the symbolic claim of "fleetingly revealed" unity.

The challenge is to the value and authenticity of the critical claim that the symbolic glimpse into the mystery of nature reveals a necessary unity, a claim equivalent to the Saussurean idea that the symbol is motivated (distinguishing it from the sign, which is not). As Fletcher puts it, "By identifying Symbol with synecdoche, Coleridge is assuming a sort of *participation mystique* of the Symbol with the idea symbolized" (1964, 17–18). For Benjamin, however, allegorical details are unimportant in themselves. They are raised onto a higher plane by the fact that they point to something else and thus appear to achieve transcendence.[3] Yet paradoxically, Benjamin emphasizes subjectivity: "If the object becomes allegorical under the gaze of melancholy . . . it is now quite incapable of emanating any meaning or significance of its own; such significance as it has, it acquires from the allegorist" (1977, 183–84). Benjamin's conclusion is that the allegorical process is arbitrary: "Any person, any object, any relationship can mean absolutely anything" (1977, 175). The battle lines are drawn here at the opposition between the symbol's extended hand toward a desired or transcendental unity and allegory's gesture of arbitrary semiotic endowment.[4]

Correspondences

In contradistinction to the views that privilege either symbol or allegory, Baudelaire's theoretical writings level the playing field between the two. Neither symbol nor allegory springs from a logical sequencing of system and illustration; rather, they are both part of a correspondential view of the world produced during certain states of mind. Baudelaire's aesthetic statements, including the sonnet "Correspondances," indicate that metaphoric thought mobilizes both the senses and the mind. While they transcend nature as they gravitate around the vertical of a spiritual world, correspondential relations possess a sensory appeal that makes them inherently valuable. Instead of canceling each other, immanence and transcendence function as goal oriented coordinates geared to respond to a more promising desire for renewal and unity. Correspondential relations spring from memory, produce echoes in a mnemonic space, and bear traces of mnemonic urgencies. Precisely for that reason, though moving under the guidance of the poet's subjective impulse, they are not arbitrary: any relation *cannot* mean any other. The new insights may be obtained during moments necessarily limited in time; or they may take the form of whole new metaphoric fields generated by vast mnemonic upheavals. Either way, they enter into the constitutions of new texts and, thus, survive the temporal limits of their origin.

The Affinity with Painting and Sculpture

In Baudelaire's art criticism, appropriately enough, the first thing that strikes us is that the word "allegory" is often used in reference to painting and sculpture. Thus, speaking in praise of a painting by Victor Robert, in which each figure represents respectively a people of Europe, Baudelaire asks, how can one make critics understand that "l'allégorie est un des plus beau genres de l'art?" 'allegory is one of the most beautiful genres of art?' ("Salon de 1845" 2: 368) In the "Salon de 1859," describing a *Petite Danse macabre*, he adds: "Les artistes modernes négligent beaucoup trop ces magnifiques allégories du Moyen Âge . . ." 'Modern artists neglect too much these magnificent allegories of the Middle Ages . . .' (2: 652). He appears to have in mind allegory as a genre, allegory which in the traditional view consists of "une proposition à double sens, à sens littéral et à sens spirituel tout ensemble" 'a proposition with a double meaning, a literal meaning and a spiritual meaning together' (Fontanier 1977, 114) or which in Fletcher's terms "says one thing and means another" (1964, 2) or in Wing's excellent formula, "relays meaning from one semantic level to another, within a limited polyvalence" (1986, 9). Baudelaire's poems have probably the richest collection of figures that betray their kinship with the allegorical figures in painting and sculpture: "ma Douleur" and "le Regret souriant," "le Repentir," "la Débauche et la Mort," and many others. They are stylized figures representing forces on a spiritual level and, thus, bear out the idea of a relay from one level to another. How is this relay or transfer to be understood?

When Baudelaire describes his experience of seeing the sculpture of "l'éternelle Mélancolie" 'eternal Melancholy' whose face is reflected in the waters of a basin or "la figure prodigieuse du Deuil" 'the prodigious figure of Mourning' ("Salon de 1859" 2: 669), one would tend to see a transfer from a visual image to a state of mind, from a perceivable figure to the experience of a concept. But for an observer with Baudelaire's anticipation, the human figure may present itself simultaneously as a figure and as a concept, the literal and the spiritual appearing as one in the interaction of an allegorical dynamic pattern. This is even clearer in his poetry where, for example, "ma Douleur" appears at the same time as a living childlike figure ("Sois sage, ô ma Douleur" 'Be good, my Sorrow') and as the concept of the poet's suffering. The concept becoming vivid experience moves toward the level of personification, while the figure being stylized offers a hand to the concept. This allegory relies more on an exchange than on a simple transfer, on an interaction, between image and concept that is correspondential and metaphoric in its function and effect.

Under the Umbrella of Metaphoric Thought

We should not be surprised, then, by the fact that in the important passage from "Le Poème du hachisch," Baudelaire makes no distinction among or between allegory, symbol, analogy, and correspondences.[5] An ordinary sight becomes symbol; Fourier and Swedenborg embodied in nature teach analogies and correspondences; and "L'intelligence de l'allégorie prend en vous des proportions à vous-même inconnues" 'The understanding of allegory takes on in your mind proportions unknown to yourself' (1: 430). Although what he describes here is the experience of the individual taking hashish, it is clear that for him symbol, analogies, correspondences, and allegory are all procedures of the creative impulse, which, becoming operational during privileged states of mind, metamorphose the ordinary and familiar into the unexpected and new, and facilitate the poet's understanding of "the depth of life." Baudelaire's apparently innocent gesture endows not only the symbol but all other tropes, including allegory, with metaphoric power. He, thus, goes beyond the initial Romantic doctrine and intimates a more comprehensive aesthetics of figural language.

Are Correspondences the World's or the Poet's?

Clearly for Baudelaire correspondences are a means of affirming or reestablishing the primary unity of the world. Imagination "a créé, au commencement du monde, l'analogie et la métaphore" 'created, at the beginning of the world, the analogy and the metaphor' ("Salon de 1859" 2: 621). But it has to repeat that performance again and again to renew the world and, Atlas-like, hold and maintain its unity. The central question emerges as a critical desire to determine the exact status of this unity. Does it exist in the world itself or is it a poetic construct?

The issue has been debated at length. Ruff and Adam both stress respectively the mystical and metaphysical nature of correspondences. Ruff cites the well-known sentence, "La première condition nécessaire pour faire un art sain est la croyance à l'unité intégrale" 'The first condition necessary for creating a healthy art is the belief in the integral unity' ("Les Drames" 2: 41), and Adam points out that Baudelaire never ceased repeating that the universal analogy is the great law of creation.[6] On the other hand, Prévost, Hubert, and Leakey, for example, place correspondences on an aesthetic level. Prévost suggests that the poet only "imagines" that things correspond among themselves; Hubert, while admitting Baudelaire's belief in the universal analogy, is convinced that instead of discovering them in nature, the poet himself invents his analogies; and Leakey, while admitting the ambiguously "spiritual" character of correspondences, denies their transcendental nature.[7] Others, among them Pommier, Austin, Blin, and Eigeldinger, perhaps more interested in the aesthetic aspect than in the mystical, occupy an intermediary position between the two extremes.[8] Eigeldinger stresses the active role of the poet, who is more than a decipherer. Allegory is an instrument that allows the poet to perform certain operations: "L'allégorie établit des rapports analogiques entre l'esprit et la matière . . ." 'Allegory establishes analogical relations between spirit and matter . . .' (1951, 110). But can one bracket the question of the nature of analogies? Eigeldinger answers that for Baudelaire "L'état originel fait d'unité et d'harmonie, pour l'homme tout au moins, n'est pas un donné, il doit se conquérir par la volonté de dépouillement et de concentration" 'The original state made of unity and harmony, at least for humankind, is not a given, it must be conquered by the will to self-discipline and concentration' (1951, 103).

We are here at the center of the problem. Is this original state the Edenic time? Or is it a historical stage, the starting gate of an evolutionary descending curve?[9] Should one conceive of this primordial unity as preexisting? If, as Van Dyke says, allegory "envisions human life as a continual interchange between temporal event and eternal pattern" (1985, 63), is time the primary text that has to be read and interpreted? Or is it the eternal pattern that has to be deciphered? While Baudelaire believes that poetry is what is completely true only in another world ("Puisque réalisme" 2: 59), and while he intimates that figural constructs can only derive their ultimate truth from an eternal pattern, in his practice, he exploits to the full the sensory experience of the world and explores, with as great an intensity as any of the moderns, the ravages of time on the human condition. He celebrates both the immanent richness of the visible objects and their transcendental orientation. Correspondences exist in the visible world, but the poet has to identify them, activate their transcendental virtues in a situation that is analogous to the relation between a critic and the text he or she has to read and interpret. This may be one reason for the disagreements about their nature and site. And it is also the reason the cognitive view points to memory as the answer to our basic questions.

The Intervention of Memory

Baudelaire's theory and practice leave no doubt that his allegorical patterns are neither deliberate personifications of concepts in the service of an ideology nor divine revelations on a mystical path, but epiphanies in a mnemonic continuum. We know, says Baudelaire, since all relations between the spiritual and the natural are hieroglyphic, that "les symboles ne sont obscurs que d'une manière relative, c'est-à-dire selon la pureté, la bonne volonté ou la clairvoyance native des âmes" 'symbols are obscure only in a relative way, that is, in accordance with the purity, the good will or the native clearsightedness of souls' ("Victor Hugo" 2: 133). This lucidity of the soul is in fact the ability of memory to possess the dictionary of the language. For the poet, correspondences are both a text to be read and a repertoire of analogies (in cognitive terms, dynamic patterns) to be mastered. They are neither a matter of religion nor a product of a purely aesthetic impulse; rather, they are strength of memory, magic of the language, more akin to the power of ritual than to the balm of prayer. What is the source of this strength?

Everything that happens happens in the mind, in memory. But having said that, we are faced with the next question, which is the one that cannot be easily answered. In what way does what happens in memory correspond to what happens in the world in nature or beyond? Clearly, in Baudelaire's view, nature is im-

portant, at least as a starting point, as a catalyst. Whatever organization nature has, however, cannot be apprehended without a
decipherer, and to that extent it is dependent on his or her good
will and clearsightedness. By the same token, a poet, a seer, Kalchas at Aulis, interpreting the sign of the snake and sparrows,
Cassandra before the palace in Argos, prophesying Agamemnon's
death and her own, and the modern poet in a Parisian street,
where a swan helps him interpret Andromache's destiny and his
own, all need reality, need to face some physical manifestation of
nature, which will awake the prophetic strain and guide them to
the sign's or allegory's primal event. Figural language depends on
the organs of perception and ultimately on the seer's or poet's
memory, memory as an organizational principle of the things that
are, as the legatee of a tradition, possessing knowledge of the past,
and as divination of the things to come.[10] We thus do not know
how much of nature and reality can be captured and how great
is the residue after processing. It may be that the organization of
the world differs from the one intimated by Baudelairean aesthetics and that the ultimate reality will always elude us. What is not
beyond human means is to go on a quest for that reality. In that
search, memory, relying both on the literary tradition and on the
senses, creates metaphors, and allegories as a subspecies, to ex-
pand and deepen whatever knowledge we have. We thus face
Baudelairean allegorical figures, possible truths, limited in scope,
with meager salaries, but salaries paid in mnemonic and sensory
coins that allow them to have a better life-style than a severance
pay ever would.

Allegory as Fable or as Ballet

When an allegorical figure is called by its name, it points to
reality where it began and speaks to the issues that preoccupy
those who need to interpret its meaning. It speaks, but in the
language of signs that have to be read by an interpreter, or as in
"Le Masque," the language of the statue's real face behind the
mask of appearances, the allegorical language of tears caused by
the consciousness of living. And at the end, like a fable, the poem
states the moral, that life in whatever form appears is subject
to suffering.

In "L'Irrémédiable," the various images, an angel, a poor soul,
a damned person, a ship, all are emblems that illustrate the skill
of the devil, who "Fait toujours bien tout ce qu'il fait!" 'Does always

well all that he does!' (line 32). They are allegories that demonstrate, in the manner of a fable, a certain truth ("Vérité" with a
capital letter) and do not pass up the chance to explain it, to leave
no room for doubt about their own significance and meaning.
What is remarkable about this procedure is that each image taken
independently does not necessarily suggest anything diabolical. It
is the movement of the narrative, the way the narrator choreo-
graphs the dance of the protagonists, and finally the vision of the
eternal pattern behind the individual glimpses that complete the
effect of a universe, resembling a puppet show where the devil
holds the strings. The movement is captured, like that on Keats's
urn, in the moment of stasis. The emblems or allegories drive
home the moral of the done that cannot be undone, of a destiny
that cannot be remedied, the destiny that is the poet's own.

In the fourth "Spleen," the allegories, lining up on the same
dynamic and metaphoric floor, resemble dancers in a symbolic
ballet. From the first fairly realistic image of "le ciel bas et lourd"
'the low and heavy sky,' the poem moves gradually but resolutely
toward a high degree of stylization, consequently away from a
realistic representation of the world. Justifiably, Auerbach points
out that "the image of spiders in the brain is unrealistic and symbolic" (1962, 151). By way of stylization, the key images become
allegories or metaphors. Yet, what makes them Baudelairean is
the fact that they never relinquish all claim to the reality of their
origin. The liquidity of the day, as the sky "pours" it for "us"
(indicating that as in a fable the image has normative value for
all humankind), the mimetic power of the rain when it transforms
the world into a prison, and the slowing down of vital functions,
illustrated by the bat that touches rotten ceilings, display a very
high perceptual index. Even the spiders, certainly symbolic, set
or spread their webs (they do not spin them) in the brain, in the
manner of new owners who take possession of their new dwelling.
Having become a dynamic pattern of the potential, in which the
spiders are one in intent and purpose but many in their capacity
to accomplish it, having thus advanced toward a highly metaphoric and stylized state, this image turns back toward its possible
origin to simulate a visually perceptible taking over of the
brain's estate.

A ballet performance is by its very nature stylized movement,
and so is the poem. Hope, who now weeps, defeated, after the
wandering souls have yielded to the forces of Spleen, and Anguish, who plants the black flag on the poet's skull, are both highly
stylized, that is, stripped naked of the aggregate of detail that

accompanies them in (psychological) experience. But at the same
time, they retain certain links with reality: the figures can weep
or plant a flag. They mimic at the dynamic level, in balletic fashion,
not necessarily actions that have taken place in real life, but behavior that makes manifest a (real) state of mind, the victory of
spleen.[11]

Literature Begets Literature

Clearly allegory has the capacity to reveal truth and to make it
pertinent to the human condition and, specifically, to the poet
himself. Nowhere is that more evident than in "Un Voyage à Cythère." The poem is given as an account of an event in the poet's
experience and appears as a voyage of discovery. But while the
first ten stanzas bear out this initial impression, the last two in
particular speak of "cette allégorie" and "un gibet symbolique" 'a
symbolic gibbet tree' and cast doubts on the realism of the voyage.
As far as we know, Baudelaire never traveled to the island of
Cythera, and he may not have seen a man hanging on a gibbet.
The interesting circumstance associated with the poem is the fact
that the manuscript sent to Gautier has this note: "Le point de
départ de cette pièce est quelques lignes de Gérard [de Nerval]
(Artiste) qu'il serait bon de retrouver" 'The point of departure of
this piece is in a few lines by Gérard (Artiste) which it would be
good to find' (qtd. 1: 1069). A note on another manuscript speaks
of the same lines of prose that served as program for the poem.
And, in fact, articles by Nerval published in L'Artiste, which will
later be part of his Voyage en Orient, contain the passage with the
hanged man. The story is based on another story.
    Since the source of Baudelaire's story is not nature, this evi-
dence demonstrates that literature issues from literature. Nevertheless, in a cognitive perspective, if the idea, or program as
Baudelaire calls his intention, comes from reading, the process of
identifying the hanged man as significant is mnemonic, and as
such has a great deal to do with Baudelaire's life and experience.
The real source of the poem is in the poet's mnemonic potentials,
which bear deep traces of previous interpretations of both literature and reality.[12] What is new is the analogy the poet makes
between Nerval's image (pattern) and his own destiny.

The Continuity of Renewal

The mnemonic potentials are continually renewed by new interpretations and memory is not a static store of accumulated knowledge, but rather a dynamic agency, which never ceases to
interpret, seek new analogies and correspondences, and renew or
transform those that have already been used. The creative impulse
reaches its high level of effectiveness only "Dans certains états de
l'âme presque surnaturels" 'In certain states of mind which are
almost supernatural' ("Fusées" 1: 659) and in which the long-
filling visionary potential overflows into consciousness. It is significant, then, that the cumulative experience the poem relates,
though tempered by metaphoric thought, takes place in a realistic
setting. Even the rise of the final vision is foreshadowed by the
poet's realistic, physically brutal sensation when he feels "Comme
un vomissement, remonter vers mes dents / Le long fleuve de fiel
des douleurs anciennes" 'Like a vomit, rise to my teeth / The long
river of gall of past sorrows' (lines 47–48). This feeling is the
signal that the correspondence has become operational, that the
spiritual has invaded the physical, and that the two are locked in
a power struggle over the narrator's estate.

Literature and language meet perception and vision. If Baudelaire did not travel to Cythera in "real" life, he undertook to re-
construct such a voyage with details of his own experience of life
and literature. If he paraphrases Nerval, he interprets and "cor-
rects" him. The time of allegory coincides with the moment of
vision; the poem coincides with the experience it relates. Again
and again, in "Le Masque" or in "Le Cygne," or here, the catalyst
may be a sculpture, a literary text, but the epiphany, the revelation,
is experienced through and within the new organization of signifiers. The error here could be illustrated by two extremes: to
believe, on the one hand, that the poem's story in its totality pre-
ceded this organization or, on the other, that the narrative, the
poem, has nothing to do with the reality of Baudelaire's interpretation of life and literature. Allegory harks back to a previous text
or rather to the interpretation of previous texts.[13]

Truth and the Void

De Man and others have been impressed by Benjamin's conclusion that allegory "means precisely the non-existence of what it

presents" (1977, 233). De Man quotes his version of the statement, "signifies precisely the non-being of what it represents," and interprets it in the sense that it defines "allegory as a void" (1971, 35). Introducing de Man's and Fineman's essays, Greenblatt explains that, in their view, allegory fails to recover "the pure visibility of truth" and fails "to present Reality." It may dream to do so "but its deeper purpose and its actual effect is to acknowledge the darkness, the arbitrariness, and the void that underlie, and paradoxically make possible, all representation of realms of light, order, and presence" (1981, vii–viii). Unquestionably, these studies have to be counted among the most serious investigations into the nature of figural language in contemporary critical theory. They contain valuable insights, yet ultimately they appear to be misleading for two fundamental reasons.

The first is that they cut off allegory's lifeline to reality, opening an unnecessary gap, an abyssal void, between its mnemonic origins and representation. The second difficulty is that they blur the distinction between allegory in its essential ontology as image or dynamic pattern and the entity to which it points. That is to say, Baudelaire's image of a swan bathing in the dust, his allegory, points to the absence of the native lake, which is essential to the tension of exile; but the image itself, far from approximating an absence, is a mnemonic reality, the truth of exile, the plenitude of a heroic stance in the face of adversity. The poet may be aware of the vanity of all spiritual longing for an Edenic harmony with one's environment, but his allegorical poem is as real as any text that can be processed. The truth it presents and represents is there to be interpreted and perhaps questioned, but it is not absent. What the poem shows is that metaphors and allegories are ways to obtain knowledge about those elements of reality that would be difficult to process in perceptually direct fashion. With reference to the eternal, this knowledge may in the end prove to be illusory, to the extent that all our knowledge is vanity before the power of death. Indeed there are allegories whose goal is precisely to propose as much; but neither arbitrariness nor a void underlies their representation. At the origin of such undertaking is the all-too-human need to know and to speak. The philosophically crucial difference between a void and the statement that such a void exists has the corollary that the statement may be true or false, the void may or may not exist, but the statement itself is there as a text to be interpreted. Truth is thus a matter of interpretation; the reality of the text is not.

That the recovery of truth is allegory's purpose is borne out by the revelation at the end of "Un Voyage à Cythère." The anguish and anxiety that overwhelm the speaker, the revulsion he experiences in seeing the degradation of the body, the intense realization of the specular ties that bind him to the hanged man, are not caused by a void or by the failure to present reality, but by an oppressing and depressing presence of truth. The disgust, the memory of past suffering that feels like physical vomiting, and the anguish that emerges from his prayer, "Ah! Lord! give me the strength and the courage" (line 59) leave no doubt that the metamorphosis of Cythera's incense of love into the horror of castration reflects the narrator's own drama and destiny. What propels his identity into sharp focus is not so much the feeling that this mutilation may correspond to a specific sexual trauma: it is the recognition of his mirror image, the physical and mental distress he experiences, that constitutes evidence of a unified self.[14]

The Visionary Tradition

And again, as in Saint-Amant or Nerval or Dante, the incredibly powerful effect of allegory issues from its visionary character. Saint-Amant's poem entitled "Les Visions" presents a state of affairs in which visions are the inescapable signs of a melancholy, a mind dominated by a profound sense of loss, the death of a friend assassinated in the prime of his life. The poet sees things transformed and metamorphosed by his melancholy into omens: a deer reminds him of the death of Acteon, the Louvre becomes an asylum, and the swans on a peaceful pond turn into ravens swimming in blood. In similar fashion, Baudelaire in his journey sees, instead of a temple dedicated to Venus, a gallows tree, and says that for him "tout était noir et sanglant désormais" 'all was henceforth dark and bloody.' The poet of "Un voyage" who at the end has "le coeur enseveli dans cette allégorie" '[his] heart shrouded in this allegory' (line 56) echoes Saint-Amant's beginning: "Le coeur plein d'amertume et l'ame ensevelie / Dans la plus sombre humeur de la melancolie" 'My heart filled with bitterness and my soul shrouded / In a most somber mood of melancholy' (lines 1–2).

There are differences, of course, and important ones. While Saint-Amant's visions are taking place in a rambling narrative, in the context of an abnormal state of mind caused rather than occasioned by a specific event, and are akin to hallucination,

Baudelaire's allegory here, while being prompted by an encounter, is more unique and intuitional. Its cerebral energy reminds us perhaps that it is part rhetorical construct and part vision.

On the other hand, the allegory in "Les Sept vieillards" moves toward the hallucinatory end of the spectrum. So much so that Pichois in his notes specifies that the poem offers "une hallucination—non une allégorie" 'a hallucination—not an allegory' (1: 1011). As one can imagine, there is a thin line beyond which hallucination ceases to be allegory (but perhaps all vivid images border on hallucination). Here the moment of allegory coincides with that of hallucination, the sudden, unexpected realization that the old man in rags, the pupils of his eyes steeped in gall, his back not bent but broken at a right angle, is not an ordinary human being but an apparition, a manifestation of some moral evil at the foundation of the universe.

Note that although the opening stanza, in standard poetic fashion, prepares the reader for a narrative containing dreams, specters, and mysteries, and that what follows may not be ordinary, the man is first seen in a perceptually normal way, and it is only after several disturbing details, the gall in his eyes and the comparison with a crippled quadruped, at the moment when he appears to crush the dead under his old shoes, that his hostility becomes manifest, the literal "m'apparut" retrospectively acquires figurative meaning, and his appearance becomes apparition. The accumulation of similes and metaphors corresponds to a gradual increase in the contribution of the mnemonic potentials to the interpretation of the outside stimuli, indicating the way the spiritual from memory invades the perceptual. Only when the invasion reaches a critical stage does the specter become ominous and terrifying, his meanness evolves into a reflection of evil, and he is ready to begin to multiply. These textual circumstances show that the critical moment, the moment of transcendence, has its sources in the collision of memory and perception and that transcending the world is a consequence of interpretation, but that the visionary event cannot happen without a text to be interpreted, a reality to be transcended.

Transcendence: Going beyond the Limits

The poem is, thus, exemplary because it illuminates the concept of transcendence that may occur at three levels. To begin with, the vision takes place in Paris, but a Paris that has been processed

by the poet's mind and through the medium of language trans-
ported to a text. This is the first level of transcendence: the sensory experience becomes language, the mnemonic potentials
become correspondences, the event transcends the real city, the
city as a natural text, to become a literary text. The second level
of transcendence occurs when the poem echoes other allegorical
visions and enters the internet of a long tradition.

Finally, a third level of transcendence, with metaphysical implications, opens within the poem itself: the visionary elements transcend the aggregate of the real to intimate a terrifying spiritual
reality at the foundation of the world. All our critical concerns
converge on the status and meaning of this reality. The cognitive
view opposes "spiritual" to the material and thus stresses that
the sensory data to be meaningful have to be modulated by the
contribution of the mnemonic potentials, which is, as we have
seen, figural or metaphoric in its function and design. The metaphoric impulse, including allegory, emerges as a remedy to the
inability of the senses to have information about certain areas of
reality. Instances of the moral force of evil may be observed in
everyday life, but the embodiment of evil is rarely seen. Baudelaire
proposes an allegory or hallucination to show that embodiment.

What is fundamental is the fact that both the knowledge from
previous interpretations and the sensory data combine to construct a coded model of the world that is then projected onto the
outside reality. Our neural circuits cannot show the vision they
possess at the site of its emergence, at its biological origin, but
instead project it onto the world.

When memory intervenes to evaluate the sensory data, as it
does in every act of interpretation, the stimuli (already coded
in peripheral processes) become "spiritual," transcending their
origin. But real transcendence, in the sense it is generally understood, occurs only if the new knowledge is modulated by the belief
that the metaphoric field created by memory has correspondential links and reflects the existence of a spiritual reality outside
the individual mind. When one talks about religious or simply
extrasensory spiritual forces without believing in them, appre-
hending them logically as constructs of the mind, there is no real
transcendence.

Transcendence as belief may help explain the sentence that
accompanied an earlier version of the poem entitled "Fantômes
parisiens" sent by Baudelaire to Jean Morel, a sentence that ac-
quired fame but remains difficult to interpret: "je crains bien
d'avoir simplement réussi à dépasser les limites assignées à la Poé-

sie" 'I am really afraid of having simply succeeded in going beyond the limits assigned to Poetry' (1973, 1: 583). Perhaps what Baudelaire suggests is that in believing he crossed the frontiers of the natural world and into the realm of the spiritual, where hallucination gets the upper hand, he has gone beyond the ordinary limits of poetry. This belief would also be an additional reason why he dedicated the poem to Victor Hugo, a poet who had begun to explore the spiritual domain (in "La Pente de la rêverie" for example).

Does the narrator believe in the authenticity of what he sees? He suggests in a defensive move, another example of Baudelairean irony addressed to the skeptics, that perhaps he is a victim of a plot (demons or friends playing a practical joke?) to humiliate him. Although worried that some of his readers might laugh at him, he is terrified and profoundly affected by the satanic apparition. Was it caused by the use of opium? Pichois suggests it as a possibility (1: 1011). Or by loneliness, as Adam intimates in his notes (1961, 382)? Or is it, as Jackson proposes, the embodiment of the poet's own hatred turning against him?[15] Or, I would add, could it be a nightmare adapted to daylight scrutiny? The fact that we have no way of knowing if, or to what extent, it ocurred in a specific previous experience should not prevent us from accepting the seriousness of the close encounter in the poem. Whatever the actual scenario that accounts for its origin, the vision emanates from Baudelaire's fears and is strengthened by his belief, here and elsewhere, in the existence of evil.

One can assume that in "Les Sept vieillards" Baudelaire believes his correspondences transcend the world, that the signifiers simply formulate a concept of transcendence, or, finally, that the reader believes such transcendence to occur. According to one's belief, one may choose to accept all of these conditions, reject them all, or choose some and reject the others.[16]

My belief is that Baudelaire's allegories propose a unified ontology, a view of a world dominated by evil, including degradation and decomposition of the body, but also leavened by the possibility of a redemptive move toward the unity that human desire cannot allow the poet to renounce and that allegory cannot allow him to forget: "Aussi devant ce Louvre une image m'opprime" 'And so before this Louvre an image oppresses me' ("Le Cygne" line 33). His allegories proceed from the belief that metaphoric imagination, obeying the injunction that the world must be renewed again and again, can name things, transform them, endow them with semiotic attributes and thus confirm their correspondential unity.

Allegories are moved by belief, the belief that they can call forth the world out of the chaos of the unformed. If there is a void, then that void exists where there are no texts to interpret; it exists outside the metaphoric fields of the mind. If some would question the need for faith, that is because they are distracted by the word's religious connotations. But faith is central to the operation of correspondences and allegory: the faith that they are invaluable links not only to the visible world but also to the ultimate reality that is its foundation. Baudelaire's whole creative enterprise is marked by the struggle (one may be able to trace its progress or regress) to gain and maintain that faith.

8

The Dynamics of Transmutation

Identity as a Function of Perspective

In the cognitive view, identity is the nodal center of decision making, the vision-controlling agency, and the point where the interpretive forces of an observer converge. What makes someone tick is a question of capital interest not only because it expects fundamental answers about who the individual is, but also because it implies that those answers cannot come easily, that the evidence-constituting signs are not transparent and need to be interpreted. They need an observer, a reader, and, thus, a perspective. Whether it comes from an outsider or from the inner voice that questions and acts as an interpreter of one's own thoughts and actions, the point of view is the essential factor in the creation of meaning. Thus, it is an error to claim a particular status for an identity without indicating at the same time in whose perspective this is so. For, by themselves, neither the individual character and actions nor the social, cultural, and historical forces that modulate an identity give it meaning. It is the interpreter, activating his mnemonic potentials and employing concepts from various sources, that determines whether such an identity is fragmented, imaginary,[1] divided, unified or a combination of several possibilities. Even when plagued by divisions of will, identity remains at the center of personality, which, like any text, has to be read and interpreted.

An identity may appear straightforward, unproblematic, only when one assumes a social order in which everyone agrees to subscribe to the interpretation emitted through the dominant discourse. Certainly there are societies in which the pressure from outside, from the social order or from the state, is overwhelming and, for practical purposes, impossible to resist. In such circumstances, the interpretation of an identity is already given and cannot be challenged. An individual called to answer for offending public morality, or for being a saboteur, for example, may not be able to shake loose the imposed label. But permitting the freedom to protest against it is equivalent to allowing the shadow of a doubt to intervene.

The question that has to be asked is this: Does mid-nineteenth-century France under Napoleon III delineate itself as a unique social order whose consequences would inevitably produce *Les Fleurs du mal,* poems like "Femmes damnées" or "Le Cygne," or behavioral patterns like that of Baudelaire? We associate Baudelaire with this particular historical period and are reluctant to place him anywhere else in history. But situations like the one in which Baudelaire was taken to court for writing a book that undermined moral and religious standards can occur in societies with very different political systems and at various periods in history. It is not so much that the authorities or the prosecutors were offended by the book: rather, if Foucault's interpretation of history can be taken as a guide, the publication of the book represented an occasion for them to exercise their power. Secondly, and perhaps more importantly, historical and contemporary examples show that there are always dissenting voices, which prove that labeling someone is a matter of judgment and point of view. Saying that the dissenting voices are few is not an argument. Who knows how many more would dissent if the herd instinct would not be so strong and fear were not thwarting their better judgment?

Herd instinct, sheer blindness, and perhaps some degree of stupidity modulated the attacks on Baudelaire's poetry. For while the authorities prosecuted him, many nineteenth-century critics proclaimed his lack of imagination, the aridity and banality of his poetry.[2] According to them, Baudelaire, who extolled the virtues of imagination, owned no stock in its powers. It is true that today no one reads these critics. Nevertheless, the conclusion one can draw from reading some of their statements is unavoidable: Baudelaire's identity, as a human being and as a poet, depended heavily on the critic's adopted perspective. For that reason it is imperative not only to ascertain what Baudelaire thought about himself but also to avoid misreadings, or blurring the distinction between certain peripheral tendencies and the central preoccupations, the dominant forces and urgency, in his life and work.

The Authority of the Poet

Baudelaire himself must bear some responsibility for the legend he created, the reputation of dabbling in satanism and social aberrations and the tendency to shock (telling the Belgians that he was a spy for the French government, for example) by his behavior those who were not close enough to know him. It is not so much that these tendencies were not there; they were, however, outward manifestations of a fundamental need that was neither aberrant nor shocking and that most of his contemporaries could not or would not understand. In this context, we are fortunate to have at our disposal his correspondence, letters in which Baudelaire speaks more directly, cutting through the ambiguities that characterize so much of his ironic stance. These texts reveal Baudelaire as he sees himself, laboring under increasing pressure to assert his identity in the interaction with others. He conceives of himself first and foremost as a human being, but a human being who is a poet, who has dedicated his life to poetry, and whose one authority, when all other authorities fail, is to speak as a poet.

This comes through especially in his differences with various editors. To Alphonse de Calonne (28 April 1860) he repeats his admonition about poems submitted to the *Revue contemporaine:* "Je suis désolé de vous faire observer pour la dixième fois qu'*on ne retouche pas MES vers*. Veuillez les supprimer" 'I am sorry to point out to you for the tenth time that *you do not alter MY poems*. You can reject them' (1973, 2: 33). Clearly he accepts the editor's prerogatives to reject whole poems but not to make changes and then publish them—not *HIS* poems. In the context of the letter "on ne retouche pas mes vers" suggests the tone of someone's warning, "on ne touche pas à mes vers" 'don't touch (tamper with) my poems.' On 20 June 1863, after seeing two of his prose poems ("Les Tentations" and "La Belle Dorothée") published in the *Revue nationale* with changes he did not approve, he expresses his displeasure to the editor, Gervais Charpentier:

Je vous avais dit: supprimez *tout un morceau*, si *une virgule* vous déplaît dans le morceau, mais ne supprimer pas la virgule; elle a sa raison d'être.

J'ai passé ma vie entière à apprendre à construire des phrases, et je dis, sans crainte de faire rire, que ce que je livre à une imprimerie est *parfaitement fini*.

I had told you: delete *a whole piece*, if *a comma* displeases you, but do not delete the comma; it has its raison d'être. I have spent my entire life learning how to put together sentences, and I say, without fear of being laughed at, that what I deliver to the press is *perfectly finished*. (1973, 2: 307)

What these passages reveal is Baudelaire's last stand against the encroaching universal stupidity, "le dernier carré" of a self that will not surrender the pride of the poet, because that pride is the ultimate frontier of its identity. One has to read this letter in its entirety to appreciate the scathing irony, the anger, and yet the will to control this anger, to bring the outburst of feeling within the bounds of propriety, within the province of the dandy. This struggle reveals the fundamental needs of the self that are as powerful as hunger and thirst, as basic as love and hate. Among them is the need to be understood to be appreciated, to be given his due, for, as he says, "Paris n'a jamais été juste envers moi" 'Paris has never been fair to me' (1973, 2: 553). And as he becomes more unhappy about it and about everything else, both his pride and his anger against the others increase (see 1973, 2: 99).

Certainly a different view emerges when we enter into the equation the reactions and opinions of the people who were the objects of Baudelaire's scorn. While he felt wronged, felt that others had no right to change what he wrote, the editors for their part considered him stubborn or worse. Pichois notes that "Calonne jugea cette lettre «très impertinente»" 'Calonne considered this letter "very impertinent"' and threatened to publish the poems "«tels quels» avec les «chevilles»: «tant pis pour vous»" "'as they were" with the "chevilles": "too bad for you"' (1973, 2: 656). Edouard Le Barbier from the *Revue libérale,* who incurred Baudelaire's wrath in connection with two prose poems ("Le Joueur généreux" and "Les Vocations"), complains that he thought Baudelaire was going to strangle him when he proposed to suppress some lines: "Baudelaire n'a été ni loyal ni poli" 'Baudelaire was neither fair nor polite' and concludes: "tout cela est d'une *vanité insensée*" 'All that is *demented vanity*' (in a letter to Taine, qtd. by Kopp, 1969, LXII). Where is Baudelaire in all this? Clearly his identity not only depends on a point of view, it cannot be even conceived outside somebody's point of view.

The Defining Factor: "Le Conseil judiciaire"

The proposition that ultimately it is Baudelaire's work, *Les Fleurs du mal,* his art criticism, his prose poems, that counts or should count does not invalidate the connection with his life, which remains essential. He never stopped believing in the defining properties of this connection. Certainly in the temporal distance that separates us from him, his work appears all the more impressive as it was done under difficult conditions. But it is important to note that Baudelaire himself recognized the severity of the struggle to ward off debts and to resist the fear of losing his creative powers. In 1855, speaking to his mother about his financial difficulties, Baudelaire concludes that what worries him even more than physical pain is the fear of losing his creative power.[3] He links in a chain of causes and effects lack of money, physical pain, lack of heat ("je t'écris avec mes deux dernières bûches, et les doigts gelés" 'I write to you with my last two logs and my frozen fingers' 1973, 1: 210), loss of time, and, finally, the loss of the creative faculty that is central to the ambition of his life. And beyond a shadow of a doubt, that ambition is to produce "quelques beaux vers" 'a few beautiful poems' ("À une heure du matin") to prove to himself that he is not inferior to other men and to attain the improvement of his mind and "la gloire," the literary fame he considered "le bien le plus positif et le plus solid du monde" 'the most positive and solid possession in the world' (1973, 2: 489). And the most difficult.

Throughout, Baudelaire's view of the factors that determined the trajectory of his "horrible existence" can be summed up in one phrase: "le conseil judiciaire" 'the legal guardianship.' In 1861, he repeats the message he has always tried to convey to his mother and calls "le conseil"

> Cette maudite invention! invention maternelle d'un esprit trop préoccupé d'argent, qui m'a déshonoré, poussé dans les dettes renaissantes, qui a tué en moi toute amabilité, et a même entravé mon éducation d'artiste et d'homme de lettres, restée incomplète.

> This accursed invention! this maternal invention of a mind too preoccupied with money, which dishonored me, pushed me into recurring debts, which killed in me all kindness, and even hampered my education as an artist and a man of letters, which remained incomplete. (1973, 2: 142)

Clearly, in this view, the "conseil judiciaire" acquires the magnitude of the original sin, the scene of the decree of damnation and exile, where his destiny was predetermined by heredity and circumstances outside his control. Precisely because of the belief in its mythic attributes, Baudelaire did not think it possible to change it or to avert its consequences. This is the meaning of his statement to his mother, in December 1854, in connection with the possibility of asking the courts to lift the "conseil judiciaire." He confesses that he would not have any chance of success and

adds: "En somme, je crois que ma vie a été *damnée* dès le commencement, et qu'elle l'est *pour toujours*" 'In short, I believe my
life has been *damned* from the beginning and that it will be so
forever' (1973, 1: 303).

Idleness and Leisure

It remains to be seen, then, what effect this primal event had
on his mission as a poet. Baudelaire's view is unequivocal: it had
harmful consequences. But the matter is not as clear-cut. Another
factor intervenes to render judgment difficult. Already in 1847,
he speaks to his mother about it: "Supposez une oisiveté perpé-
tuelle commandée par un malaise perpétuel, avec une haine pro-
fonde de cette oisiveté, et l'impossibilité absolue d'en sortir, à cause
du manque perpétuel d'argent" 'Suppose a perpetual idleness
governed by a perpetual malaise accompanied by a deep hatred
for this idleness and the absolute impossibility of getting over it,
because of the perpetual lack of money' (1973, 1: 142). Again, the
root cause is lack of money that can be traced back to the "conseil,"
but now, in the tension of unremitting idleness, he feels trapped
and on the point of a breakdown. In the same letter, he asks his
mother for a certain sum of money: "Or voici ce que je vous
demande *à mains jointes,* tant je sens que je touche aux dernières
limites, non seulement de la patience des autres, mais aussi de la
mienne" 'Now here is what I am asking you *with clasped hands,*
because I feel that I have reached the ultimate limits, not only of
the patience of others but of my own as well' (1973, 1: 143). Yet,
if in 1847 he sees idleness as a trap, in his later years in "Mon
coeur mis à nu," in a more reflective mood, he becomes an even-
handed judge:

> C'est par le loisir que j'ai, en partie, grandi.
> À mon grand détriment; car le loisir, sans fortune, augmente les
> dettes, les avanies résultant des dettes.
> Mais à mon grand profit, relativement à la sensibilité, à la médita-
> tion, et à la faculté du dandysme et du dilettantisme.

> It is through leisure that I have, partly, grown.
> To my great detriment; for leisure, without money, increases one's
> debts, the snubs that are the consequence of debts.
> But to my great benefit, concerning my sensibility, meditation, and
> the faculty of dandyism and dilettantism. (1975, 1: 697)

Granted that "oisiveté" and "loisir" do not mean the same thing, they are in Baudelaire's case inextricably related in a chain of situations that we are familiar with. Idleness is simply the negative pole of leisure. He admits here that his leisure entailed disadvantages but even more significantly that it also was the path to his growth intellectually and socially.

At this point, one has to ask if the logic of the chain of events, beginning with the "conseil," has the coherence of a demonstration. Did the "conseil" have a wholly negative effect on his life? When it comes to placing blame, Pichois suggests that rather than accusing the general, the mother, Ancelle, or even "l'injuste Justice française" 'the unjust French Justice,' we should thank them perhaps, "dans un esprit maistrien, avec Baudelaire lui-même, s'il pouvait contempler son oeuvre entière en fonction de son existence" 'in a Maistrian spirit, with Baudelaire himself, if he could contemplate his entire work in relation to his existence' ("Introduction" 1973, 1: 11).[4]

Perhaps then the important question is whether the extreme difficulties Baudelaire encountered, physical suffering, debts, and social miscommunication and misunderstanding, were necessary to his literary creation. The fact that he had to work hard to accomplish what he did undoubtedly contributed to the tension of his texts. As Eliot said some time ago, it is "the intensity of the artistic process, the pressure, so to speak, under which the fusion takes place, that counts" (1960, 8).

Destiny and Damnation

Such as the texts reveal them, in "Bénédiction," but also as early as 1842 or 1843 in "Le Mauvais moine," idleness and leisure are registered in his consciousness as two poles of the same damnation that is the corollary to his identity as a poet. On the temporal level, damnation receives its official stamp of approval in 1844 with the dation of the "conseil judiciaire" as an event that takes away his initiative and freedom. But in the perspective of the eternal, damnation appears as the divinely inspired overdetermination of his life from the beginning, as the letter says or "depuis l'éternité" 'since eternity' as in "Le Mauvais moine" and one that has been instituted by fate, the "puissances suprêmes" 'supreme powers' ("Bénédiction") and cannot be deleted or overturned. That may explain perhaps why Baudelaire did not appeal, did not do anything to oppose the measure taken by his family, even though he considered it degrading and shameful.[5]

One cannot agree with Sartre that Baudelaire chose his destiny. However, once damnation enters his consciousness, he accepts it as a challenge, as one of the fundamental limits that has to be both preserved and overcome. He must overcome damnation to fulfill his mission, and must preserve it because it manifests itself through suffering, which is a remedy for the impurities of human nature and which prepares the strong for spiritual elevation. In this context, the importance of "Bénédiction" is twofold: the poem metamorphoses damnation into blessing and also links idleness and leisure in the activity of the poet-child who "plays with the wind and talks with the clouds." This idleness, which surfaces as "la féconde paresse" 'the fertile idleness' in "La Chevelure," is part of the poet's strength and is central to his success. In his analysis of "L'Invitation au voyage," Benjamin notes that the hero is strong but that "[Modernism] makes him fast in the secure harbour forever and abandons him to everlasting idleness" (1973, 96). As in the first incarnation in "Bénédiction" so "in his last embodiment" "as a dandy," idleness or leisure is one of his fundamental attributes and part of his greatness. "C'est par le loisir que j'ai, en partie, grandi."

Can we say, then, that without damnation, without the tension between idleness and hatred of this idleness, without the debts that were the inevitable consequence, without suffering as a mark of his difference from other men, without the pride of his exile, Baudelaire would not have become a great poet? Would some of his formulas have been less shocking, some of his angers less traumatic, some of his allegories less haunting? These are hypothetical questions that will remain unanswered. We will never know.

In the Beginning was the Metaphor

Baudelaire's works appear neither as a mirror of his life nor as a refracting prism in which events are given a new direction but as a ritual transmutation producing correspondential, therefore sacred, relations. The distortion the events of his life undergo is not simply the result of a change in their dynamics, as in a dream for example, but the consequence of a profound integration with tradition. A more accurate analogy may be with the transformations that occur in the Djanggawul songs, narrating the voyage of the Ancestral Beings of the Aborigines, during which the animals and birds they meet acquire sacred significance. The ritual re-enacts "the primal birth" (Berndt, 1953, 23) of the ancestors of the Aborigines and thus indicates that the accompanying songs, words, rhythm, and meaning are generated by a tradition. In Baudelaire's case, the "certain états de l'âme presque surnaturels" 'certain states of mind which are almost supernatural' ("Fusées" 1: 659), which reveal the depth of life, occur in ordinary circumstances, but they have been prepared by the words and images of a tradition. This is why memory is central to Baudelaire's creation and to his aesthetics.

As a memory function, imagination "a créé, au commencement du monde, l'analogie et la métaphore. Elle décompose toute la création, et, avec les matériaux amassés et disposés suivant des règles dont on ne peut trouver l'origine que dans le plus profond de l'âme, elle crée un monde nouveau, elle produit la sensation du neuf" 'created, at the beginning of the world, the analogy and the metaphor. It breaks up the whole creation, and, with the constituent elements accumulated and arranged according to rules, whose source can be found only in the depths of the soul, it creates a new world, it produces the feeling of something new' ("Salon de 1859" 2: 621). Memory is "résurrectionniste, évocatrice, une mémoire qui dit à chaque chose: «Lazare, lève-toi!»" 'resurrectionist, evocative, a memory that says to each thing: Lazarus, come forth!' ("Le Peintre" 2: 699). To the question, "What is this crying?" one of the ancestors in the Djanggawul songs identifies a sacred tree, a sacred bird: "*Waridj*, it is a parakeet, / Calling softly from the sacred tree" (Berndt, 1953, 97). Naming the parakeet is equivalent to saying, "Parakeet, come forth!"; it is concurrent with discovering the relation between the red glow of the sun and "the sacred feathers," simultaneous with the unfolding of the sacred dimension of things, at the beginning of time, at the beginning of a tradition or as Baudelaire puts it, "at the beginning of the world." And for Baudelaire, everything began with *The Iliad* and *The Odyssey*, and also with *The Aeneid*, with Homer and Virgil, who created the analogy and the metaphor. The depths of the soul are in fact the depths of memory. And each time the birth of metaphor is re-enacted, each thing is resurrected, and correspondences are forged, analogies made according to rules that have been laid down by tradition. When Baudelaire says that they come from the depths of the soul, he indicates that unlike the Djanggawul songs, which have communal sources, his view emphasizes the individual contribution. But the process of metaphoric creation is similar. In the first case, its goal is to re-enact, with the help of ritual songs, the birth and voyage of the ancestors and to account for the presence of the Aborigines in their land, the Australian mainland. For Baudelaire the purpose is to use "une espèce de sorcellerie évocatoire" 'a sort of evocative witchcraft' to celebrate the birth of a tradition and his own presence in the land of imagination. In both cases the song or the poem fulfills a fundamental need, and the connection with life is strong.

The Alchemy of Art

On the one hand, there is no one-to-one relation between texts and the life of the historical personality that produced them; and on the other, at the opposite extreme, one cannot sever all links to the forces that governed that life.[6] The lesson of resisting the lure of the two extremes, of avoiding them, has to be relearned by each generation. One cannot, for example, reduce a textual figure or allegory to the value of a specific person in the life of the poet. Some people or even some emotions that play a significant role in the life of the author, as T. S. Eliot pointed out long time ago, may not enter into the textual equation at all or be only an indirect influence, part of a greater creative impulse. And even those that are at the center of the creative drive are changed, transmuted, genetically programmed to obey the dynamics of the new metaphoric fields.

Thus, to discern, in various texts, patterns that bear the inevitable resemblance to their counterparts in life, one must look hard and exercise caution. As the examples that follow show, the affinities are mostly on the level of pattern dynamics. The tension between the two allegiances to God and Satan, as it is exemplified on the metaphoric level of some of his poems or prose poems, has some affinity with the tension in the poet's life between good and evil, between love and hate, between the desire to dominate the others and the need to be loved. Idleness becomes "spleen," the boredom of "the limping days," but its complementary part "le loisir" is glorified in "La Chevelure" and later channeled into the activity of "flânerie." Consciousness of time, "il est *grandement temps* d'agir" 'it is *high time* to act' ("Hygiène," 1: 668), is reflected in the metaphoric field of the interrupted performance in "Une Mort héroïque." The desire to create a family for himself reaches deep in the past with Andromache of "Le Cygne" and Marguerite of "Sonnet d'automne" or in the surrounding reality with "la négresse, amaigrie et phtisique" and "les petites vieilles." The despair of "je ne crois pas que je puisse devenir fou" 'I don't believe I will become mad' may in fact explode in the fourth "Spleen." And the attempts to finalize his view of tradition, to transform it, to humble it, but also to obey its commands, appear in "Le Voyage."

Tradition and its Sources

It would be difficult to assess the character of Baudelaire's texts without the recognition that tradition is everywhere in them. One is struck, for example, by the fact that Baudelaire's three women to whom he dedicates the three major cycles of his love poetry correspond in number to Ronsard's "inspiratrices," Cassandre, Marie, and Hélène. One cannot fail to note the many figures from the classical antiquity, the Middle Ages, and the Renaissance, who march on the stage of his poems, bringing with them the aura of depth and vast horizons: Andromache, Electra, Pylades, Sapho, Don Juan, Faust, Marguerite, and of course the many artists of "Les Phares."

Some of his poems, Baudelaire acknowledges, were influenced by Gray, Poe, Longfellow, Statius, and Virgil; but there are hundreds of lines that show affinities with other poets.[7] For Baudelaire fragments from the works of Gautier, De Quincey, Balzac, Hugo, Poe, Saint-Amant, Barbier, Musset, Hoffmann, Lamartine, and others represented "une espèce de pâture que l'imagination doit digérer et transformer" 'a sort of food that imagination must digest and transform' ("Salon de 1859" 2: 627). He submitted those fragments to high heat and intense creative pressure and transformed them almost beyond recognition to meet the demands of new metaphoric fields. Baudelaire's achievement emerges from the extraordinary fusion that he performed at the center of Western tradition.

This performance, however, bears the marks of a radical departure, both at the dynamic or metaphoric level and at the level of the treatment of subject matter or theme. For although Gautier, Balzac, and Hugo, for example, had already begun vital exploratory probes into the realm of correspondences, their attempts had remained subordinated to descriptive, narrative, philosophical, and other concerns. For Baudelaire, on the other hand, exploring the metaphoric domain becomes the main goal, so much so that in some important poems, the fourth "Spleen" for example, the

tenor has been catapulted on the allegorical level and the distinction between tenor and vehicle is no longer operative. Moreover,
Baudelaire's tendency is to exploit much more consistently images
for their shock value, to render them more dramatic, dynamically
more powerful. Thus, Gautier's image comparing the poet, a
wound in his heart, to a pine tree, which has been cut for its resin
and which does not regret "son sang qui coule goutte à goutte"
'his blood flowing in drops' (1862, 309) becomes in "La Fontaine
de sang" the haunting line: "Il me semble parfois que mon sang
coule à flots" 'Sometimes I feel my blood streaming out.'[8]

Though the French Renaissance poets had also practiced a similar technique of assimilation, the process in Baudelaire's "Le
Cygne," for example, appears more deliberate and akin to the
one in music exemplified by the similarity of themes in the
Brahms's first symphony and Beethoven's ninth. Although obviously possible, it would be difficult to imagine the mastery with
which Pound and Eliot transform tradition and employ quotations without Baudelaire's example.[9]

Modernism and "Le Cygne"

The second way in which Baudelaire's departure from tradition
manifests itself is linked to Baudelaire the poet-hero of modernism. Because of the deep ideological divisions in contemporary
criticism, this is the most difficult issue that one can undertake to
discuss. There are two areas that have become fertile grounds
for the study of the poet's modernity: one is the section entitled
"Tableaux parisiens," "Le Cygne" in particular, and the other the
prose poems.

In spite of the agreement that "Le Cygne" is about a form of
exile, the poem is many things to many people. I have tried to
show that it springs from the memory of other interpretations
and that its purpose is to transcend exile by the creation of the
myth of exile. The rise and fall of urban cultures, Troy, Rome,
and Second Empire Paris, have to be viewed in a perspective in
which cities rise to fame and go down in ruin to fulfill the exigencies of myths and history. War and peace and the inevitable ebb
and flow of civilizations will make many more exiles "bien d'autres
encor," in a future that repeats itself, mimics, and fulfills *The Iliad's*
mythic present. The poem may offer a lesson in historical pessimism then.

But to politicize this achievement, to define, for example, exile exclusively in terms of the opposition to Napoleon III, is to substitute other textual parameters for the existing ones. Although by dedicating the poem to Victor Hugo, the author of "Le Cygne" implicitly cast in his lot with the banished and contested the legitimacy of the tyrant's power, there is no justification for seeing in Baudelaire, as German Marxist critics appear to do, a revolutionary, a secret agent intending to destroy the bourgeoisie from within. Pichois is right to point out, in a compelling assessment of this tendency, that a good part of the French writers are intellectual aristocrats, who belong to no class and feel above all that they are different. He writes: "Je réclame pour Baudelaire le droit d'avoir été à son époque un réprouvé et d'exprimer pour nous le scandale d'un révolté qui ne veut pas plus du juste milieu que de la dictature du prolétariat" 'I claim on Baudelaire's behalf the right of having been in his time an outcast and of expressing for us the scandal of a rebel who has no more use for the middle of the road than for the dictatorship of the proletariat' (1981, 232–33).[10]

The Prose Poems: A Program of Experimentation

As far as the prose poems are concerned, Baudelaire has given us a clue to their interpretation. Explaining to his mother (9 March 1865) what he hopes to accomplish, he speaks of "un ouvrage singulier, plus singulier, plus volontaire du moins, que Les Fleurs du mal, où j'associerai l'effrayant avec le bouffon, et même la tendresse avec la haine" 'a singular work, more singular, more deliberate at least, than Les Fleurs du mal, in which I will combine the frightful with the farcical, and even tenderness with hate' (1973, 2: 473). Both this passage and the dedication to Houssaye confirm that this work is experimental in nature, not just in the sense of this poetic prose adapted to the lyrical movements of the soul, but also in the sense of a more consistent focus on urban experience, which was already in "Tableaux parisiens" generated by the activity of the flâneur. Chesters stresses "the relationship between experimentation and urban theme" (1978, 429). And it is in the context of the urban experience in "Les Sept vieillards" that Baudelaire claims to have succeeded in "dépasser les limites assignées à la poésie" 'going beyond the limits assigned to poetry' (1973, 1: 583). The poet's claim comes from the realization that the hallucinatory experience, somehow linked to the big city, is indeed communicating "un frisson nouveau" 'a new shudder' (see

Hugo's letter). But it would be useful to recall here that a hallucinatory experience of this kind is a theme in "Les Visions" of Saint-
Amant, for whom the swans in a peaceful pond become ravens
swimming in blood; and the Louvre, in the middle of Paris, becomes an asylum. Thus, it would be inexact to say with Benjamin
that it is with Baudelaire that "Paris for the first time became the
subject of lyrical poetry" (1973, 170); nor would it be fair to say
that hallucination bordering on allegory had not been presented
before in a lyric poem. Baudelaire surpasses others not because
many of his poems have a Parisian setting but because their vision
challenges the limits that people tend to associate with lyric poetry.
It is the total effect that is new.

In the prose poems, what is also new is the relentless pursuit
of paradoxes and the single-minded intention to push the possibilities, offered either by experience itself or by experimental hy-
pothesis, to their ultimate consequences on the existential, social,
philosophical, and aesthetic levels. One also has to point out that
although most of these possibilities spring from an urban setting,
some do not. A modest example is the short piece entitled "Déjà!"
After being at sea for many days, the passengers welcome the
sight of a magnificent shore and the chance to be back on land
with the word "Enfin!" 'Finally!' while the poet, overcome with
sadness at being separated from the sea, "si monstrueusement
séduisante" 'so monstrously seductive' could cry "Déjà!" 'Already!'
Can this sea be the same sea Baudelaire abandoned, by returning
home before reaching his destination, in his voyage toward the
Indies? It both is and is not. It is in fact a paradox of the mind,
of memory. If one possibility is to be happy at the end of the
voyage, the other is to regret that it had an end. The poem reflects
the dynamics of the opposition between the two. It is generated
by Baudelaire's experience at the tropics, as the description of the
sea and shore indicates, yet it is also not this experience but a
hypothetical experiment, pushing the two possibilities to their
logical consequences.

One can see this experimentation everywhere. It is deliberate
and it follows the programmatic intention to combine the frightful with the farcical and tenderness with hatred. This is evident
in sketches of wry or grim humor, such as "Un Plaisant," "Le
Mauvais vitrier," "La Femme sauvage et la petite-maîtresse," and
"La Corde." In "Une Mort héroïque," "une experience physiolo-
gique d'un intérêt *capital*" 'a physiological experiment of *capital*
interest' (1: 320; Kaplan 1989, 64) is carried to its ultimate conse-

quences, that is, the death of the protagonist, and it represents the model for what Baudelaire himself is doing in the prose poems.[11]

The Price of Concluding

One cannot conclude without saying that no satisfactory conclusion is possible. It is not because we as critics have different ways of seeing Baudelaire's achievement. A conclusion is difficult because the historical perspective in which we locate our points of view is constantly changing, advancing, pointing to the need for another assessment at the very moment in which one is given. Yet each period exacts its own ever changing kaleidoscope of portraits. We cannot escape the desire to approach the poet and bring him closer to us. This is perhaps his greatest success: the constant imperative to formulate our view of him, to proclaim our own identity in the process of defining his.

Baudelaire already intimated some of the discoveries of our own time. In making a vast synthesis of so many sources, he took into account the considerable power that resides in the ways language circulates. How else can we explain his cryptic remark: "Profondeur immense de pensée dans les locutions vulgaires, trous creusés par des générations de fourmis" 'Vast depth of thought in the vulgar idiom, holes made by generations of ants' (1: 650)? But he went beyond the limitations of twentieth-century classical structuralism by his commitment to memory and thus his recognition of perceptual forces operating at the level of the text. The creation of correspondences, dynamic patterns, and the implicit understanding of what they represent, for literature, are Baudelaire's finest achievement and insight. In that sense, by preparing the way for the cognitive view, he was not only far ahead of his time, but perhaps a step ahead of ours as well. He showed the decisive impact that point of view and perspective have, and implicitly pointed to our present understanding that truth in poetry, or criticism, or history depends on who is writing it.

Notes

The epigraph, "I am very much afraid of having simply succeeded in going beyond the limits assigned to poetry," comes from a letter sent by Baudelaire to Jean Morel, May 1859 (see 1973, 1: 583). The letter accompanied the manuscript of "Fantômes parisiens," whose title was subsequently changed to "Les Sept vieillards."

All Baudelaire quotations come from two main sources: The first is Pichois's Pléiade edition of Baudelaire's *Oeuvres complètes,* in 2 volumes, published by Gallimard in 1975–76. Since these references occur frequently, I will omit the year of publication and indicate only the volume and page numbers. This procedure will enable the reader to distinguish them from the references to a second important source, which is Pichois's (in collaboration with Ziegler) Pléiade edition of *Correspondance,* in 2 volumes, published in 1973. These references will include the year of publication. The translations of the prose poem passages come from Kaplan's *The Parisian Prowler.* Unless attributed to a source, the other translations are mine.

Introduction

1. For my analysis of the structure of dynamic patterns and a more extensive discussion of their importance see 1992, 50–51, 74–81, and 85–104.

2. See Neisser 1967, 20; Haber 1971, 37, 45; and Forgus and Melamed 1976, 217.

3. The excerpts quoted by Foley come from the Parry Collection published in the series *Serbo-Croatian Heroic Songs,* edited by Milman Parry and Albert Lord (Cambridge: Harvard University Press, 1953).

4. This should not be surprising, when one considers that processing the texts of reality follows a similar path. Haber points out that the duration of a fixation in reading is about the same as that of a fixation in visual explorations and writes: "an integrated view of a continuous world that we perceive must be *constructed* out of many glances, and all that we know about the visual world around us is constructed out of information contained in icons" (1971, 47).

5. One has to distinguish between intertextual echoes and actual sources. Since the reader can mnemonically recognize both through thematic, lexical (semantic), and dynamic affinities, they do overlap; but echoes, often rich in sensory material, reflect the fundamental mnemonic character of reading, while sources, either thematic or in the form of fragmentary traces, betray the mnemonic character of writing.

6. It is perhaps surprising that contemporary critics have not shown a greater interest in Baudelaire's own view of the function of correspondences, especially when it comes to their discussion of allegory.

7. In a similar view, which may suggest perhaps the degree to which Baudelaire's aesthetics has been absorbed by French tradition, Dufrenne maintains that "lorsque l'oeuvre est faite, on connaît s'il y a unité au sentiment que l'on éprouve d'accéder à un monde cohérent, à un monde qui soit vraiment monde" 'when the work is done, one knows if there is unity by the feeling one experiences of having access to a coherent world, to a world that is really a world' (1967, 1: 246).

8. The cognitive view of literature and deconstruction, which is formalist in its philosophy, oppose each other in a schismatic relation. What they appear to have in common is a modern insight, emerging from the ruins of structuralist ambitions, the idea expressed by Leitch: "we ponder the possibility that there is only always interpretation" (1983, 250). Formalist critics, however, do not see meaning as a relation between an interpreter and a text: "Meaning is not an individual creation but the result of applying to the text operations and conventions which constitute the institution of literature" (Culler 1975, 30). The system oriented critics transform readers into "empirical subjects" (Eco 1976, 317) or role playing actors, and refuse to admit that the individual performing these operations interprets the text under scrutiny in the light of his or her previous interpretations of "the institution of literature," in terms of the unique mnemonic potentials at his or her disposal. This refusal is tantamount to a contradiction of the principle that "there is only always interpretation." For who is going to "make explicit the operations and conventions which will account for a range of acceptable readings and exclude those which we would agree to place outside the normal procedures of reading" (Culler 1975, 29)?

9. See Lattimore 1951, 12.200–229. The merit for selecting the Homeric passage to serve as an interpretive model belongs to Vincent Leitch, who in the "Prologue" to his book on Deconstruction offers a marvelous analysis of the bird sign and of the difficulties of interpretation (see 1983, 3–6).

10. Terdiman also speaks of an outside text used in interpretation, but he conceives it in a different way: "To explain a text at all," he writes, "there must always be a *hors-texte*, an *other* of the text's own expression" (1993, 174). For him, however, this "other" is a contextual "adversary," Sainte-Beuve's and Taine's determinism in the case of Proust, against which the text struggles: "The text can neither speak nor silence it" (1993, 174). The question remains: In what way is interpretation "its bearer" or how can criticism make "such knowledge functional" (1993, 175)? That is, to find such a "hors-texte," the critic must first interpret the text he or she is reading. By virtue of what critical concept or imported text does the critic locate and identify such force in the text under scrutiny? Wold it be found in a text by Marx, or a text by Freud? Terdiman does not say.

However, in analyzing the contextual method practiced by Greenblatt and others, which is not unlike Terdiman's approach, Perkins does give us an answer, pointing out the difference between what critics do and what they claim to be doing:

The ideas by which the literary works are explained and interpreted are not derived from the contexts or the texts so much as they are imposed upon them. They are formed by other sources, in other experiences (for example, the experience of reading Harold Bloom), and applied to construct the contexts and read the texts. (1992, 138)

11. Brés cites Hume, who attributes the notion of identity to pride and shows that it does not correspond to anything real. See Brés 1983, 17–18. As for

Nietzsche, Brugière writes: "Le romantisme prépare la voie à cette destructura-
tion du sujet qu'accompliront Nietzsche et la psychanalyse et qui fait actuellement partie de la modernité" 'Romanticism prepares the way for this
destructuring of the subject that will be accomplished by Nietzsche and psychoanalysis and that is at present part of modernity' (1983, 254).

12. The approach is neither formalist nor psychological. It is not formalist
because it accepts intertextual evidence from biographical and historical sources.
And since it does not rely on any psychological theory or ideas from psychology,
it would be even more inappropriate to call it psychological. Psychobiology, psycholinguistics, the neurosciences, and personal interpretations based on language, which are its sources, are not psychology.

Chapter 1. Baudelaire and the Unity of the Self

1. In his 1968 essay, "The Death of the Author," Barthes explains that "As
soon as a fact is *narrated* . . . outside of any function other than that of the very
practice of the symbol itself, this disconnection occurs, the voice loses its origin,
the author enters into his own death, writing begins" (1977, 142).

2. If, for his part, Lacan does not speak of death in this context, it is only
because from the beginning, as early as the pre-mirror stage, the infant does
not see itself as one. According to Ragland-Sullivan, Lacan describes the pre-
mirror stage "as a period in which an infant experiences its body as fragmented
parts and images" (1986, 18).

3. When they profess this belief in the priority of language, twentieth-
century critics appear to follow in the footsteps of Mallarmé and Nietzsche.
Barthes cites Mallarmé, who saw the necessity "to substitute language itself for
the person" (1977, 143). For Foucault, if one can speak of man's disappearance
it is because "with Nietzsche, and Mallarmé, thought was brought back, and
violently so, towards language itself" (1970, 306). More recently, speaking about
Baudelaire's "Le Mauvais vitrier," Wing links the shattering glass to "the disappearance of the speaking voice" (1979, 26) as defined in Mallarmé's well-known
statement on the "elocutionary disappearance of the poet" and the self-
reflexivity of language (see 1945, 366). Thus, Mallarmé more than Baudelaire
should be given credit (or blamed) for introducing these ideas. On the other
hand, while fragmentation and the disappearance of the self may be regarded
as signs that define our contemporary criticism, the denial of the self is not
necessarily new. Hume apparently had attributed the notion of identity to pride
and had showed or tried to show that it does not correspond to anything real.
See Brés's introduction 1983, 17–18. And the idea of a self-reflexive language
may go back to Petrarch. See Freccero (1975, 38) and Waller (1980, 53–54).

4. After assessing Lacan's psychoanalysis of the child, who "fashions a self-
image on the basis of statues," Marshall concludes: "The very fact that the coherent self can be created only by the use of an external mediating image undoes
its coherence" (1993, 109–110). For Collier, the "series of substitutive images" in
"La Cloche fêlée" "restructure the narrator's thoughts, swamping his mnemonic
consciousness, and the poet drowns in his own suffocating inability to distance
himself from them" (1990, 31). The attempt "to represent an ideal self in symbolic form" ends in failure (see 1990, 27). Chambers speaks of a similar mediating process when he says that Baudelaire's narrator, the man of the crowd, as
"the agent of mediation loses all identity but that of a purely discursive subject"

(1991, 147). And even as such, his identity is problematic because it is linked to the indeterminacy of discourse.

5. For MacInnes (in "Un Voyage à Cythère") "a far-flung dispersion of the self" is achieved "through the rhetoric of likening" (1988, 14). In Mehlman's view, what is at stake in the incarnations of the prince-dandy may be "a certain violence of metaphoricity, as it *exceeds* and decenters individual consciousness" (1974, 9). Intentionality may also contribute to the dismantling of the self. Wing suggests that "Texts such as 'Une Mort héroïque,' 'Le Mauvais vitrier,' ... 'Assommons les pauvres,' and others can be read as scenes in which subjectivity, in the assertion of control, self-destructs" (1979, 26). Bersani, for his part, speaks of "self-scattering" but at one point expresses some skepticism about "psychic fragmentation" and "partial selves" that "have become ideological tenets of much contemporary thought" (1977, 4).

6. Although they see "vaporisation" and "centralisation" in different contexts, both Meitinger and Harrington point out the interdependence of the two tendencies. The first emphasizes that, in projecting himself toward others, the poet risks dissipation, but then, in a movement of double posture, brings the self back "dans ses propres limites" 'within its own limits' (1989, 119). According to the second, the results are uneven: Sometimes "the loss or absence of the self creates a positive extension of the poetic act" at other times, however, "this interaction points to an impasse" and it is disruptive (1991–92, 177).

7. Brombert expresses a similar view about the dialectics of intoxication: "egocentricity and depersonalization remain interlocked" (1974, 58). The two parallel the "opposites of the creative method" (1974, 57).

8. For a different view of the mask function see Walker, "Persona Criticism." For her the (author-)persona "is a mask"; but this persona or "author-mask" "is almost precisely opposite to the historical subject-author in that it functions like an outline, a potentiality, rather than a fullness ..." (1991, 115).

9. Pichois is, thus, amply justified in saying: "C'est avec Baudelaire que la conscience de soi entre impérieusement dans la poésie française ..." 'It is with Baudelaire that self-consciousness enters French poetry in compelling fashion ...' (1983, 302).

10. Some of these expressions reappear in "Le Peintre de la vie moderne" to portray Constantin Guys, the painter: "Sa passion et sa profession, c'est d'*épouser la foule*" and "c'est une immense jouissance" 'His passion and his profession are to *espouse the crowds*' and 'it is an immense pleasure' (2: 691).

11. The relation between the moral and the aesthetic drives is defined by Kaplan as "This tension between ethical pathos versus a compelling passion for ideal Beauty" (1990, 17).

12. The visionary text, the acrobat's "regard profond, inoubliable" 'deep, unforgettable look,' is fulfilled in Asselineau's 1867 letter, containing a description of Baudelaire's impairment: "il ne m'a reconnu que par un regard d'une fixité navrante" 'the only sign that he recognized me was a look of a distressing steadiness' (qtd. by Pichois and Ziegler, 1987, 586).

13. Here is the passage in question:

Un oeil expérimenté ne s'y trompe jamais. Dans ces traits rigides ou abattus, dans ces yeux caves et ternes, ou brillants des derniers éclairs de la lutte ... il déchiffre tout de suite les innombrables légendes de l'amour trompé, du dévouement méconnu, des efforts non récompensés, de la faim et du froid humblement, silencieusement supportés.

A practiced eye is never wrong. In those rigid or dejected features, in those hollow and dull eyes, or eyes shining with the battle's final flares . . . it immediately deciphers innumerable legends of love deceived, of unrecognized devotion, of unrewarded efforts, of hunger and cold humbly, silently endured. (1: 292, Kaplan 23)

14. In his analysis of "Le Vieux saltimbanque," Thélot stresses the total domination of the creator over the other: "[L]e saltimbanque—autrui—est aboli, vidé de sa réalité personnelle, ne survivant désormais, idéalement, que par ce qu'il permet de refuser: pour que de ce vide rayonne l'irréelle plénitude de l'artiste, de ce Néant l'Etre fictif du créateur" 'The acrobat—the other—is abolished, emptied of his personal reality, surviving henceforth, ideally, only through what he can refuse: so that from this emptiness may radiate the unreal plenitude of the artist, from this Void the fictional Being of the creator' (1993, 65).

15. In his analysis of "Le Peintre de la vie moderne," Bersani rightly emphasizes the role of memory: "The external stimuli that gravely, and erotically, 'shake' us are those that reactivate . . . memory traces of other stimuli" (1990, 74).

16. The poet, though male, may acquire the mother principle when in contact with the other, with women in particular. Kaplan rightly points out that in "Les Veuves" "Baudelaire becomes a widowed mother, incorporates her pain and joy, and engenders poetry" (1980, 241). Describing the poet's relation to his allegorical figures, which are mostly women, Gasarian writes: "L'allégorie s'annonce comme un moyen d'effraction dont le poète jouit, d'une jouissance qui est aussi naissance, car cette pénétration d'autrui vient en retour le féconder" 'Allegory appears as a means of entering that the poet enjoys, an enjoyment which is also a birth, for this penetration of the other in return impregnates him' (1991, 180).

17. Whether the poem is disclosure or invention would depend on the way in which the fictional blend is a reflection of the other or a reflection of the self. In his analysis of Baudelaire's "hysteria," Gasarian believes that the poet "se découvre en train de devenir autre, en train d'excéder ses limites" 'discovers himself in the process of becoming other, in the process of exceeding his limits' (1991, 182). Godfrey tips the balance in favor of subjectivity: "The fiction [on the surface of the window] grows out of a self-conscious, mirroring subjectivity which it must then efface" to allow Baudelaire "to embrace the aesthetic fiction as wholly other" (1982, 97). But this movement is short-lived, and Godfrey finally agrees with Sartre that "the image Baudelaire sees in the windows of Paris is ultimately always his own" (1982, 98). Similarly, Prendergast sees more invention than disclosure, "less a window than a mirror reflecting back not the 'truth' of the other, but an enabling fiction of the self" (1991, 187).

18. Speaking about the Oedipus myth, Felman defines truth as a promise that is not kept, a promise that is in fact untenable (1982, 14). And she adds: "En effet, à aucun moment, le mythe ne *nomme* pas la vérité: l'oracle lui-même n'énonce, strictement parlant, qu'un mythe—rhétorique (métaphorique, énigmatique) et invérifiable" 'Indeed, at no time does the myth *name* the truth: the oracle itself, strictly speaking, sets forth only a myth—a rhetorical (metaphorical, enigmatic) and unverifiable myth' (1982, 18). Is the legend of the woman in "Windows" unverifiable, in the manner of the ancient myth?

19. Here is Baudelaire's description: "De temps en temps la personnalité disparaît. L'objectivité qui fait certains poètes panthéistiques et les grands comédiens devient telle que vous vous confondez avec les êtres extérieurs" 'From time to time your personality disappears. Objectivity, which makes pantheistic poets and great comedians, becomes such that you merge with (the beings of) external

reality' ("Du vin et du hachisch" 1: 393). He repeats the idea in "Le Poème du hachisch" 1: 419.

Chapter 2. The Mnemonic Text: "Le Mauvais vitrier" and "Mademoiselle Bistouri"

1. Ruff defines the subject of "Le Mauvais vitrier" as "une manifestation d'angélisme, le refus d'une condition imparfaite où manquent les «vitres de paradis»'" 'a manifestation of angelism, the refusal of an imperfect condition in which there are no «panes of paradise»' (1955, 362). Hiddleston speaks of "black humour," which "has in an exaggerated form something of the diabolical laugh of Melmoth" (1987, 96). Kaplan calls the poem "a double polemic directed against contrary standards: complacent didacticism or naive hedonism bereft of sensitivity" (1990, 47). Pizzorusso invokes psychoanalysis and speaks of "fantasmes conscients" 'conscious phantasms' (1976, 171). Fairlie summarizes what appears to be true for *Petits poëmes en prose* as a whole, when she speaks of the ambition to reach "the Tree of Knowledge" (1967, 457–58). In a departure from the more traditional approaches, Johnson proposes that the prose poems "can be read as ironic reflections of the nature of poetic language as such" (1983, 79). And there is a tendency to establish parallels between the level of narrative and the level of drives or desire. Thus, commenting on the narrator's question at the end of "Mademoiselle Bistouri," Maclean explains: "The narrative of lack and of obsession in each case returns compulsively and inevitably to the lack which underlies desire" (1988, 157). In exploring the scene of destruction, the narrator's folly, at the end of "Le Mauvais vitrier," Wing concludes: "In several ways, then, the poem invites reflection on the problem of how meaning is generated in the text and of the relation between the narrating voice to that process" (1979, 26). In his commentary on "Une Mort héroïque," Mehlman states that "what is at stake in the diverse incarnations of the prince-dandy may be less a series of metaphors for violence . . . than a certain violence of metaphoricity, as it *exceeds* and decenters individual consciousness" (1974, 9). Discursive relations, including the relation of text to reader, tend to acquire the potency to mirror narrative action. For a critique of Johnson and Mehlman, see Cohn (1986, 116–19).

2. Mauron quotes the narrator's asking for "des vitres qui fassent voir la vie en beau" and comments: "Jugement qui rabaisse deux fois l'art, car, avant de le déclarer inefficace, il le classe parmi les drogues" 'Judgment that twice reduces the value of art, for, before pronouncing it ineffective, it classifies it as a drug' (1966, 117). Pizzorusso is even more explicit: "Le narrateur-protagoniste reproche au vitrier de ne pas posséder ces vitres merveilleuses. Or la vision colorée du monde qu'elles produiraient est sans doute une des illusions qui s'inscrivent sur la rétine de l'homme pris de haschisch" 'The narrator-protagonist reproaches the glazier for not having these marvelous panes. Now, the colored vision of the world that they would produce is undoubtedly one of the illusions which appear on the retina of man under the influence of hashish.' (1976, 164).

3. Wing calls "these confrontations with the double" in "Le Mauvais vitrier" and elsewhere "an impasse which the narrator goes about dismantling, even if he does not precisely resolve it" (1986, 25). For the idea of self-destruction, see Wing 1979, 26.

4. Baudelaire may have known and may have been inspired by a story enti-

tled "La Mère Bistouri," published by *L'Epoque*, 30 January 1866, in Paris. See Kopp 1969, 347–48, and Maclean 1988, 158–60.

5. Baudelaire describes a similar reasoning in favor of God in "Mon coeur mis à nu":

> *Calcul en faveur de Dieu.*
> Rien n'existe sans but.
> Donc mon existence a un but. Quel but? Je l'ignore.
> Ce n'est donc pas moi qui l'ai marqué.
> C'est donc quelqu'un, plus savant que moi.
> Il faut donc prier ce quelqu'un de m'éclairer. C'est
> le parti le plus sage.

> *Calculation in favor of God.*
> Nothing exists without a purpose.
> Consequently my existence has a purpose. What purpose?
> I don't know.
> Clearly then it is not I who set that purpose.
> It must be someone who has more knowledge than I.
> I must therefore pray that someone to enlighten me.
> That is the wisest course.

(1: 678)

6. Prévost speaks of a velleity of blasphemy: "[Le poète] est tout près de demander à la divine Providence le pourquoi du crime et du châtiment. Un pas de plus, cette ferveur serait doute, et presque blasphème" 'The poet comes very close to asking the divine Providence the reason for crime and punishment. Another step and this fervor would become doubt and almost blasphemy' (1964, 100).

7. Hiddleston categorically affirms the ambiguity of the prayer, which is for him "both a cry of distress and a veiled indictment of the justice of an omniscient God" (1987, 60). In his view the prayer "points not to providence but to a moral anarchy at the heart of the universe" (1987, 61). Kaplan points out that the modern poet's "thinking is free of idolatry," but he also cautions that the "religious content of this anguished prayer remains ambiguous" (1990, 150). In Aynesworth's view, the prayer can be regarded as "the equivalent of physical pain" (1982, 215). Maclean for her part believes that just as "Mademoiselle Bistouri addressed the account of her obsession to a phantasm created by her own mind, the *surgeon* she imagines," the narrator "addresses his text and his prayer to a construct of his own mind" (1988, 156).

8. Both Kaplan and Maclean preserve the ambiguity of the original. Kaplan translates, "comment ils *se sont faits* et comment ils auraient pu *ne pas se faire*" into "how *they were made* and how they might have been able *not to be made*" (1989, 118). Maclean's translation reads: "how they *came into being* and how they might *not have come into being*" (1988, 157).

9. "C'est peut-être la grandeur de Baudelaire, que cette prise de conscience de la condition humaine *dans sa contradiction,* et de l'avoir vécue *dans sa totalité*" 'Perhaps Baudelaire's greatness is in this awareness of the human condition *with its inherent contradiction,* and in having lived it *in its totality*' (Ruff 1955, 373).

10. See Homer 1951, 12.200–250. In the Prologue to his book on Deconstruction, Leitch quotes the Homeric passage as paradigmatic of the act of inter-

pretation (see 1983, 3–6). As one would expect, Leitch's concerns are to elucidate Deconstruction, but the example has important cognitive implications.

Chapter 3. The Realignment of the Love Lyric

1. Blin draws the main lines of the argument: "Ici les lèvres de la plaie, par leur pouvoir d'analogie sexuelle, le conduisent à une forme de sadisme plus intérieur, plus profond, plus troublant" 'Here the lips of the wound, by the power of the sexual analogy, lead him to a more interior, deeper, more troubling form of sadism' (1948, 29). And he emphasizes the relation to Sade and the erotic perversion of the desire to poison. Bersani picks up the train of thought: "This ecstatic punishment is a simulacrum of 'normal' sex" (1977, 73). In a view that is as dogmatic as it is condescending, Bersani explains: "Blin wrote his book before the French discovered Freud" (1977, 89n.19) and the French critic's "limited" discussion has to be completed by psychoanalysis. More recently, Graham Robb in a new twist poses the question, "Baudelaire ne traite-t-il pas ici le thème stendhalien du *fiasco?*" (1992, 74) In his view, the ending of the poem may be better explained by supposing the violent reaction of a poet who had been humiliated and embarrassed as a consequence of a sexual weakness (impotence?).

2. On this point Conio's statement is helpful: "Le plaisir des sens et l'extase spirituelle, loin de s'opposer, s'engendrent réciproquement" but one cannot follow him when he adds, "et forment un cercle vicieux, une impossibilité logique" (1992, 97).

3. One would think that those who attach some importance to Maistrian influence would tend to accept the viability of the intercessory role, and those who do not would prefer to dwell on the human aspect of the poet's appeal. But the situation is more complicated. Pointing out Maistre's concept of prayer as the dynamics granted to human beings to augment their natural forces (see Blin 1948, 88) and its influence on Baudelaire, Blin is still convinced that "même quand [Baudelaire] se donne l'air de sommer, par la mise en application de formules ou par l'utilisation d'intercesseurs bien placés, quelque mystérieuse transcendance, c'est lui-même qu'il sollicite" 'even when [Baudelaire] appears to summon, by the implementation of formulas or by the use of well placed intercessors, some mysterious transcendance, it is himself he is soliciting' (1948, 89). Thus, Blin feels that for the poet, prayer is more a matter of hygiene than of worship. At the same time, however, being forced to justify Maistrian influence, Blin writes: "[Baudelaire] conserve en aveugle et paradoxalement la théorie maistrienne du sacrifice et le principe de la réversibilité" '[Baudelaire] retains blindly and paradoxically the Maistrain theory of sacrifice and the principle of reversibility' (1948, 67). But why blindly, if Maistrian theory of the existence of evil is at the core of Baudelaire's view of the world? Milner, on the other hand, maintains that prayer for Baudelaire is not intercession on behalf of the sinner "mais bien plutôt une sorte d'infusion magique de santé et de force qui fait exactement pendant à l'infusion de venin sur laquelle s'achevait A *celle qui est trop gaie*" 'but rather a sort of magic infusion of health and force which is the exact counterpart to the infusion of venom at the end of À *celle qui est trop gaie*' (1967, 99). One could not describe more appropriately the link between the two poems; but why deny the intercessory value of the prayer?

4. One can recall here Marcel Raymond's observation that breaking with

the conventional psychology, Baudelaire accepted as a fact and exploited the consequences of "l'étroite relation du physique et du spirituel" 'the tight relation between the physical and the spiritual' (1940, 18).

Chapter 4. "Une Mort héroïque": Martyrdom and Tradition

1. Among the earliest critics is Mauron, who adopts a psychoanalytical perspective and sees the prince and the mime as two manifestations of Baudelaire's own personality (see 1966, 136–40). Reworking Mauron's thesis and reversing the values, Mehlman contends that in his reading the prince, "would have a privileged access to reality" (1974, 13). In a traditional article, Starobinski explores Baudelairean conception of art (1967). Chambers analyzes and defines nineteenth-century themes of the poet as comedian (1971). Wing identifies the issue of the textual status of narration (see 1979, 25). Kaplan explores and enriches the various implications of the word *faveur* (1990, 54). Pichois, Lemaitre and Kopp, in the notes to their editions, give us valuable historical and intertextual information.

2. Kaplan stresses the philosophical implications: "The Fool [the mime] and the Prince reenact the inevitable duel between nature and art, spirit and matter . . ." (1990, 55). Starobinski suggests that in this poem and in "Le Vieux saltimbanque," "Baudelaire semble vouloir mettre en évidence l'envers mortel de la réussite esthétique" 'Baudelaire, it seems, wishes to underscore the fatal reverse of artistic success' (1967, 405). Chambers expresses the belief that "tout artiste, même le plus accompli, est voué à la catastrophe du sifflet" 'every artist, even the most skillful, is doomed to the disaster of the catcall' (1971, 247). In the last two views, the artist's failure looms large. Starobinski dwells on the ephemeral character of the artist's success (1967, 409), while Chambers stresses the poet-comedian's failure to achieve the desired synthesis between life and art and to realize "les conditions d'un art véritable" 'the conditions of a true art' (1971, 245). The clown dies either because of a necessarily brief success or because of an ultimate failure. While emphasizing the rhetorical aspects of the poem and its potentially political significance, Wing also stresses the role of death in the conflict between the two rivals: "The text also makes it very clear that this performance confronts the source of despotism's power: death" (1990, 10). And Rubin, seeing the mime's death as necessary, argues that "when the real world, in the form of the whistle, interrupts and so destroys the creation with which he has identified, which he himself incarnates, he is himself necessarily also destroyed . . ." (1985–86, 58).

3. The queen mother tells her son: "Vous avez contre cet homme une rancoeur qui n'est ni saine ni virile! . . . Thomas Becket serait une femme qui vous aurait trahi et que vous aimeriez encore, vous n'agiriez pas autrement" 'You have against this man a resentment which is neither healthy nor manly! . . . Had Thomas Becket been a woman who had betrayed you and whom you still loved, you would not behave differently' (1959, 179–80). There is, of course, some irony for the contemporary reader when, in Eliot's play, the first tempter refers to Becket with the words "Old Tom, gay Tom" (1952, 183); but it is not certain how, or if, the homosexual implications can be transferred from Anouilh to Eliot or to Baudelaire.

4. As Schofer puts it: "The theater reeks of death for the narrator even

before the ominous whistle" (1988, 51). It may be useful here to recall the two different ways of looking at the metaphoric level espoused by deconstructive and cognitive theorists. Nealon quotes Hartman on the interest of deconstructors in "'figurative language, its excess over any assigned meaning'" and also Miller who speaks about "the undecidability of figurative language (see Nealon 1992, 1273). Yet it can be demonstrated that the longer mnemonic sequences needed in coding metaphors produce greater precision and depth rather than excess and undecidability.

5. It is interesting to note that in the English pantomime Baudelaire saw, Pierrot was eventually guillotined. See the passage in "De l'essence du rire" 2: 538–40. That experience may have provided knowledge and material for envisaging some aspects of the performance and for describing the narrator's reactions.

6. In a similar reading of the fatal whistle in "Une Mort héroïque," Mehlman stresses that it causes "death *before the end* of the performance" and relates it to Nietzsche's concept of untimeliness (1974, 10). Nietzsche, of course, speaks about his classical studies, which are "untimely—that is to say acting counter to our time and thereby acting on our time and, let us hope, for the benefit of a time to come" (1983, 60). The context is different, but the reference has explanatory power.

7. The narrator's foreknowledge and awareness of the abyss may reflect Baudelaire's own apprehensions before his tragic fall in the Saint-Loup church in 1866. There are very few thoughts that preoccupy him during the years of the prose poems more than the fear of the abyss, premonitions and warnings that soon his time may be up: "Au moral comme au physique, j'ai toujours eu la sensation du gouffre . . . Maintenant j'ai toujours le vertige, et aujourd'hui 23 janvier 1862, j'ai subi un singulier avertissement . . ." ("Hygiène" 1: 668) 'Mentally as well as physically, I have always had the sensation of the abyss . . . Now I experience dizziness all the time and today 23 January 1862, I was subject to a singular warning.' In other "Hygiène" fragments, he speaks of "pressentiments" 'premonitions' and "signes envoyés déjà par Dieu" (1: 668) 'signs already sent by God,' and a bit further on: "Rêves sur la Mort et avertissements" (1: 672) 'Dreams about death and warnings.' In the light of these passages, the pantomime on the stage and its capacity to veil the terrors of the abyss acquire added significance.

8. For the similarity between the mime's triumph on the stage and the death scene in *Madame Bovary*, see my article, 1986–87, 253. At the moment when Emma's initial visions of eternal beatitude appear to give her hope of salvation, unexpectedly, the beggar intervenes. Mocking her cherished dreams, his song has all the characteristics of the "coup de sifflet" pattern.

9. Cohn rightly points out that at the decisive moment "an artist naturally sides with the artist" (118).

10. In noting that "the narrator [in "Une Mort héroïque"] is reduced to concluding his analysis with a series of 'suppositions non exactement justifiées, mais non absolument injustifiables,'" Margery Evans tips the balance in favor of the difficulty of knowing: "Far from probing the depths of another person's soul with macho Balzacian acuity, in the *Petits Poèmes en prose* Baudelaire's references to eyes invariably suggest that communication with the Other is problematic, if not impossible" (1993, 50).

11. This is brought out by at least two critics. Jones stresses the relation between chorus and audience: "With and through the Chorus, we of the audience

are invited to participate in the celebration of the act of martyrdom and to accept the sacrifice of Thomas as made in our behalf" (1971, 96). Similarly, in explaining that neither chorus nor audience is allowed "to be entirely spectators," Ward writes: "the drama is shaped toward ritual purposes, and ritual inevitably involves participation: it is the way in which the tribe or the community reaffirms and re-creates the consciousness of its identity—and the struggle, the suffering and the triumph of the hero are its own agon, pathos and theophany" (1988, 75).

12. Starobinski calls "Une Mort héroïque" and "Le Vieux saltimbanque" "deux paraboles" (1967, 405); Kaplan calls the prose poems "fables of modern life" (1990, ix).

Chapter 5. Andromache and Baudelairean Exile in "Le Cygne"

1. Leakey notes with justifiable wonder that the poem begins "so arrestingly and mysteriously" (1990, 255n17). And Burton observes with similar admiration that "[the poem] emerges *ex nihilo* with the force of an absolute beginning . . ." (1988, 155).

2. Houston believes "Baudelaire amused himself in 'Le Cygne' by writing the poem twice: the same material is first presented in a radically free-associative pattern . . . and is then reintroduced in part two, following a neat reverse chronological order . . ." (1991, 128).

3. I have indicated elsewhere the resemblance between SaintAmant's allegories in "Les Visions" and Baudelaire's poem. See "Baudelaire in the Circle of Exiles," 126–28. The following lines show strong affinities with "Le Cygne":

> Le coeur plein d'amertume et l'ame ensevelie
> Dans la plus sombre melancolie
>
> . . . .
>
> Si je rencontre un cerf, ma triste fantaisie
> De la mort d'Actéon est tout soudain saisie;
> Les cygnes qu'on y void dans un paisible estang
> Me semblent des corbeaux qui nagent dans du sang;
>
> . . . .
>
> Le Louvre, dont l'éclat se fait si bien parestre,
> N'est à mes yeux troublez qu'un chasteau de Bicestre;
> Le fleuve qui le borde est à moi l'Acheron. . . .
>
> . . . .
>
> O belle Polixene! amante infortunée!

> My heart full of bitterness and my soul buried
> In a most somber mood of melancholy
>
> . . . .
>
> If I encounter a deer, my gloomy fantasy
> Is suddenly struck with the death of Acteon;
> The swans I see in a peaceful pond
> Appear as ravens swimming in blood;
>
> . . . .
>
> The Louvre, whose brilliance is so clearly seen,
> Is in my eyes no more than a Bicetre asylum;

The river which borders it is for me the Acheron. . . .
. . . .
O beautiful Polyxena! unlucky in love! (87–90)
"Les Visions" 1855, 1: 83

4. For a critical assessment of Burton's association between Hector in "Le Cygne" and Baudelaire's father, François Baudelaire, see Robb 1991–92, 17–20.

5. But Emmanuel also stresses the temporal influence of experience and the poet's difficulties with women (see 1967, 142).

6. The mention of Milton's Satan betrays the Romantic sources of this association and may remind one of Chateaubriand's *Atala* and Lamartine's "L'Automne," but the passage also shows Baudelaire's greater awareness of the concept's aesthetic function.

7. See Bush's thesis in "'Le Cygne' or 'El cisne': The History of a Misreading"; but also Thélot, who writes: "l'immense premier vers du «Cygne» est aussi un hommage à Racine—autant qu'à Virgile—" 'the immense first line of "Le Cygne" is also a tribute to Racine—as much as to Virgile—' (1993, 145).

8. In his letter (7 December 1859) of dedication to Hugo, Baudelaire speaks of the sight of a suffering animal and what it may suggest (see 1973, 1: 623).

9. This is how Terdiman must see them to write that "the language-fragments that materialize within "Le Cygne" can turn up anywhere, but for now they turn up *here*" (1993, 140) and to conclude that the "mnemonics of dispossession opens the text to limitless relation, and hence to the limitless migration of other texts" (1993a, 184).

10. Although de Man argues against allegory's links to memory and experience, he remains aware of the ambivalence of his position: "To claim that the loss of representation is modern is to make us again aware of an allegorical element in the lyric that had never ceased to be present, but that is itself necessarily dependent on the existence of an earlier allegory and so is the negation of modernity" (1971, 186). This admission, instead of counterbalancing his idea of allegory as a void, contradicts it. Something that had never ceased to be present is not a void.

Chapter 6. "Le Voyage": The Dimension of Myth

1. "Le Voyage" (1: 129–134) As in the earlier chapters, the source for Baudelaire quotations is Pichois's Pléiade edition of *Oeuvres complètes*. The parenthesis references to the poem will be limited to line numbers.

2. Here are some judgments on Electra's character: "Except for her loyalty and devotion to her brother, Electra is a piece of complete viciousness, stubborn in spite and malice with the bitterness born of envy and resentful virginity" (Arrowsmith, "Introduction to *Orestes*" 1958, 109). In speaking about Sophocles's Electra, Banks writes: "The only thing that qualifies this harsh impression [of Electra] is her love for Orestes. He is not merely her instrument of vengeance but the child she tenderly remembers nursing" (1966, xiv).

3. See, however, the intriguing suggestions put forward by Burton about the identity of Pylades and several other figures. He sees Poulet-Malassis "standing as an improbable Pylades-figure to Baudelaire's decidedly unheroic Orestes" (1988, 28).

4. In this context, it is instructive to recall the text of Baudelaire's prose

poem "Le Joueur généreux," cited by several critics for its resemblance to the stanzas of the enticing voices. In that passage, the narrator is invited by the devil to a house in the middle of Paris. He compares the atmosphere of "somber beatitude" in the house to the happiness of the lotus-eaters living in the light of an eternal afternoon.

5. Galand takes his cue from Campbell, who speaks of "night visitants from the mythological realm that we carry within" (1968, 8). Campbell's claim that this realm is the Unconscious erases the distinction between myth and dreams and is incompatible with a cognitive view.

6. In speaking about Odysseus's trip to the Underworld, Tracy calls the journey "a well-established metaphor for the acquisition of self-knowledge" (1990, 55). Although general in scope, this is perhaps the best answer we have. Another way to answer the question is to invoke the imperatives of a tradition. Clarke points out that the protagonists of all great myths, Gilgamesh, Odysseus, Theseus, Heracles, Orpheus, Christ, Aeneas, and Dante and Virgil, make the trip to the Underworld. And he adds: "Perhaps, then, it is pointless to talk of why Odysseus goes to the Underworld": "Odysseus goes because all heroes go" (1967, 60). Yet Clarke's excellent discussion of this matter (58–60) promotes a strategy that only postpones the question, nudges it to the end of the list.

7. Underlining the differences between "Le Voyage" and Nerval's *Voyage en Orient*, Betz concludes: "Unlike Nerval, Baudelaire's hero will never return home" (1991, 406).

8. Ruff offers a religious interpretation. In his view the travelers' "joy" at the end can be explained by "l'espoir de la vie future, «de cette après-midi qui n'a jamais de fin», et où nous retrouverons les êtres aimés . . ." 'the hope of the afterlife, «of this endless afternoon», and where we will find those we love . . .' (1955, 348).

9. The original: "Faut-il le mettre aux fers, le jeter à la mer, / Ce matelot ivrogne, inventeur d'Amériques" 'should he be cast in irons and hurled into the sea, / this drunken sailor who invents Americas' (lines 42–43; Scarfe 1964, 184). In an ironic twist, Columbus, who "invented" America and was at one point brought back to Spain in irons, is assimilated to the profile of a lowly sailor. For another interpretation of the figure of the drunken sailor, see Burton 1988, 274.

10. In defining the affinity between Baudelaire and Conrad, Putnam points out that both in "Le Voyage" and in *Heart of Darkness*, "Time will be no more chronological than space will prove geographical" (1989, 334).

11. Perhaps Poulet goes too far when he concludes that Baudelaire is "incapable of a clear conceptualization of any future whatever" (1984, 14). But in quoting "Elévation," Poulet formulates an assessment that should not surprise us: "Thus the elsewhere and the future are above all centrifugal in function; a pure *beyond (au-delà)*, characterized by the total absence of characteristics" (1984, 14).

Chapter 7. Allegory and Correspondences

1. In summarizing Coleridge's view Fletcher writes:

With Symbol the mind perceives the rational order of things directly, by an 'unmediated vision,' without any logical extrapolation from the phenomena of our material world, whereas in allegory there is always (as Coleridge sees it) an attempt to categorize logical orders first, and fit them to convenient phenomena second, to set forth ideal systems first, and illustrate them second. (1964, 18)

2. Moreau traces the origin of the "symbol" to the context of ancient hospitality, where the Greek "Sumbolon," a fragment of a broken object, becomes a sign of recognition. In the context of Baudelaire's poetry, Moreau distinguishes three stages of recognition: the world recognizes its cosmic unity; the external universe and the inner life see themselves in each other; and the unconscious self sees itself in the creative self, the self of sleep in the self of waking, the human self in its divine essence (see 1951, 91–92).

3. That they appear thus to be invested with transcendental attributes is confirmed by Cowan's explanation: "In becoming a world of allegorical emblems, the profane world is robbed of its sensuous fullness, robbed of any inherent meaning it might possess, only to be invested with a privileged meaning whose source transcends this world" (1981, 116).

4. Among contemporary critics, Benjamin's views simply strengthen Saussure's idea of the arbitrariness of the sign. Terdiman, for example, quotes from Umberto Eco's essay on memory to the effect that "anything can be the sign of anything" (qtd. 1993, 142), and then in discussing "the limitless migration of *other* texts" in "Le Cygne," he affirms: "In the mode of anamnesis, anything can suggest anything" (1993, 143).

5. MacInnes makes the same point when he defines "Allégorie," the poem, as a meditation "on *allégorie, symbole, emblème, image,* or *correspondance,* since Baudelaire makes no functional distinction among these terms" (1988, 101).On this issue, Dufour points out that as soon as a symbol needs to be accompanied by an interpretation to be understood, "on voit mal ce qui le distingue d'une allégorie" 'it is difficult to see what distinguishes it from allegory' (1989, 144).

6. See Ruff 1955, 240; and Adam 1961, 274–75.

7. See Prévost 1964, 62–63; Hubert 1953, 272; and Leakey 1969, 245.

8. See Pommier 1932, 100; Blin 1939, 108; Austin 1956, 55; and Eigeldinger 1951, 63–65. Fischer-Lichte points out that for Benjamin "The meaning which the allegorist ascribes to a thing has, of course, nothing to do with its original meaning, its idea, that it was able to express 'before the Fall'" (1986, 160). The new meaning that the rescue operation performs is arbitrary and subjective.

10. In this context, it is worth noting Spariosu's remark about the link between allegory and divination: "In ancient Greece, allegory was clearly related to the birth of the science of interpretation or hermeneutics, which was in turn based upon the old science of divination . . ." (1987, 59).

11. One critic suggests that the poem translates a real headache: "while the conscious interest of the reader has been directed by the poet toward the allegory of Psychomachia he has been all the while appealing to our unconscious associations in order to infect us with the physical sensation [the headache] which he is surrepticiously describing" (Spitzer 1959, 290).

12. On the subject of painting memories in the *Salon of 1846,* Fried reaches similar conclusions about the role of tradition. He suggests that Baudelaire's "thematics of memory" "reflects a fundamental characteristic of paintings in the Western tradition, namely, that in one way or another, or in a variety of mutually reinforcing ways, they are made from previous paintings, which in turn are made from still previous ones . . ." (1984, 518).

13. To that extent, de Man is right, "an allegorical element in the lyric . . . is itself necessarily dependent on the existence of an earlier allegory" (1971, 186);

but does it then follow that "Modernity exists in the form of a desire to wipe out whatever came earlier" (1971, 148)? Nietzsche's philosophy notwithstanding, modernity and history are not so much diametrically opposed to each other as they are in a position to feed on each other. We can at least agree that one cannot be conceived without the other.

14. Even MacInnes, who opts in favor of the fragmentation of the poet's voice, is moved to write at the end of an analysis of the poem: "Having said this, I must at the same time disavow any attempt on my part to reduce the text to the too innocent state of 'play.' There is too much density in the poem's history, too much seriousness about the way it sets out *as if* toward truth, and too much anguish in its final polylogue to allow for such trivialization" (1988, 42). Finally, however, MacInnes concludes that "any given statement concerning the sense of the text . . . creates only a momentary stoppage of a continual flow" (1988, 84).

15. See Jackson's perceptive comments. He stipulates that Baudelaire when he writes the poem "ne *sait* pas que ce vieillard vengeur, c'est lui qui s'en inflige la rencontre, bien qu'il prête à celui-ci un caractère hallucinatoire . . ." 'does not *know* that it is he who inflicts on himself the encounter with this vengeful old man, though he lends him a hallucinatory character . . .' (157). But the idea of "not knowing" can be ambiguous. It may leave room for an actual hallucination.

16. Chambers appears to preempt any transcendence, since for him "the poem is an allegory of itself, in the sense that what it says it does, what it speaks of is simultaneously a self-description" (1993, 101).

Chapter 8. The Dynamics of Transmutation

1. Eugene Holland is right to point out that the statement, "I am King Louis XVI, son of Louis XV, legitimate heir to the throne of France" "constitutes an individual identity in fixed relation to a certain form of socio-symbolic order" (1993, 21). But his statement that in modern society "individual personality is largely imaginary" can only make sense in the context of psychoanalysis, or schizoanalysis; that is, its validity is dependent on a psychoanalytical point of view. If Baudelaire were to speak in the manner of Louis XVI, the effect would be different not only because of the difference between the two societies, not only because the requirements for being a poet are different from those of being a king, but also because neither Baudelaire nor we as his readers think in those terms. This does not preempt the existence of solid relations in the constitution of Baudelaire's identity. That this constitution is a function of perspective emerges also from the converse proposition: Consider the King's identity in June 1789 as defined by Simon Schama: "[The King] was increasingly incapable of deciding whether he could indeed become some sort of King of the People as Mirabeau wanted or the anointed of Rheims, armed with the *oriflamme*" (1989, 364). On the eve of the Revolution, his identity, in his own eyes, was far from having a fixed relation; his hypothetical statement has the aura of "a fixed relation" only if it is taken in a specific context, only if we are looking at it in the perspective of the momentous events that were about to unfold. A different perspective changes the picture.

2. Brunetière, one of his most relentless critics, writes: "C'est qu'aussi bien le pauvre diable n'avait rien ou presque rien du poète, que la rage de le devenir. Non seulement le style, mais l'harmonie, le mouvement, l'imagination, lui manquent" 'It is also the case that the poor devil had nothing of what makes a poet

except the rage to become one. Not only does he lack style but he lacks harmony, movement, imagination' (1889, 266). And Faguet assures us that Baudelaire has no imagination: "C'est le poète aride de la banalité" 'He is the arid poet of triteness' (quoted by Vivier 1926, 302).

3. In this letter, Baudelaire speaks of his need to have a sum of money, which would result in an immediate benefit, enabling him to avoid loss of time, and concludes:

> car il y a quelque état plus grave encore que les douleurs physiques, c'est la peur de voir s'user et péricliter, et disparaître, dans cette horrible existence pleine de secousses, l'admirable faculté poétique, la netteté d'idées, et la puissance d'espérance qui constituent en réalité mon capital.

> for there is an even more serious state than physical pain, that is the fear of seeing wear out and decline and disappear, in this dreadful existence full of jolts, the admirable poetic faculty, the clearness of ideas, and the power of hope, which constitute in reality my capital. (1973, 1: 327)

4. Arguing for the centrality of "le conseil" in Baudelaire's outlook, Raser proposes a terse and memorable assessment of the relation between life and work: "I am tempted to see in the *conseil judiciaire* an origin of Baudelaire's works" (1991–92, 188).

5. After noting this fact Pichois concludes "Comme s'il avait cherché cette infamie . . ." 'As if he had sought this infamy' (1987, 168). This remark is pregnant with meaning. It may imply that Baudelaire not only accepted the "conseil judiciaire" as inevitable but may also have secretly welcomed it, either as granting of a wish tainted by masochistic intentionality or in the sense that it would confirm damnation and his destiny as a poet.

6. Speaking about "Mon coeur mis à nu" to his mother (1 April 1861), Baudelaire envisages it as a book and compares it with Rousseau's autobiography: "Ah! si jamais celui-là [the book] voit le jour, les *Confessions de J[ean]-J[acques]* paraîtront pâles" 'Ah! if this book is ever published, *Jean Jacques's Confessions* will appear pale beside it' (1973, 2: 141. Qtd. in 1: 1467). Although relying much more on factual data, the process of creating biographical texts is governed by the same kind of forces that govern the generation of fictional ones. And this is a fortiori true when autobiographical texts are in question. The texts that Baudelaire has given us in "Mon coeur mis à nu" (intended for publication) and in his correspondence (not intended for publication) offer valuable intertextual links with his poetry.

7. Barthes believes that a text in general is constructed from "quotations without quotation marks" (1979, 77). However, the changes that those "quotations" undergo are of capital importance, and that is what Barthes would never acknowledge because it would mean reinserting the author into the text.

8. One can see that this correspondence, loss of blood-poet, had become a traditional dynamic pattern. Impressed by "La fontaine de sang," Crépet and Blin write: "Ce sonnet . . . rend avec une terrible netteté une sensation voisine de celles du cauchemar et de l'hallucination" 'This sonnet . . . renders with terrible clarity a feeling akin to feelings of nightmare and hallucination' (1942, 496–97).

9. *Les Fleurs du mal* was, according to Marcel Raymond writing in 1940, the source of the contemporary poetic movement: one channel led to the *artistes*, such as Mallarmé and Valéry, the other to the *voyants*, such as Rimbaud (see

1940, 11). But one can also see two (or more) legacies: one bequeathed to the French, having, as Raymond indicates, two channels; the other left to the English speaking poets, Pound and Eliot in particular, that of turning toward a tradition, transforming it, reviving it, and quoting it. In both cases, the turn was away from romanticism and toward a new conception or conceptions of tradition.

10. Undoubtedly Baudelaire would have been pleased by Pichois's conclusion: "Son royaume n'est pas de ce monde" 'His kingdom is not of this world' (1981, 233). For another view of Baudelaire's attitude toward revolution see also T. J. Clark. In his commentary on "Assommons les pauvres," Clark defines Baudelaire's philosophy of revolution as "bitter, illiberal, absolutely anti-utopian; scorning the dreams of February . . ." (1973, 177).

11. Without the recognition of the experimental character of "Assommons les pauvres," for example, one can easily be led to see in it an illustration of a political theory. Not everybody can, of course. Clark points out, and rightly so, that the prose poem is not "prescriptive." "It is among other things a joke—but a joke which takes on its own life in the telling, over which the joker's voice breaks and falters" (1973, 177). And Diamond, recalling the beginning where the narrator speaks about reading all kinds of books on how to be happy and rich in twenty-four hours, writes: "What is being caricatured by Baudelaire is the instant transformation promised by the self-help manuals. Equality through conquest emerges as another slogan and it is deconstructed by the pathetic but farcical scene of urban violence" (1991, 176). This is a valuable insight, which confirms again the experimental nature of the prose poem.

References

Adam, Antoine, ed. 1961. *Les Fleurs du mal,* by Charles Baudelaire. Paris: Garnier Frères.

Aeschylus. 1953. *Agamemnon. Aeschylus I: Oresteia.* Translated by Richmond Lattimore. Chicago: University of Chicago Press.

Alighieri, Dante. 1954. *The Inferno.* Translated by John Ciardi. New York: Mentor-New American Library.

Anouilh, Jean. 1959. *Becket.* [Paris?]: La Table Ronde.

Arnold, Paul. 1972. *Esotérisme de Baudelaire.* Paris: Librairie Philosophique J. Vrin.

Arrowsmith, William. 1958. "Introduction." In *Orestes. Euripides-IV,* by Euripides. Edited by David Grene and Richmond Lattimore. Chicago: University of Chicago Press.

Auerbach, Eric. 1962. "The Aesthetic Dignity of *Les Fleurs du mal.*" In *Baudelaire: A Collection of Critical Essays.* Edited by Henri Peyre. Englewood Cliffs, N.J.: Prentice Hall.

Austin, Lloyd J. 1956. *L'Univers poétique de Baudelaire: Symbolisme et symbolique.* Paris: Mercure de France.

————. 1961. "Baudelaire: Poet or Prophet?" In *Studies in Modern French Literature.* Presented to P. Mansell Jones. Edited by L. J. Austin, Garnet Rees, and Eugène Vinaver. Manchester: Manchester University Press. 18–34.

Aynesworth, Donald. 1982. "Humanity and Monstrosity in *Le Spleen de Paris:* A Reading of 'Mademoiselle Bistouri.'" *Romanic Review* 73: 209–21.

Babuts, Nicolae. 1977. "Structure and Meaning in Baudelairian Images of Immersion." *Symposium.* 31 (Fall): 185–95.

————. 1979. "Baudelaire et J. G. F." *Bulletin Baudelairien* 14.2 (Winter): 3–6.

————. 1986–87. "Flaubert: Meaning and Counter Meaning." *Symposium* 40 (Winter): 247–58.

————. 1992. *The Dynamics of the Metaphoric Field: A Cognitive View of Literature.* Newark: University of Delaware Press.

————. 1993–94. "Baudelaire in the Circle of Exiles: A Study of 'Le Cygne.'" *Nineteenth-Century French Studies* 22 (Fall–Winter): 123–38.

Banks, Theodore Howard, trans. 1966. *Electra. Four Plays by Sophocles.* New York: Oxford University Press.

Barthes, Roland. 1970. *S/Z.* Paris: Seuil.

————. 1977. "The Death of the Author." In *Image Music Text.* Translated by Stephen Heath. New York: Hill and Wang. 142–48. (The volume presents selected essays by Barthes.)

Baudelaire, Charles. 1961. *Les Fleurs du mal.* Edited by Antoine Adam. Paris: Garnier Frères.

———. 1962. *Petits poèmes en prose: Le Spleen de Paris.* Edited by Henri Lemaitre. Paris: Garnier Frères.

———. 1964. *Baudelaire.* Translated by Francis Scarfe. Baltimore: Penguin Books.

———. 1968. *Petits poèmes en prose.* Edited by Melvin Zimmerman. Manchester: Manchester University Press.

———. 1969. *Petits poëmes en prose.* Edited by Robert Kopp. Paris: José Corti.

———. 1973. *Correspondance.* Edited by Claude Pichois and Jean Ziegler (Pléiade). 2 vols. Paris: Gallimard.

———. 1975–76. *Oeuvres complètes.* Edited by Claude Pichois (Pléiade). 2 vols. Paris: Gallimard.

———. 1982. *Les Fleurs du mal.* Translated by Richard Howard. Boston: David R. Godine.

———. 1989. *The Parisian Prowler: Le Spleen de Paris, Petits Poèmes en prose.* Translated by Edward K. Kaplan. Athens: University of Georgia Press.

———. 1993. *The Flowers of Evil.* Translated by James McGowan. Oxford: Oxford University Press.

———, trans. 1932. *Histoires Extraordinaires par Edgar Poe.* Edited by Jacques Crépet. Paris: Conard. Vol. 12 of *Oeuvres complètes de Charles Baudelaire.*

Bénichou, Paul. 1985. *Le Sacre de l'écrivain 1750–1830: Essai sur l'avènement d'un pouvoir spirituel laïque dans la France moderne.* Paris: Corti.

Benjamin, Walter. 1973. *Charles Baudelaire: A Lyric Poet in the Era of High Capitalism.* London: NLB.

———. 1977. *The Origin of German Tragic Drama.* London: NLB. Translation by John Osborne of *Ursprung des deutschen Trauerspiels.* Frankfurt am Main: Suhrkamp Verlag, 1963.

Berndt, Ronald M. 1953. *Djanggawul: An Aboriginal Religious Cult of North-Eastern Arnhem Land.* New York: Philosophical Library.

Bersani, Leo. 1977. *Baudelaire and Freud.* Berkeley and Los Angeles: University of California Press.

———. 1990. *The Culture of Redemption.* Cambridge, Mass.: Harvard University Press.

Betz, Dorothy M. 1991. "Nerval's *Voyage en Orient* and Baudelaire's Imagined Orient." *Romance Quarterly* 38: 399–406.

Blin, Georges. 1939. *Baudelaire.* Paris: Gallimard.

———. 1948. *Le Sadisme de Baudelaire.* Paris: Corti.

Bonnefoy, Yves. 1959. *L'Improbable.* Paris: Mercure de France.

Brés, Yvon. 1983. "Introduction: Ambiguïtés de la conscience de soi." In *Genèse de la conscience moderne: Études sur le développement de la conscience de soi dans la littérature du monde occidental.* Publications de la Sorbonne. Edited by Robert Ellrodt. Paris: Presses Universitaires de France. 13–22.

Brombert, Victor. 1973. "'Le Cygne' de Baudelaire: Douleur, Souvenir, Travail." In *Études baudelairiennes 3.* Hommage à W. T. Bandy. Neuchatel: À la Baconnière. 254–61.

————. 1974. "The Will to Ecstasy: The Example of Baudelaire's 'La Chevelure.'" *Yale French Studies* 50: 55–63.

Brooks, Peter. 1994. "Aesthetics and Ideology: What Happened to Poetics." *Critical Inquiry* 20 (Spring): 509–23.

Brugière, Bernard. 1983. "Aspects de la conscience de soi dans le romantisme." In *Genèse de la conscience moderne: Études sur le développement de la conscience de soi dans la littérature du monde occidental.* Publications de la Sorbonne. Edited by Robert Ellrodt. Paris: Presses Universitaires de France. 233–54.

Brunetière, Ferdinand. 1889. *Questions de critique.* Paris: Calmann Lévy.

Burton, Richard D. E. 1988. *Baudelaire in 1859: A Study in the Sources of Poetic Creativity.* Cambridge: Cambridge University Press.

————. 1991. *Baudelaire and the Second Republic: Writing and Revolution.* Oxford: Clarendon Press.

————. 1991a. "A Note on 'Le Cygne' and the *Iliad.*" *French Studies Bulletin* 38 (Spring): 7–9.

Bush, Andrew. 1980. "'Le Cygne' or 'El cisne': The History of a Misreading." *Comparative Literature Studies* 17 (December): 418–28.

Campbell, Joseph. 1968. *The Hero with a Thousand Faces.* Bollingen Series XVII. 2nd ed. Princeton: Princeton University Press.

Chambers, Ross. 1971. "«L'art sublime du comédien» ou le regardant et le regardé: autour d'un mythe baudelairien." *Saggi e ricerche di letteratura francese.* New series 11. Rome: Bulzoni. 189–260.

————. 1987. "Are Baudelaire's 'Tableaux Parisiens' about Paris?" In *On Referring in Literature.* Edited by Anna Whiteside and Michael Issacharoff. Bloomington: Indiana University Press. 95–110.

————. 1987a. "Mémoire et mélancolie." In *Mélancolie et opposition: Les Débuts du modernisme en France.* Paris: José Corti.

————. 1990. "Perpetual Abjuration: Baudelaire and the Pain of Modernity (Review Article)." Rev. of *Baudelaire in 1859,* by Richard Burton and of *Narrative as Performance,* by Marie Maclean. *French Forum* 15: 169–88.

————. 1991. "The *Flâneur* as hero (on Baudelaire)." *Australian Journal of French Studies* 28 (May-August): 142–53.

Chesters, Graham. 1978. "Baudelaire and the Limits of Poetry." *French Studies* 32:420–31.

Clark, T. J. 1973. *The Absolute Bourgeois: Artists and Politics in France 1848–1851.* London: Thames and Hudson.

Clarke, Howard W. 1967. *The Art of* The Odyssey. Englewood Cliffs, N.J.: Prentice-Hall.

Cohn, Robert Greer. 1986. "Baudelaire's Beleaguered Prose Poems." In *Textual Analysis: Some Readers Reading.* Edited by Mary Ann Caws. New York: Modern Language Association. 112–20.

Collier, Peter. 1990. "Baudelaire and Metaphor: Work in Regress." *Forum for Modern Language Studies* 26 (January): 26–36.

Collins, Christopher. 1991. *The Poetics of the Mind's Eye: Literature and the Psychology of Imagination.* Philadelphia: University of Pennsylvania.

Conio, Gérard. 1992. *Baudelaire: Étude de Les Fleurs du mal.* Alleur (Belgium): Marabout.

Cowan, Bainard. 1981. "Walter Benjamin's Theory of Allegory." *New German Critique* 22 (Winter): 109–22.

Crépet, Jacques, ed. 1932. *Histoires Extraordinaires par Edgar Poe.* Translated by Charles Baudelaire. Paris: Conard, 1932. Vol. 12 of *Oeuvres complètes de Charles Baudelaire.*

Crépet, Jacques, and Georges Blin, eds. 1942. *Les Fleurs du mal.* Paris: Corti.

Cuadra, Pablo Antonio. 1979. *Songs of Cifar and the Sweet Sea.* New York: Columbia University Press.

Culler, Jonathan. 1975. "Stanley Fish and the Righting of the Reader." *Diacritics* 5: 26–31.

De Man, Paul. 1971. *Blindness and Insight: Essays in the Rhetoric of Contemporary Criticism.* New York: Oxford University Press.

———. 1979. *Allegories of Reading: Figural Language in Rousseau, Nietzsche, Rilke, and Proust.* New Haven: Yale University Press.

———. 1981. "Pascal's Allegory of Persuasion." In *Allegory and Representation: Selected Papers from the English Institute, 1979–80.* Edited by Stephen J. Greenblatt. Baltimore: Johns Hopkins University Press. 1–25.

———. 1984. "Intentional Structure of the Romantic Image." In *The Rhetoric of Romanticism.* New York: Columbia University Press. 1–17.

———. 1986. *The Resistance to Theory.* Vol. 33 of *Theory and History of Literature.* Minneapolis: University of Minnesota Press.

De Quincey, Thomas. [1856?]. *Confessions of an English Opium-Eater and Selected Essays.* New York: A. L. Burt.

Derrida, Jacques. 1967. *De la grammatologie.* Paris: Éditions de Minuit.

———. 1992. *Given Time: I. Counterfeit Money.* Translated by Peggy Kamuf. Chicago: University of Chicago Press.

Diamond, Josephine. 1991. "Paris, Baudelaire and Benjamin: The Poetics of Urban Violence." In *City Images: Perspectives from Literature, Philosophy, and Film.* Edited by Mary Ann Caws. New York: Gordon and Breach. 172–78.

Dillon, George L. 1978. *Language Processing and the Reading of Literature: Toward a Model of Comprehension.* Bloomington: Indiana University Press.

Dufour, Pierre. 1989. "Formes et fonctions de l'allégorie dans la modernité des *Fleurs du mal.*" In *Baudelaire* Les Fleurs du mal: *L'Intériorité de la forme.* Edited by Société des Études Romantiques. Np: SEDES. 135–47.

Dufrenne, Mikel. 1967. *Phénoménologie de l'expérience esthétique.* Vol. 1. Paris: Presses Universitaires de France.

Eco, Umberto. 1976. *A Theory of Semiotics.* Bloomington: Indiana University Press.

Eigeldinger, Marc. 1951. *Le Platonisme de Baudelaire.* Neuchâtel: A la Baconnière.

Eliot, T. S. 1952. *Murder in the Cathedral.* In *The Complete Poems and Plays 1909–1950.* New York: Harcourt, Brace. 173–221.

———. 1960. "Tradition and Individual Talent." In *Selected Essays.* New York: Harcourt, Brace, and World. 3–11.

Emmanuel, Pierre. 1967. *Baudelaire.* N.p.: Desclée de Brouwer.

Esrock, Ellen J. 1994. *The Reader's Eye: Visual Imaging as Reader Response.* Baltimore: Johns Hopkins University Press.

Euripides. 1958. *Orestes. Euripides IV.* Translated by William Arrowsmith. Edited by David Grene and Richmond Lattimore. Chicago: University of Chicago Press.

———. 1986. *Trojan Women.* Translated by Shirley A. Barlow. Wiltshire, England: Aris and Phillips.

———. 1993. *The Trojan Women.* Translated by Brendan Kennelly. Newcastle upon Tyne, England: Bloodaxe Books.

Evans, Margery. 1993. *Baudelaire and Intertextuality: Poetry at the Crossroads.* Cambridge: Cambridge University Press.

Fairlie, Alison. 1967. "Observations sur les «Petits poèmes en prose.»" *Revue des Sciences Humaines* 127: 449–60.

Felman, Shoshana. 1982. "Le Scandale de la vérité." In *Discours et Pouvoir.* Edited by Ross Chambers. Ann Arbor: Michigan Romance Studies. 1–28.

Fineman, Joel. 1981. "The Structure of Allegorical Desire." In *Allegory and Representation: Selected Papers from the English Institute, 1979–80.* Edited by Stephen J. Greenblatt. Baltimore: Johns Hopkins University Press. 26–60.

Fischer-Lichte, Erika. 1986. "Walter Benjamin's 'Allegory.'" *American Journal of Semiotics* 4: 151–68.

Fitzgerald, Robert, trans. 1990. *The Aeneid Virgil.* New York: Vintage Classics.

Fletcher, Angus. 1964. *Allegory: The Theory of a Symbolic Mode.* Ithaca: Cornell University Press.

Foley, John Miles. 1990. *Traditional Oral Epic: The Odyssey, Beowulf, and the Serbo-Croatian Return Song.* Berkeley and Los Angeles: University of California Press.

Fontanier, Pierre. 1977. *Les Figures du discours.* Paris: Flammarion.

Forgus, Ronald H., and Lawrence E. Melamed. 1976. *Perception: A Cognitive Stage Approach* [1966]. New York: McGraw-Hill.

Foucault, Michel. 1970. *The Order of Things: An Archaeology of the Human Sciences.* A Translation of *Les Mots et les choses.* New York: Pantheon Books—Random House.

———. 1977. "What is an Author?" In *Language, Counter-Memory, Practice.* Edited and translated by Donald F. Bouchard. Ithaca: Cornell University Press. 113–38.

———. 1980. *Power/Knowledge: Selected Interviews and Other Writings 1972–1977.* Translated by Colin Gordon, Leo Marshall, John Mephan, and Kate Soper. New York: Pantheon Books.

Frank, Joseph. 1945. "Spatial Form in Modern Literature." *Sewanee Review* 53: 221–40, 433–56, and 643–53.

Freccero, John. 1975. "The Fig Tree and the Laurel: Petrarch's Poetics." *Diacritics* 5 (Spring): 34–40.

Fried, Michael. 1984. "Painting Memories: On the Containment of the Past in Baudelaire and Manet." *Critical Inquiry* 10 (March): 510–42.

Galand, René. 1969. *Baudelaire: Poétique et poésie.* Paris: Nizet.

Gasarian, Gérard. 1991. "La figure du poète hystérique ou l'allégorie chez Baudelaire." *Poétique* 86 (April): 177–91.

Gautier, Théophile. 1862. *Poésies complètes.* Paris: Charpentier.

Godfrey, Sima. 1982. "Baudelaire's Windows." *L'Esprit Créateur* 22 (Winter): 83–100.

———. 1991. "From Memory Lane to Memory Boulevard: *Paris change!*" In *City*

Images: Perspectives from Literature, Philosophy, and Film. Edited by Mary Ann Caws. New York: Gordon and Breach. 158–71.

Goldbaek, Henning. 1990. "A l'ombre du voyage: Une interprétation du «Voyage» de Baudelaire." *Revue Romane* 25:73–91.

Greenblatt, Stephen J. 1981. "Preface." In *Allegory and Representation: Selected Papers from the English Institute, 1979–80.* Edited by Stephen Greenblatt. Baltimore: Johns Hopkins University Press. vii–xiii.

Haber, Ralph Norman. 1971. "Where are the Visions in Visual Perception?" In *Imagery: Current Cognitive Approaches.* Edited by Sidney J. Segal. New York: Academic Press. 33–48.

Hambly, P. S. 1971. "Notes sur deux poèmes de Baudelaire: 'Réversibilité' et 'Châtiment de orgueil.'" *Revue d'Histoire Littéraire de la France* 71 (May-June): 485–88.

Hampton, Timothy. 1982. "Virgil, Baudelaire and Mallarmé at the Sign of the Swan: Poetic Translation and Historical Allegory." *Romanic Review* 73:438–51.

Harrington, Karen A. 1991–92. "Fragmentation and Irony in *Les Fleurs du mal.*" *Nineteenth-Century French Studies* 20 (Fall-Winter): 177–86.

Hartman, Geoffrey H. 1954. *The Unmediated Vision: An Interpretation of Wordsworth, Hopkins, Rilke, and Valéry.* New Haven: Yale University Press.

Hiddleston, J. A. 1987. *Baudelaire and Le Spleen de Paris.* Oxford: Clarendon Press.

Holland, Eugene W. 1993. *Baudelaire and Schizoanalysis: The Sociopoetics of Modernism.* Cambridge: Cambridge University Press.

Holland, Norman N. 1992. *The Critical I.* New York: Columbia University Press.

Homer. 1951. *The Iliad.* Translated by Richmond Lattimore. Chicago: University of Chicago Press.

———. 1967. *The Odyssey of Homer.* Translated by Richmond Lattimore. New York: Harper Torchbooks.

Houston, John Porter. 1969. *The Demonic Imagination: Style and Theme in French Romantic Poetry.* Baton Rouge: Louisiana State University Press.

———. 1991. "Two Versions of *Les Fleurs du mal.*" In *The Ladder of High Designs: Structure and Interpretation of the French Lyric Sequence.* Edited by Doranne Fenoaltea and David Lee Rubin. Charlottesville: University Press of Virginia. 110–37.

Hubert, Judd. 1953. *L'Esthétique des Fleurs du mal: Essai sur l'ambiguïté poétique.* Geneva: P. Cailler.

Isherwood, Christopher, trans. 1977. *Intimate Journals.* By Charles Baudelaire. New York: Howard Fertig.

Jackson, John E. 1989. "L'Économie de la haine." In *Baudelaire Les Fleurs du mal: L'Intériorité de la forme.* Edited by Société des Études Romantiques. Np: SEDES. 149–59.

Jarvella, Robert J. 1971. "Syntactic Processing of Connected Speech." *Journal of Verbal Learning and Verbal Behavior* 10: 409–16.

Johnson, Barbara. 1983. "Disfiguring Poetic Language." In *The Prose Poem in France: Theory and Practice.* Edited by Mary Ann Caws and Hermine Riffaterre. New York: Columbia University Press. 79–97.

Jones, David E. 1971. "The Temptation of the Audience." In *Twentieth Century*

Interpretations of Murder in the Cathedral: *A Collection of Critical Essays.* Edited by David R. Clark. Englewood Cliffs, NJ: Prentice-Hall. 96–97.

Kaplan, Edward K. 1980. "Baudelaire's Portrait of the Poet as Widow: Three Poëmes en Prose and 'Le Cygne.'" *Symposium* 34:233–48.

———. 1990. *Baudelaire's Prose Poems: The Esthetic, the Ethical, and the Religious in* The Parisian Prowler. Athens: University of Georgia Press.

———, trans. 1989. *The Parisian Prowler: Le Spleen de Paris, Petits Poèmes en prose.* By Charles Baudelaire. Athens: University of Georgia Press.

Kopp, Robert, ed. 1969. *Petits poëmes en prose.* By Charles Baudelaire. Paris: José Corti.

Lacan, Jacques. 1968. *The Language of the Self: The Function of Language in Psychoanalysis.* New York: Dell Publishing.

———. 1977. *Écrits: A Selection.* Translated by Alan Sheridan. Seuil 1966. New York: W. W. Norton.

———. 1977a. *The Four Fundamental Concepts of Psycho-Analysis.* Edited by Jacques-Alain Miller, translated by Alan Sheridan. Seuil, 1973. New York: W. W. Norton.

Lakoff, George, and Mark Johnson. 1980. *Metaphors We Live By.* Chicago: University of Chicago Press.

Lattimore, Richmond. 1953. "Introduction." In *Aeschylus I: Oresteia.* Chicago: University of Chicago Press. 1–31.

———, trans. 1951. *The Iliad of Homer.* Chicago: University of Chicago Press.

———, trans. 1965, 1967. *The Odyssey of Homer.* New York: Harper and Row.

Leakey, F. W. 1969. *Baudelaire and Nature.* Manchester: Manchester University Press.

———. 1990. *Baudelaire: Collected Essays, 1953–1988.* Edited by Eva Jacobs. Cambridge: Cambridge University Press.

———. 1992. *Baudelaire: Les Fleurs du Mal.* Cambridge: Cambridge University Press.

Leitch, Vincent B. 1983. *Deconstructive Criticism: An Advanced Introduction.* New York: Columbia University Press.

Lemaire, Michel. 1978. *Le Dandysme de Baudelaire à Mallarmé.* Montréal: Presses de l'Université de Montréal.

Lemaitre, Henri, ed. 1962. *Petits poèmes en prose.* By Charles Baudelaire. Paris: Garnier Frères.

Lettvin, J. Y., H. R. Maturana, W. S. Mc Culloch, and W. H. Pitts. 1959. "What the Frog's Eye Tells the Frog's Brain." In *Proceedings of the Institute of Radio Engineers* 47: 1940–51.

MacInnes, John W. 1988. *The Comical as Textual Practice in* Les Fleurs du mal. Gainesville: University of Florida Press.

Maclean, Marie. 1988. *Narrative as Performance: The Baudelairean Experiment.* London: Routledge.

Maistre, Joseph de. 1993. *St Petersburg Dialogues: Or Conversations on the Temporal Government of Providence.* Trans. Richard A. Lebrun. Montreal: McGill-Queen's University Press.

Mallarmé, Stéphane. 1945. "Crise de vers." In *Oeuvres complètes.* Edited by Henri Mondor and G. Jean-Aubry (Pléiade). Paris: Gallimard. 360–68.

References

Marshall, Donald G. 1993. *Contemporary Critical Theory: A Selective Bibliography.* New York: Modern Language Association.

Mauron, Charles. 1966. *Le Dernier Baudelaire.* Paris: José Corti.

Mehlman, Jeffrey. 1974. "Baudelaire with Freud: Theory and Pain." *Diacritics* 4 (Spring): 7–13.

Meitinger, Serge. 1989. "La Double posture projective-reflexive de Baudelaire." In *Baudelaire* Les Fleurs du mal: *L'Intériorité de la forme.* Edited by Société des Études Romantiques. N.p.: SEDES. 119–34.

Milner, Max. 1967. *Baudelaire: Enfer ou ciel qu'importe!* Paris: Plon.

Moreau, Pierre. 1951. "Le Symbolisme de Baudelaire." *Symposium* 5: 89–102.

Musset, Alfred de. 1962. *Poésies nouvelles.* Edited by M. Allem. Paris: Garnier Frères.

Nash, Suzanne. 1976. Les Contemplations *of Victor Hugo: An Allegory of the Creative Process.* Princeton: Princeton University Press.

Nealon, Jeffrey T. 1992. "The Discipline of Deconstruction." *PMLA* 107: 1266–79.

Neisser, Ulric. 1967. *Cognitive Psychology.* New York: Appleton-Century-Crofts.

Nelson, Jr., Lowry. 1961. "Baudelaire and Virgil: A Reading of 'Le Cygne.'" *Comparative Literature* 13 (Fall): 332–45.

Nietzsche, Friedrich. 1983. *Untimely Meditations.* Translated by R. J. Hollingdale. Cambridge: Cambridge University Press.

Perkins, David. 1992. *Is Literary History Possible?* Baltimore: Johns Hopkins.

Peyre, Henri. 1960. "Le Balcon." In *The Poem Itself.* Edited by Stanley Burnshaw. Cleveland: World Publishing. 12–13.

Pichois, Claude. 1973. "Introduction." In *Correspondance.* By Charles Baudelaire. Edited by Claude Pichois with Jean Ziegler. (Pléiade) 2 vols. Paris: Gallimard. vii–xv.

———. 1981. "Baudelaire devant la sociocritique ouestallemande." In *Études baudelairiennes IX.* Nouvelle série-I. Neuchatel: À la Baconnière. 226–33.

———. 1983. "Remarques sur Baudelaire et la conscience de soi." In *Genèse de la conscience moderne: Études sur le développement de la conscience de soi dans la littérature du monde occidental.* Publications de la Sorbonne. Edited by Robert Ellrodt. Paris: Presses Universitaires de France. 302–304.

———, ed. 1975–76. *Oeuvres complètes.* By Charles Baudelaire. (Pléiade) 2 vols. Paris: Gallimard.

Pichois, Claude, and Jean Ziegler. 1987. *Baudelaire.* Paris: Julliard.

Pizzorusso, Arnaldo. 1976. "'Le Mauvais vitrier' ou l'impulsion inconnue." *Études baudelairiennes VIII.* Neuchatel: À la Baconnière. 147–71.

Pommier, Jean. 1945. *Dans les Chemins de Baudelaire.* Paris: José Corti.

———. 1967. *La Mystique de Baudelaire.* 1932. Geneva: Slatkine Reprints.

Poulet, Georges. 1984. *Exploding Poetry: Baudelaire/ Rimbaud.* Translated by Françoise Meltzer. Chicago: University of Chicago Press.

Prendergast, Christopher. 1991. "Framing the City: Two Parisian Windows." In *City Images: Perspectives from Literature, Philosophy, and Film.* Edited by Mary Ann Caws. New York: Gordon and Breach. 179–95.

Prévost, Jean. 1964. *Baudelaire: Essai sur la création et l'inspiration poétiques.* 1953. Paris: Mercure de France.

Proust, Marcel. 1954. *A la Recherche du temps perdu.* Edited by Pierre Clarac and André Ferré (Pléiade). 3 vols. Paris: Gallimard.

Putnam, Walter C. 1989. "Baudelaire's 'Le Voyage' and Conrad's *Heart of Darkness.*" *Revue de Littérature Comparée* 63: 325–39.

Ragland-Sullivan, Ellie. 1986. *Jacques Lacan and the Philosophy of Psychoanalysis.* Urbana: University of Illinois Press.

Raser, Timothy. 1989. *A Poetics of Art Criticism: The Case of Baudelaire.* Chapel Hill: North Carolina Studies in the Romance Languages and Literatures.

———. 1991–92. "The Traumatic Origins of Baudelaire's Poetics: Criticism out of Crisis." *Nineteenth-Century French Studies* 20 (Fall-Winter): 187–95.

Raymond, Marcel. 1940. *De Baudelaire au surréalisme.* Paris: José Corti.

Rimbaud, Arthur. 1960. *Oeuvres.* Edited by Suzanne Bernard. Paris: Garnier Frères.

Robb, Graham. 1991–92. "Baudelaire and the Case of the Empty Grave: Another Corpse Goes Missing." *French Studies Bulletin* 41 (Winter): 17–20.

———. 1992. "Érotisme et obscénité des «Fleurs du mal»." *Europe* 70 (no. 760–61, August-Sept.): 69–78.

Rubin, Vivien L. 1985–86. "Two Prose Poems by Baudelaire: 'Le Vieux saltimbanque' and 'Une Mort héroïque,'" *Nineteenth-Century French Studies* 14: 51–60.

Ruff, Marcel A. 1955. *L'Esprit du mal et l'esthétique baudelairienne.* Paris: Armand Colin.

Saint-Amant, Marc-Antoine de Gérard, de. 1855. *Oeuvres complètes.* Edited by Ch.-L. Livet. Vol. 1. Paris: P. Jannet.

Sandars, N. K. 1972. *The Epic of Gilgamesh: An English Version with an Introduction.* New York: Penguin Books-Harmondsworth.

Schama, Simon. 1989. *Citizens: A Chronicle of the French Revolution.* New York: Alfred A. Knopf.

Schofer, Peter. 1988. "'Une Mort héroïque': Baudelaire's Social Theater of Cruelty." In *Theater and Society in French Literature.* Vol. 15 of French Literature Series. University of South Carolina. 50–57.

Shakespeare, William. 1972. *King Lear.* Edited by Kenneth Muir. London: Methuen.

Spariosu, Mihai. 1987. "Allegory, Hermeneutics, and Postmodernism." In *Exploring Postmodernism.* Selected Papers presented at a Workshop on Postmodernism at the XIth International Comparative Literature Congress, Paris, 20–24 August 1985. Edited by Matei Calinescu and Douwe Fokkema. Amsterdam/Philadelphia: John Benjamins. 59–78.

Spitzer, Leo. 1959. "Baudelaire's 'Spleen.'" In *Romanische Literaturstudien 1936–1956.* Tubingen: Max Niemeyer Verlag. 286–93.

Starobinski, Jean. 1967. "Sur quelques répondants allégoriques du poète." *Revue d'Histoire Littéraire de la France* 67: 402–12.

Sutton, Walter. 1957. "The Literary Image and the Reader: A Consideration of the Theory of Spatial Form." *Journal of Aesthetics and Art Criticism* 16: 112–23.

Tennyson, Alfred Lord. 1951. "Ulysses." In *Selected Poetry.* Edited by Douglas Bush. New York: Random House. 88–90.

Terdiman, Richard. 1993. *Present Past: Modernity and the Memory Crisis.* Ithaca: Cornell University Press.

———. 1993a. "The Mnemonics of Dispossession: 'Le Cygne' in 1859." In *Home and its Dislocations in Nineteenth-Century France*. Edited by Suzanne Nash. Albany: State University of New York.

Thélot, Jérôme. 1993. *Baudelaire: Violence et poésie*. Paris: Gallimard.

Thomas, Dylan. 1952. *Collected Poems 1934–1952*. London: J. M. Dent.

Tracy, Stephen V. 1990. *The Story of* The Odyssey. Princeton: Princeton University Press.

Turner, Mark. 1987. *Death is the Mother of Beauty: Mind, Metaphor, and Criticism*. Chicago: University of Chicago Press.

Van Dyke, Carolynn. 1985. *The Fiction of Truth: Structures of Meaning in Narrative and Dramatic Allegory*. Ithaca: Cornell University Press.

Virgil. 1990. *The Aeneid*. Translated by Robert Fitzgerald. New York: Vintage Books-Random House.

Vivier, Robert. 1926. *L'Originalité de Baudelaire*. Bruxelles: L'Académie Royale.

Walker, Cheryl. 1991. "Persona Criticism and the Death of the Author." In *Contesting the Subject: Essays in the Postmodern Theory and Practice of Biography and Biographical Criticism*. Edited by William H. Epstein. West Lafayette, Indiana: Purdue University Press. 109–21.

Wall, Anthony. 1986. "Parody Without Markers: Baudelaire's 'Le Mauvais vitrier.'" In *Essays on Parody: Monographs, Working Papers and Prepublications of the Toronto Semiotic Circle*. Edited by Clive Thomson. Toronto: Victoria University. 60–75.

Waller, Marguerite R. 1980. *Petrarch's Poetics and Literary History*. Amherst: University of Massachusetts Press.

Ward, David. 1988. "*Murder in the Cathedral:* The Pain of Purgatory." In *T. S. Eliot's* Murder in the Cathedral. Edited by Harold Bloom. New York: Chelsea House. 69–85.

Wing, Nathaniel. 1979. "Effects and Affects of Theory: Reading Bersani on Baudelaire and Freud." *Diacritics* 9: 13–27.

———. 1986. *The Limits of Narrative: Essays on Baudelaire, Flaubert, Rimbaud and Mallarmé*. Cambridge: Cambridge University Press.

———. 1990. "Poets, Mimes and Counterfeit Coins: On Power and Discourse in Baudelaire's Prose Poetry." *Paragraph: A Journal of Modern Critical Theory* 13: 1–18.

Index

Abyss, the: and death, 156 n. 7; the terrors of, 85

"À celle qui est trop gaie": analysis of, 69–74; and the chosen and the damned, 71; and "Réversibilité," 64; and the venom, 71, 72, 74–75; as a warning, 73. *See also* Mme Sabatier

Adam, Antoine: on correspondences, 120; on "Les Sept vieillards," 130; on "Le Voyage," 106

Aeneid, The: and Andromache and Polyxena, 92–93; and Andromache in time, 99–100; and metaphor, 140; time in, 100

Aeschylus: and Baudelaire, 20; and the chorus, 82

aesthetic accomplishment: and moral purity, 39

allegiances: prison of, 55–56; the two allegiances, 52, 61–62

allegory: achievement of, 103–4; the allegorical other, 41–43; and Baudelaire's allegorical figures, 101–3; and death, 126; as fable or ballet, 122–24; and hallucination, 127–28; and life, 141–52; and melancholy, 127; and painting and sculpture, 118–19; and reality, 125–26; and symbol, 116–17; and truth, 126–27. *See also* "L'Irrémédiable"; "Les Sept vieillards"; "Spleen"; "Un Voyage à Cythère"

Andromache: and accessibility, 96–97; an apostrophe to, 90–92; and desire, 97; in time, 99–100; and Polyxena, 92–93; Racine's, 97, 98; and the swan, 94; and the widow, 94

Anouilh, Jean: and *Becket,* parallel with "Une Mort héroïque," 77–84

aphasia: the old acrobat prophetic of, 41, 42–43

Arrowsmith, William: on Electra, 158 n. 2

art: the triumph of, 77–78

artist, the: and death, 79–80, 82, 83–85; and nature, 43–45

Auerbach, Eric: on "Spleen," 123

"À une heure du matin," 39

"À une passante": desire and refusal in, 43

Austin, Lloyd J.: on correspondences, 120; on "Le Voyage," 106, 107

Aynesworth, Donald: on "Mademoiselle Bistouri," 153 n. 7

"Balcon, Le": and "Le Voyage," 110

Balzac, Honoré de: and Baudelaire, 20, 142

Banks, Theodore Howard: on Electra, 158 n. 2

Barbier, Edouard Le, 135

Barthes, Roland: on death of the author, 34, 149 n. 1; on Mallarmé, 149 n. 3; on text and quotations, 162 n. 7

Baudelaire, Charles: achievement of, 142–44; 146; on the artist's truth, 47; and the cognitive view, 146; on Constantin Guys, 22, 44; on correspondences, 20–21, 117–18; on *Les Fleurs du mal,* 70; on Gautier, 20–21; on generative idea, 22–23; on Hugo, 21; on idleness and leisure, 139; and language, 146; and Lavater, 21; his life and work, 139, 141–42; on martyrdom and the artist, 77–78; as a poet, 133–34; on his poetic faculty, 162 n. 3; and Ronsard, 142; and Swedenborg, 21; and tradition, 140, 142–43

beauty: and misfortune, 96

"Bénédiction": damnation in, 138–39

Benjamin, Walter: on allegory, 116–

175

Foucault, Michel: on history and meaning, 88; on Nietzsche and Mallarmé, 149 n. 3; on subject as function of discourse, 34
"Foules, Les," 37–39, 48
Frank, Joseph: on "space logic," 17
Freccero, John: on self-reflexive language, 149 n. 3
Fried, Michael: on source of paintings, 160 n. 12
"Fusées": depth of life in, 93, 140

Galand, René: on "Le Voyage," 111; 159 n. 5
Gasarian, Gérard: on allegory, 151 n. 16; on becoming other, 151 n. 17
Gautier, Judith: on Mme Sabatier, 70–71
Gautier, Théophile: and Baudelaire, 20–21; and "La Fontaine de sang," 143; the monks seen by, 69; "Thébaïde," 69, 71
Gilgamesh: journey to cross the waters of death in, 112
Godfrey, Sima: on subjectivity, 151 n. 17
Goldbaek, Henning: on "Le Cygne," 98
grace: state of, 66
Greenblatt, Stephen J.: on allegory, 126

Haber, Ralph Norman: on perception, 147 n. 4
Hambly, P. S.: on the innocent in "Réversibilité," 71; against the mystical connection in "Réversibilité," 66–67
Hampton, Timothy: on "Le Cygne," 92
Harrington, Karen A.: on the self, 150 n. 6
Hiddleston, J. A.: on black humor, 152 n. 1; on "Mademoiselle Bistouri," 153 n. 7
history: as ebb and flow, 143; as interplay between power and meaning, 88–89; and irony, 79, 88; and martyrdom, 77–78; and tradition, 88–89
Holland, Eugene: on identity, 161 n. 1
Holland, Norman N.: on identity, 48
Homer: and metaphor, 140. See also Iliad, The; Odyssey, The

Houston, John Porter: on "Le Cygne," 91, 157 n. 2
Hubert, Judd: on correspondences, 120
Hughes, Ted: the English of, 30
"Hygiène": and "Une Mort héroïque," 141
Hugo, Victor: and the amnesty, 98; and Baudelaire, 20; "La Pente de la rêverie," 130

iconic memory, 14
identity: of Baudelaire's narrator, 36; of Baudelaire as a poet, 133–35; the issue of, 31; and perspective, 31, 132–35; and the social order, 132–33; struggle for, 63; and transfer of energies, 40–41; and widowhood, 99. See also self; speaking subject
idleness: and leisure, 137–38
Iliad, The: Andromache and Hector in, 96–97; and metaphor, 140; Pouly-damas and Hector, 24–25, 26, 60; time in, 100
imports (imported concepts): and mnemonic potentials, 25–26
interpretation: efficacy of, 29; and figural language, 62; an Iliad passage as model of, 24–25, 26
intertextual sources: need for, 28–29; validity of, 29–30
irony: in Becket, 79; in "Une Mort héroïque," 80
"Irrémédiable, L'": the moral of, 122–23

Jackson, John E.: on "Les Sept vieillards," 130, 161 n. 15
Jarvella, Robert J.: on speech processing, 14
Johnson, Barbara: on the prose poem, 86, 152 n. 1
Jones, David E.: on Murder in the Cathedral, 156–57 n. 11

Kalchas (The Iliad), 122
Kaplan, Edward K.: on Andromache, 94; on the ethical and the aesthetic, 150 n. 11; on "Mademoiselle Bistouri," 153 n. 7; on "Le Mauvais vitrier," 152 n. 1; on "Une Mort hér-

182   **BAUDELAIRE**

Turner, Mark: on kinship metaphors, 14

Van Dyke, Carolynn: on allegory, 120
"Vieux saltimbanque, Le": the dynamics of exchange in, 40–41
venom: and sending poems to Mmᵉ Sabatier, 73; and the primal scene of temptation, 74; and syphilis, spleen, and melancholy, 71
"Veuves, Les": a category of women, 41
"Victor Hugo": on symbols, 121
"Vieux saltimbanque, Le": as visionary text, 150 n. 12
violence: and rape in "À celle qui est trop gaie," 72; and sexual act, 74
Virgil: and Baudelaire, 20; and metaphor, 140. See also *Aeneid, The*
"Voyage, Le": and "Chacun sa chimère," 106; Circe and Electra in, 110; death and the unknown, 114; echoes of epic in, 105; Electra and Orestes in, 109–10; the explored and the unexplored in, 113–14; the eyes of memory in, 115; parallel between Ann-Margaret-Electra and J. G. F.-Jeanne-Electra in, 110; parallels with Ulysses' last voyage in, 107–8; the search for knowledge in, 112; Siren-like voices in, 108–9, 111; spectral Electra and Pylades in, 111; time and death in, 106–7; and tradition, 115; and a two-voyage interpretation, 106
"Voyage à Cythère, Un": and allegory, 127–28; and identity, 127; Nerval as source of, 124; reality and vision in, 125; and truth, 126–27

Walker, Cheryl: on "author-mask," 150 n. 8
Wall, Anthony: on Pascal's wager and the end of "Le Mauvais vitrier," 54
Waller, Marguerite R.: on self-reflexive language, 149 n3
Ward, David: on *Murder in the Cathedral*, 156–57 n. 11
widows: and suffering, 96; as victims, 41
windowpanes of paradise, 53–54
Wing, Nathaniel: on the division of the subject, 56, 150 n. 5; on "Le Mauvais vitrier," 149 n. 3, 150 n. 5, 152 n. 1, 152 n. 3; on "Une Mort héroïque," 77, 150 n. 5, 155 nn.1 and 2